T5-ASL-673

Rights & Liberties
in the World Today

Studies in Comparative Politics

PETER H. MERKL, EDITOR

Studies in Comparative Politics is designed to make available to students and teachers comparative studies of substantive interest and innovative approach. Written for classroom use, they range over a broad spectrum of topical subjects and lend themselves in particular to supplementing course content in a comparative direction.

Rights & Liberties in the World Today: Constitutional Promise & Reality

Ivo D. Duchacek

Santa Barbara, California

Oxford, England

© 1973 by Ivo D. Duchacek

All rights reserved.
This book or any part thereof may not be reproduced in any form
without the written permission of the publishers.

Library of Congress Catalog Card Number 72–95263
ISBN Clothbound Edition 0–87436–112–5
Paperbound Edition 0–87436–113–3

American Bibliographical Center—Clio Press, Inc.
2040 Alameda Padre Serra
Santa Barbara, California

European Bibliographical Center—Clio Press
30 Cornmarket Street
Oxford OX1 3EY, England

Designed by Barbara Monahan
Composed by Datagraphics Press
Printed and bound by Halliday Lithograph
in the United States of America

LIBRARY
ALMA COLLEGE
ALMA, MICHIGAN

TO Las 70

Contents

Illustrative Documents

Preface

This is a comparative study of political, economic, and social rights and liberties that are expressed in the national constitutions of the Western, Communist, and Third worlds. My analysis of over 100 bills of rights compares constitutional promise against actual practice and examines the political motives and ideological assumptions of modern constitution makers.

The book is divided into seven chapters that, in sequence, examine and compare the political role of modern constitutions (Chapter 1); the guarantees of personal liberty, privacy, thought, minority rights (including the right to one's own language), and the status of women (Chapter 2); the right to social progress, economic equality, and education (Chapter 3); impartial justice (Chapter 4); the freedom of expression, including the right to be informed (Chapter 5); participatory rights: suffrage and political parties (Chapter 6); and the right to influence: interest groups (Chapter 7). The Introduction and Conclusion deal with the contemporary avalanche of new constitutional texts and their violations, and attempt to determine why ruling elites continue to suspend and rewrite national constitutions.

The text includes verbatim quotes from constitutional bills of rights and other official sources grouped into thirty-eight illustrative documents, none of which exceeds two pages. Thus, without inundating the reader in legalistic detail, these documents exemplify the varied flavor and style of many national charters and permit comparison of different political cultures and the contrasting goals of various national elites. The illustrative documents also focus on some interesting similarities which are due either to an identity of political and social tasks or to imitative copying, in some instances quite unwitting. An approximate balance between continents, major ideologies, and large, small, and very small countries has been maintained throughout the book. Ideally, all the existing national constitutions and their bills of rights, including some of the older ones—such as the constitutions of the first French Republic, Czarist Russia, Meiji Japan, and Weimar Germany—should have been reproduced herein to satisfy the need for full and detailed reference. This would have required an appendix of more than 4,000 pages— patently an uneconomical undertaking.

This book is particularly suited for courses in comparative politics, introductory general courses in political science, social sciences sequences, and courses in American government and constitutional law. Accordingly, references to American constitutional theory and practice are included in all chapters and their major subdivisions for comparative purposes.

It is a pleasure to acknowledge several great debts that I have incurred during my six years of work on the comparative politics of constitutions.

My colleague, Professor John H. Herz, read the very first manuscript outline and later critiqued the penultimate draft. His detailed comments, conceptual suggestions, and encouragement were of inestimable value in preparing the final draft. He thus shares responsibility for whatever merit the book may have in its present form; any faults that remain must be attributed to me. I also want to express my sincere appreciation for the encouragement and advice given to me by Professors Gabriel A. Almond and Lucian W. Pye, who commented on the original plan of the study and later on the first drafts of the book. Professors Walter Murphy and Donald James Puchala read the final draft and provided me extremely useful suggestions concerning several basic concepts as well as the future format and utility of the book. I am indebted for their effort and help.

The final draft was read in detail by Professor Peter H. Merkl. His imaginative suggestions, searching comments and queries, detection of errors in judgment and facts, and a spirited scholarly critique are acknowledged with my warmest thanks.

This book has also been immeasurably helped by my editor, Lloyd Garrison, whose vigilance and suggestions on substance, style, and form were inestimable.

I should like also to acknowledge a special assistance received from my colleague and friend, Professor Thomas G. Karis, who, while in Zambia, introduced me to the insightful analyses of a Ghanaian scholar, Professor K. Bentsi-Enchill, the former dean of the Law School at the University of Zambia. Bentsi-Enchill's refreshingly frank papers on constitution making in Africa and the reform of the party system in Ghana are quoted in the book.

Thanks are due to the City College of New York: the first draft of the book was completed during my sabbatical leave; and a faculty grant to defray the cost of purchasing source material abroad was also helpful. My findings, doubts, and conclusions were exposed to the alert graduate and undergraduate students at the City College. That exposure proved, as always, to be stimulating and rewarding.

Finally, my special appreciation is due to Mrs. Shirley Quinn and Dave Lynch for their initial editorial help and innumerable searching queries.

I. D. D.

New York, February 1973

Rights & Liberties in the World Today

Constitutional Rights & Liberties in Jeopardy

This is an era of new aspirations, new nations, and new constitutions.[1] It is also an era in which constitutional bills of rights and liberties, new and old, are constantly violated. Two simultaneous phenomena recur in nations throughout the world—new bills of rights appear, and old ones are amended while their provisions are generally disregarded. Both the letter and the spirit of the American Constitution seem, to many citizens, to be violated by governmental methods of electronic surveillance, police actions against nonviolent protesters, and disregard for individual, minority, and women's rights. Beyond our borders, we observe even more frequent, serious, and unabashed violations of fundamental constitutional pledges and guarantees. In Mexico, France, Argentina, and Germany student protests have been brutally suppressed and followed by excessive administrative restrictions of academic freedoms. In Canada, terroristic kidnappings in Quebec resulted in the temporary suspension of major constitutional safeguards—martial law permitted the detention of persons merely suspected of conspiracy to overthrow the government. In Northern Ireland the provincial government and British troops have allegedly detained hundreds of suspected terrorists without due process of law and kept them in prison camps for long periods of time. India suspended a good portion of the constitutional bills of rights by a proclamation of emergency which remained in effect for six years (1962–1968). In neighboring Pakistan there was no need to suspend the bill of rights since it was never really implemented. In Africa a majority of nations live under a military or one-party dictatorship although their new constitutions, adopted in the wake of their liberation from colonial rule, contained liberal bills of rights or made the United Nations Declaration of Human Rights an integral part of their text. In the Soviet Union and other Communist countries the constant denial of the freedom of speech and of the press and denials of the right to impartial justice have become characteristic features of authoritarian socialism. Under Stalin's rule dissenters were sent to Siberia or were summarily executed; today dissent is most frequently punished by imprisonment or confinement to an insane asylum. The strict censorship imposed during Stalin's rule continues to eliminate all expression of thought that the party cannot approve. In Communist China any deviation from Mao's thought is repressed with extreme severity. In Communist Czechoslovakia several intellectuals were imprisoned because they advised voters that they had the constitutional right to cross out the name of any candidate for governmental office from the ballot. The ballot followed the practice of all Communist countries by providing a single list of party-approved candidates.

The general practice of frequently violating constitutional rights and liberties necessarily raises questions concerning the nature and value of constitutions and their bills of rights in this period of ferment within nations. Why do nations and their leaders insist on producing new and elaborate bills of rights if they cannot respect them? What good are those constitutional guarantees if they are discarded when political passions are aroused? How can they be preserved when governments, or their opponents, believe that rights are subservient to might which better serves their political purposes? What types of guarantees tend to be more violated than others? What kinds of rights and liberties tend to be emphasized in modern texts as opposed to the traditional texts? Is it the idealistic and absolute wording of bills of rights that makes violation inevitable? Or is it, on the contrary, their ambiguity which invites violation? Is the decline of constitutional rights and individual liberties only a mirror of the modern state's central planning for welfare and warfare? If constitutional guarantees tend to become more reliable with the passage of time as systems become better established, does the too recent vintage of most constitutions, and nations, make the constitutions vulnerable to extraconstitutional facts of life?

These and other related questions will be dealt with in this comparative study.

NEW CONSTITUTIONS: AN AVALANCHE

Over two-thirds of the existing national constitutions were drafted and promulgated in the last three decades; in the same period constitutions of many old established nations were either partly or totally revised to fit the new era and its new needs and values. Today, as in the turbulent past, many constitutions, with bills of rights, are being drafted and adopted to symbolize a leader's or his people's wish "to make a fresh start . . . to begin again."[2] As the record indicates, a fresh start is difficult in all matters involving men and nations: it is easier to write a new national charter—a certificate of birth for a new nation or a certificate of rebirth or reincarnation for an established nation—than to close a chapter of past tragedies or errors and begin a truly new life. Consequently, as we shall see, constitution making is a continuous and, despite all frustrations and disappointments, a never-ending process: a *"perpetuum constitutionale"* of sorts.

Between the 1790s and 1970s, France, for instance, had five different *republican* constitutions; in addition, there were several royal, imperial (Napoleon I and Napoleon III), and authoritarian interludes, the last one during World War II (1940–1945) when the north of France and its Atlantic coast were under direct German rule and the rest of France was under the Nazi-sponsored government of Marshal Pétain in Vichy. Neighboring Belgium decided to amend its 140-year-old constitution in the 1970s in an attempt to solve three generations of conflict between her two linguistic communities, the Dutch-speaking Flemings and the French-speaking Walloons. A new near-federal formula was designed to assure the Flemish majority, the Walloon minority, and the city of Brussels extensive autonomy as well as their respective cultural and economic development. In 1971 the Swedish Constitution of 1806—the oldest constitution on the European continent—was substantially revised; the bicameral parliament was replaced by a unicameral system, the voting age was lowered from 20 to 18, and the largely ceremonial powers of the king were further reduced.

Diligent constitution making also characterizes the Communist systems. Several new Communist nations have already written two or three national constitutions. One reason for such frequent revisions is the apparent desire of the Communist leaders to mark each stage of socialist development reached (see also chapter 1). However strange the role of constitutional founding fathers played by former guerrilla fighters or saboteurs may seem, there is a certain logic and consistency which makes all revolutionaries, from George Washington to Mao Tse-tung, desire to consolidate their revolutionary victory in a conservative constitutional form. In the case of the Communists there is the additional tendency, dating back to Karl Marx and Friedrich Engels, to translate social and political problems into solemn manifestoes and bureaucratic organizational charts. As everywhere else, the new Communist constitutions also point to the search on the part of all national leaders for a new national purpose, new methods of political and social action, and a new start which would erase past errors.

Drawing by W. Miller; © 1966 The New Yorker Magazine, Inc.

"Must you quote Mao Tse-tung at the breakfast table?"

In China, during one of the most violent phases of its Cultural Socialist Revolution in 1966, several Red Guard posters urged an immediate
revision of the 12-year-old constitution; it had been proclaimed in 1954,
five years after the Communist victory in the Chinese civil war. One
Red Guard poster, for instance, suggested an "article by article" process
of amendment. At the end of 1970 the first draft of the new Chinese
Constitution began circulating inside and outside China. The new document gave Chairman Mao a lifetime designation of "Great Leader of the
People of All Nationalities, Head of State under the Dictatorship of the
Proletariat, and Supreme Commander of the Whole Nation and the
Whole Army." The draft asked the people always to follow Mao's
thought and among the most fundamental rights and obligations of the
Chinese citizens listed support of Chairman Mao and his successor and
close comrade in arms Lin Piao, who, however, was purged in 1971. The
new Chinese draft contained only 3,400 words (in 30 articles), in contrast to the constitution of 1954 with 14,000 words in 106 articles.

In 1968 Communist East Germany adopted its second constitution.
The new East German Constitution was inspired by the other East

European models, all of which reflect many concepts contained in the Stalin Soviet Constitution of 1936, whereas the "old" East German Constitution of 1949 deliberately imitated some of the concepts and terminology of the liberal constitution of the Weimar Republic (1919–1935). The imitation of the constitution of the first German Republic was part of the initial East German effort to challenge the West German claim to be the only rightful successor to pre-Nazi democratic traditions as well as German unity. Today, on the contrary, East Germany advocates the concept of two permanently separate sovereign German states and the new constitution refers to East Germany as a "sozialistischer Staat deutscher Nation" (socialist state of the German nation or nationality).

Between 1946 and 1963 Communist Yugoslavia entirely revised its national charter three times. In 1968 the third constitution (promulgated in 1963) was revised again in order to strengthen, at least on paper, the autonomous rights of Yugoslavia's six socialist republics. In 1971 a series of twenty-one new amendments was necessitated by an increased ethnic tension among the Slavic groups composing Yugoslavia as well as by the age of President Tito (born in 1892). According to the new amendments the six component republics were entitled to approve or disapprove federal economic regulations and international obligations; local bodies were given sweeping legislative powers in fields formerly under federal control. A fourteen-man presidency was planned to succeed Tito; as in Switzerland, a different man was to be designated to head the Yugoslav collective presidency each year.

In 1969 Communist Czechoslovakia adopted its third constitution since 1948. In the wake of its ephemeral liberalization in 1968, Czechoslovakia announced a plan for a more frankly federal system in order to satisfy Slovak nationalist sensitivity (expressed in demands for greater autonomy) as well as the then popular desire for a democratic decentralization. When the new federal amendment to the unitary constitution of 1960 was finally approved on October 27, 1968, and promulgated on January 1, 1969, Czechoslovakia's movement toward democratic socialism—labeled "socialism with a human face"—was reversed back to neo-Stalinism by the Soviet armed intervention (August 21, 1968). The continuing occupation of the country by Soviet military forces formed a rather strange background for introducing a highly decentralized federal structure and for proclaiming a new constitutional system, an act usually connected with the attainment, and not the loss, of national independence.

In the Soviet Union a plan for a new constitution (the third since the Bolshevik revolution in 1917) was announced by Khrushchev in 1959 and again in 1962. At that time Khrushchev became the chairman of a commission of the Supreme Soviet, charged with the task of preparing a new constitution. In October 1964, following Khrushchev's ouster, Leonid Brezhnev assumed the role of leadership over both the party and the constitutional commission. For eight years no mention of the new constitution appeared in the Soviet press. By the end of 1972, however, the troubled state of the Soviet economy and a new fifteen-year plan for long-term development up to 1990 forced the contemplated reform back onto the stage. In a major speech, commemorating the fiftieth birthday of the Soviet federal union as the world now knows it (December 30, 1972), Leonid Brezhnev revived the 1962 proposal to replace Soviet polyethnic federalism (in which each major nationality, regardless of economic realities, administers its own ethnic republic) with a more rational regionalism. Several ethnic republics were to be combined into larger units to facilitate economic planning and territorial administration. Expecting ethnic opposition Brezhnev denounced "exaggerated or distorted national feelings," that "are . . . deeply embedded in the psychology of politically immature people," and stressed that future decision making should be for the good of the country as a whole rather than focus on the interests of ethnic republics.

Cuba's Fundamental Law of February 7, 1959, is the only Communist constitution that does not imitate the Soviet prototype but mixes socialism with Latin American constitutional traditions. Cuba's constitution is as long-winded (230 articles) as the speeches of the Founding Father, Fidel Castro. In the bill of rights (Title 4) freedom of expression is preceded by detailed criminal provisions, including the right to confiscate private property "as the government deems necessary to counteract acts of sabotage, terrorism, or any other counterrevolutionary activities" (Article 24).

LEGAL OR POLITICAL ANALYSIS

Unlike this present study, most comparative studies of national constitutions to date have been dominantly concerned with legal and institutional matters. Unlike this effort to include the constitutional theories and practices of the Third and Communist worlds, previous studies primarily focused on Western Europe, the Commonwealth, and the United States. Many previous studies were penetrating; and they greatly contributed to our knowledge of foreign institutions and comparative constitutional law. Most of them reflected the hope for a rule of law to which both public authorities and citizens were to be equally subject and which could be altered only by prescribed legitimate procedures. In that framework national constitutions were perceived and examined as a supreme law of the land, the primary legal norm or source from which, hierarchically, all other rules, e.g., statutory laws and executive orders, were derived. All secondary or tertiary norms had to conform to the supreme law and this was to be one of the major tasks of each nation's judiciary. Controversies over the meaning and application of the national supreme law sometimes produce the image of juridical minuets in which judges and constitutional lawyers dance to the melody of finely composed abstract sentences. Legal experts have been even accused of having professional vested interests in the fine print of their national supreme law for its own sake while actually maintaining a skeptical view of the impact of the constitution on politics. Such narcissistic tendencies on the part of legal experts can never be totally excluded from our perspective, although they certainly cannot explain the persistence and febrile intensity of contemporary constitution making.

The dynamic force behind all constitution making is primarily political: however legalistic a national constitution as a supreme law of the land may sound, it basically deals with the hard core of all politics, namely who leads whom, with what intent, for what purpose, by what means, and with what restraints. In such matters political leaders are not inclined to allow their legal experts to have the last word. They consider constitutions to be too serious a business to be left to constitutional lawyers alone.[3] Consequently, the task of legal and stylistic experts is to assist the ruling elite when it tries to translate its own ideological commitment and understanding of the nation's purpose, history, and political culture into bills of rights, preambles, and neatly numbered chapters, articles, and paragraphs which deal with the power, organization, and restraints of public authority. The final, finely chiseled product then reflects the way in which the ruling elite desires its national community to be governed for its own good—and for the elite's good.

National constitutions and their bills of rights can therefore be studied as dominantly political documents and political acts. This will be done so in this book.

LONG CONSTITUTIONS

Modern constitutions are generally much longer and more detailed than the short and extraordinarily succinct United States Constitution of 1789. Some are actually voluminous. Their drafters did not limit themselves to fixing the essential features of the nation's political system; rather they incorporated into their texts provisions that, in the American context, would be found in laws, executive orders, or even in municipal ordinances. The longest constitutions in the world today are those of India (395 articles, many of which extend over several pages, some dealing with such details as the regulation of pilgrimages and the slaughtering of cows); Nigeria (245 articles), Malaysia (181 articles), and Kenya (145 articles). The lengthy constitutions of these former British colonies could be facetiously interpreted as a kind of legalistic revenge against England which, except for a short time under Cromwell, has never had a written formal constitution. The length of many post-colonial constitutions seems to reflect an anxious desire on the part of drafters to codify and thus perpetuate the preliberation unity and consensus achieved in a common national struggle against foreign rule, and to protect their nation-building efforts against future internal disruptive improvisations. An attempt to translate into chapter and verse a system which has taken England many centuries to develop may lead to disappointing results, as the cases of several Commonwealth countries such as Nigeria, Pakistan, Uganda, Ghana, and Guyana amply demonstrate. Describing his experiences as a director of Nkrumah's Ideological Institute at Accra, the capital of Ghana, a Czechoslovak Communist observer made the following unabashedly patronizing comment:

> Nobody can bypass historical eras with impunity. Centuries that have been missed must be caught up with but the effort is bound to be much greater than in the case of pupils who have missed history classes at school. Unlike a student, a nation cannot say that it had headache or played hooky when the nineteenth century was assigned.[4]

No doubt, the experience of the nineteenth century—and the eighteenth as well—is still a part of contemporary constitution making. New and revised texts of national constitutions reflect the new facts of national and international life and express new political and social goals. They also reiterate and often eloquently reaffirm many older constitutional provisions which, either in spirit or actual terminology, bear the unmistakable imprint of constitutional concepts and hopes inherited from the preceding two centuries. The emphasis is again, as it was during the American and French revolutions, on popular control of government, on government's responsibility to the people's representatives and its responsiveness to the people, and on the protection of inalienable rights and liberties against governmental and other abuses. That emphasis is characteristic of constitutions in the Western as well as in the Third and Communist worlds. In contrast with nineteenth-century bills of rights two trends may be noted. First, bills of rights that propose to limit the scope of governmental powers have grown substantially in length and descriptive detail, not in effectiveness. Second, new economic, social, educational, and health rights, in tune with the welfare age, have been added. Unlike the individual rights and political liberties characteristic of the nineteenth century, the new economic and social rights do not aim at restricting governmental controls and initiative. On the contrary, the purpose is to extend the role of government. More about this will be said in chapters 4–6.

BORROWING CONSTITUTIONAL FORMULAS

The selective copying of old and modern foreign constitutional models, concepts, terminology, and slogans is general, open, deliberate, and occasionally unwitting. Most modern founding fathers seem to be constitutional copycats. They begin their work armed with verbatim copies or annotated digests of selected national constitutions (see the selected bibliography for the titles of major constitutional anthologies). Few of them search for radically new formulas, although it might be cogently argued that new formulas are really unnecessary. Popular concepts, institutions, mottos, and symbols migrate from one national charter to others, and in the process they are deprived of their original nationality to become naturalized in the country of adoption, often without modification in substance or style. A Ghanaian scholar, Kwamena Bentsi-Enchill, dean of the Law School at the University of Zambia, had this to say about the subject:

> We in Africa have no need to apologize to anyone if in our mature judgment we decide to borrow institutional arrangements from this or that foreign system. Everybody borrows and copies. Nor need anybody entertain the notion that by borrowing we will cease to be a distinctive people. . . . Even the same people, e. g. Anglo-Saxons, suffer a sea change when they settle as communities in other lands. We shall not cease to be different from the peoples from whom we may decide to borrow some institution or other —not even when we purport to adopt their language. . . . Conditioned as we are by our education and upbringing to think institutionally in terms of French or British arrangements, my call is for the comprehensive and eclectic scrutiny of foreign expedients and a hard objective look at the realities of our domestic situation and the provenance of our traditional laws and customs. Only so can we begin to do some independent thinking.[5]

A good example of domestication of a foreign motto is the French, Arabic, African, and Chinese constitutional adoption of the famous ten words from Lincoln's Gettysburg address, "government of the people, by the people, for the people" (see Document A.1).

Several African nations have adopted French constitutional symbols —a tricolor in vertical stripe, a national anthem named after a city, and the revolutionary motto of 1789: Liberté, Egalité, Fraternité. Some of the African imitators have modified the French triad to suit their needs of national unity, modernization, and work discipline.[6]

Communist founding fathers have translated Marx and Lenin into solemn "constitutionalese" using the Stalin Constitution of 1936 as a prototype. At the time of its promulgation Stalin described the Soviet Constitution as an article for export and foreign emulation. It was exported and copied throughout Eastern Europe and continental Asia after World War II. Nearly all the constitutions of the Communist world[7] contain solemn pledges and legal formulas that reflect basic Marxist-Leninist concepts,—e.g., the dialectic-materialist movement of history, class struggle, the dominant role of the working class and its vanguard, the Communist party, and the system's commitment to transition from a people's democracy[8] to socialism in which inequality still exists ("to each according to his *deeds*") and from socialism to communism ("to each according to his *needs*"[9] (see Document A.2).

Another international doctrine which has been "nationalized" through incorporation into other national constitutions is the non-Marxian social doctrine of the Catholic Church proclaimed by the famous papal encyclicals *Rerum Novarum* (1891) and *Quadragesimo Anno* (1931). The main antisocialist and anticapitalist Catholic theses may be found in the constitutions of Portugal, Spain, and several Latin American republics. The Irish Constitution of 1937 contains a Bill of Social and Economic Rights which expresses the Catholic social doctrine in appropriate constitutional articles and paragraphs; it is preceded by an invocation of the Most Holy Trinity in the preamble. Several non-Catholic former colonies of England incorporated the Irish Bill into their national constitutions with only minor changes. The British Commonwealth links evidently helped in the transmission of the Irish constitutional model to the far corners of the world. Buddhist Burma, for example, modified and "naturalized" the Irish Bill by adding state protection and support for the study of Pāli and Sanskrit scriptures. Muslim Pakistan added an expression reflecting the Islamic abhorrence of liquor (absent, of course, in the Irish model). Hindu India replaced references to the Most Holy Trinity with provisions concerning the status of sacred cows and untouchables (see chapter 4 for more statements about modern bills of social rights).

The structures of all modern constitutions follow a nearly identical pattern. All constitutions contain a bill of individual and collective rights and liberties which is the main concern of this comparative study. A basic precondition for the full enjoyment of those rights and liberties is usually found in the constitutional preamble or in a pre-constitutional declaration of independence. The right of a nation to exist as an independent sovereign territorial state may be viewed as a precondition for the enjoyment of the other rights and liberties listed and guaranteed in the bill of rights.

Nearly all constitutions provide for a traditional division of government into three branches: legislative, executive, and judicial. Most national constitutions have adopted some variant of the British cabinet system, i.e., wherein the executive branch of government issues from, is accountable to, and removable by a popularly elected chamber of the national legislature. This pattern is found in several West European constitutions, in nearly all former British colonies, and strange as it may seem, in European and Asian Communist systems, including those of the Soviet Union and the People's Republic of China. The American presidential system is favored in the Western Hemisphere but hardly anywhere else. The hybrid presidential-cabinet system introduced by de Gaulle in France was adopted by a number of African states that had formerly been French colonies.

The concept of judicial review developed in the United States (although without being explicitly part of the constitution of 1789) and has now wandered into Latin America and, in a somewhat diluted form, into Indian, West German, French, Japanese (a special case which will be discussed later), and several other constitutions.

The reciprocal borrowing and foreign imposition of constitutional concepts, organizational patterns, attractive symbols, and rousing slogans have endowed the new constitutions of the Communist, Third, and Western worlds with what, at first sight, may appear to be terminological uniformity, if not dullness. But this judgment is deceptive in many cases. Although the text of a new constitution and its bill of rights may seem routine,[10] a comparative analysis will demonstrate that the political intent of a drafting elite will clearly shine through the whole text. When value preferences, the nation's political culture, and the ruling elite's commitment to utopian or pragmatic goals are incorporated into the nation's supreme law, political leaders and not constitutional lawyers have the last ideological and editorial word.

JAPAN: A SPECIAL CASE

Selective copying appears to be a matter of free choice on the part of drafting committees, but there have been cases when such choices were severely circumscribed by international realities, especially the influence of great powers on their allies, former colonies, or puppets. This is especially the case in postwar Soviet-inspired constitutions in

Document* A.1

THE GETTYSBURG ADDRESS INTERNATIONALIZED

France, 1958
Article 2. France is a Republic, indivisible, secular, democratic and social. . . . Its principle is government of the people, by the people, and for the people.

Guinea, 1958**
Preamble. The people of Guinea by their overwhelming vote of September 28, 1958, rejected domination and, in so doing, acquired their national independence and became a free and sovereign State. . . . The principle of the Republic of Guinea is: Government of the People, by the People, and for the People.

China (Taiwan), 1947
Article 1. The Republic of China, founded on the basis of *San Min Chu I**** shall be a democratic republic of the people, by the people, and for the people.

Algeria****, 1963
Article 3. Its guiding principle is: Revolution by the people and for the people.

---

*In this and all following documents many notes and references to national constitutions have been simplified. Only the name of the country and the year of its constitution's promulgation are indicated. Thus, for example, the full title "The Constitution of the Socialist Federal Republic of Yugoslavia—as promulgated in 1963 and amended in 1965" appears simply as "Yugoslavia, 1963."

**Lincoln's words were incorporated into de Gaulle's Constitution of 1958; from there they moved into the constitutions of practically all the French-oriented African states, including the Republic of Guinea which refused to remain associated with France when given a choice.

****San Min Chu I,* as used in the English text of the Chinese nationalist constitution, means Sun Yat-sen's Three People's Principles: People's National Consciousness, People's Power, and People's Livelihood, usually rendered in English to approximately mean Nationalism, Democracy, and Socialism.

****The Algerian expropriation and subsequent nationalization of Lincoln's words is, to say the least, interesting.

East Europe, North Korea, and North Vietnam, as well as in the case of the American-inspired constitutions of South Korea and South Vietnam. It is also true of de Gaulle's influence on constitution making in French Africa.

Japan is a rather special case in that postwar leaders resisted American demands for democratization of the old Imperial Meiji Constitution of 1889. The text of the Japanese Constitution is a curious conglomeration taken from western models. The draft was conceived in detail and then imposed on the Japanese cabinet and legislators by American occu-

Document A.2

LENIN IN CONSTITUTIONAL ARTICLES

USSR, 1936

Article 12. Work in the USSR is a duty and matter of honor for every able-bodied citizen, in accordance with the principle: "He who does not work, neither shall he eat." The principle applied in the USSR is that of socialism: "From each according to his ability, to each according to his work."

Albania, 1952

Article 13. Work is both a duty and an honor for all able-bodied citizens according to the principle of "who works not, eats not."

Yugoslavia, 1963

Article 36. Whoever will not work, though he is fit to do so, shall not enjoy the rights and the social protection that man enjoys on the basis of work. [The Yugoslav Constitution seems to permit a nonworker to eat.]

Czechoslovakia, 1960

Preamble. Socialism has triumphed in our country! We have entered a new stage in our history, and we are determined to go forward to new and still higher goals. . . . We are already practicing the socialist principle: "From each according to his ability, to each according to his work." People's democracy, as a way to socialism, has fully proved its worth; it has led us to the victory of socialism. . . . All our efforts are now directed at creating the material and moral conditions for the transition of our society to communism. . . . At a later stage in which work becomes the primary necessity of life, it is our intention to expand the forces of production and multiply the wealth of the society to such a degree that it will be possible to provide for all the growing requirements of society and for the full development of each of its members. It will then be possible to proceed to the realization of the highest principle of distribution—the principle of communism: "From each according to his ability, to each according to his needs."

Rumania, 1965

Article 2. In close union, the working class—the leading class of society— the peasantry, the intelligentsia, and the other categories of working people, regardless of nationality, build the socialist system, creating the conditions for transition to communism.

---

pation forces seven months after Hiroshima. The formal procedure of enactment of the new constitution involved adoption through the amendatory process prescribed by the preceding Imperial Constitution.

In 1946 the "constitutional assembly" for new Japan was composed of twenty-five American officers under the command of General Whitney. Only four members of the group were lawyers and none was a constitutional expert. There was one specialist in public administration, one historian specializing in China, and one sociologist specializing in Japan. On February 3, 1946, General MacArthur ordered this group to prepare a draft of a new Japanese democratic constitution so that it could be "accepted" by the Japanese government (in accordance with MacArthur's taste for dramatic symbolism) on George Washington's 214th birthday. There were other reasons for the incredible speed. MacArthur was impatient with Japanese procrastination in liberalizing the Imperial Meiji Constitution (their first draft of a "new" constitution was essentially the old one). He was also afraid that further delay would result in undue Soviet and Communist influence on the new constitution. The American draft of the Japanese Constitution was completed in six days and the Japanese government accepted, at least in principle, the basic concept on February 22, 1946. There were relatively few minor changes (the only major one was the retention of a bicameral system favored by the Japanese. The American drafters wanted a unicameral legislature). Nonetheless, the American constitutional draft was formally adopted and promulgated as the new Japanese Constitution, it became effective as of May 3, 1947, and has remained in force since then without amendment.

The preamble and the bill of rights of the Japanese Constitution read better in English than they do in Japanese. The constitution had to be translated twice, once in formal bureaucratic style, then in a more popular and understandable form. Some new ideographic compounds had to be devised (e.g., for *civil rights*), because some American concepts and assumptions were so foreign to the Japanese pattern of thought and the Japanese script. The preamble and the bill of rights reflect the traditions and ideals of the American republic, rather than those of Japan. A partial listing of the allusions and literary sources of the Japanese preamble includes the American Declaration of Independence, the United States preamble and Constitution, President Roosevelt and General MacArthur. "No analogous references to the Japanese literary heritage occur."[11]

The remarkable result of the whole task of writing a constitution for a major world power was not that it was prepared by a group of young American officers and accepted by the Japanese elder statesmen and the Diet almost without change but that it worked, as constitutions and their bills of rights go, in the specific conditions of postwar Japan.

MODELS FOR THE BILLS OF RIGHTS

The principal models for the content and style of bills of rights have primarily been the English Bill of Rights of 1689, the French Declaration of the Rights of Man and Citizen (enacted on August 26, six weeks after the fall of the Bastille on July 14, 1789), and the American Bill of Rights (the first ten amendments of the constitution, enacted in 1791).

The English, French, and American bills of rights have, of course, their antecedent and model too: the English Magna Carta of 1215, the "Great Charter" of English liberties, given by King John to the English barons assembled on a meadow "which is called Runnymede, between Windsor and Staines, on the fifteenth day of June, in the seventeenth year of our reign." The fundamental rights claimed in the Magna Carta by the noblemen were those associated with justice and property. In addition, the English church insisted on freedom from royal interference. Above all, however, the Magna Carta of 1215 established the general principle that a ruler must govern not arbitrarily but according to law. It was centuries later before this principle was developed into a full-fledged concept of constitutional government, i.e., rule subject to legal restraints. While the Magna Carta and the English Bill of Rights (see Document A.3) represent lists of concessions obtained from hereditary rulers, the French Declaration of the Rights of Man, the American Declaration of Independence (see Document A.4) and the Bill of Rights of 1791 reflect the theory that men have inalienable rights given to them by nature or God.

The French Declaration of 1789 contains seventeen major themes, ranging from the assertion that "men are born and remain free and equal" (point 1) to the proclamation of property as a "sacred and inviolable right" (point 17). Many constitutions enacted in the nineteenth and twentieth centuries quote some of the 1789 formulations almost verbatim. Others alter the style but not the substance of those formulations. Still others modify their substance or scope to make them fit the ideological framework of Marxism-Leninism, Catholicism, Buddhism, Hinduism, and Islam. Many constitutional drafters, we assume, have emulated copies, unaware of the original fountains of much of their "inspiration" (see Document A.5).

The French Declaration of August 26, 1789, was made into the preamble of the first French Constitution (still recognizing the King), enacted on September 3, 1791. Two years later, the first *republican* constitution of France (June 24, 1793) incorporated portions of the Declaration of 1789 but added some new rights, reflecting the revolutionary spirit of the Jacobin era. Article 33, for instance, guaranteed the "right to resist oppression as a consequence of the Rights of Man," Article 34 stated that "there is oppression against the social body, if one of its members is oppressed; and there is oppression of every one if the social body is oppressed," and the concluding Article 35 proclaimed "the right to insurrection as the most sacred right and indispensable duty of the

Document A.3

THE ENGLISH CHARTERS

Magna Carta, 1215

(1) In the first place we have granted to God, and by this our present charter confirmed, for us and our heirs forever, that the English church shall be free, and shall hold its rights entire and its liberties uninjured. . . .

(12) No scutage or aid [taxes] shall be imposed in our kingdom except by the common council of our kingdom, except for the ransoming of our body, for the making of our oldest son a knight, and for once marrying our oldest daughter. . . .

(39) No free man shall be taken or imprisoned or dispossessed or outlawed, or banished, or in any way destroyed, nor will we go upon him, nor send upon him except by the legal judgment of his peers or by the law of the land.

(40) To no one will we sell, to no one will we deny, or delay right or justice. . . .

Bill of Rights, 1689*

[The] Lords Spiritual and Temporal, and Commons, pursuant to their respective Letters and Elections, being now assembled in a full and free Representative of the Nation, . . . Do in the first place (as their Ancestors in like case have usually done) for the vindicating and asserting their ancient Rights and Liberties,

Declare

(1) That the pretended power of suspending laws, or the execution of laws, by Regal authority, without consent of Parliament, is illegal; . . .

(5) That it is the right of the subjects to Petition the King, and all Commitments and Prosecutions for such petitioning are illegal; . . .

(6) That the raising or keeping of a Standing Army within the Kingdom in time of peace, unless it be with the consent of Parliament, is against the law; . . .

(9) That the Freedom of Speech, and Debates and Proceedings in Parliament, ought not to be impeached or questioned in any Court or place out of Parliament;

(10) That excessive Bail ought not to be required, nor excessive Fines imposed, nor cruel and unusual punishments inflicted;

(11) That Jurors ought to be duly impanneled and returned, and Jurors which pass upon men in trials for High Treason ought to be Freeholders; . . .

*The 1689 Bill also condemns the previous practices and offenses from which Englishmen would now be protected under the rule of William and Mary of the House of Orange. William and Mary replaced King James II of the House of Stuart who, as the Bill states, "by the assistance of divers evil Councellors, Judges, and Ministers employed by him, did endeavour to subvert and extirpate the Protestant Religion, and the laws and liberties of this Kingdom." It may be noted that this great English bill of rights simultaneously denied any Catholic the right to be elected Member of Parliament or to succeed to the English throne.

Document A.4

THE AMERICAN AND FRENCH DECLARATIONS

U.S. Declaration of Independence, 1776

We hold these Truths to be self-evident, that all Men are created equal, that they are endowed by their Creator with certain inalienable Rights, that among these are Life, Liberty, and the Pursuit of Happiness—That to secure these Rights, Governments are instituted among Men, deriving their just Powers from the Consent of the Governed, . . .

French Declaration of the Rights of Man and Citizen, 1789

The representatives of the French people, organized in National Assembly, considering that ignorance, forgetfulness or contempt of the rights of man are the sole causes of the public miseries and of the corruption of governments, have resolved to set forth in a solemn declaration the natural, inalienable, and sacred rights of man, in order that this declaration, being always present to all the members of the social body, may unceasingly remind them of their rights and their duties; in order that the acts of the legislative power and those of the executive power may be each moment compared with the aim of every political institution and thereby may be more respected. . . . In consequence, the National Assembly recognizes and declares, in the presence and under the auspices of the Supreme Being, the following rights of man and citizen.

(1) Men are born and remain free and equal in rights. Social distinctions can be based only upon public utility.

(2) The aim of every political association is the preservation of the natural and imprescriptible rights of man. These rights are liberty, property, security, and resistance to oppression.

(3) The source of all sovereignty is essentially in the nation; no body, no individual can exercise authority that does not proceed from it in plain terms.

(4) Liberty consists in the power to do anything that does not injure others; accordingly, the exercise of the natural rights of each man has no limits except those that secure to the other members of society the enjoyment of these same rights. These limits can be determined only by law. . . .*

(16) Any society in which the guarantee of the rights is not secured, or the separation of powers not determined, has no constitution at all.

*Point 5 and the following ones deal with impartial justice; they may be found in Document 4.1 in chapter 4 that deals with justice in civil and criminal law and proceedings.

---

people or portion of the people [right of secession?] when the government violates the rights of the people." Article 27 declared that an individual who would usurp people's sovereign rights "should be immediately executed by free men" and Article 28 guaranteed "the right to revise, reform, and change the Constitution since one generation

ECHOES OF THE AMERICAN AND FRENCH DECLARATIONS

Japan, 1946
Article 13. All of the people shall be respected as individuals. Their right to life, liberty, and the pursuit of happiness shall, to the extent that it does not interfere with the public welfare, be the supreme consideration in legislation and in other governmental affairs.
Article 14. All of the people are equal under law. . . .

USSR, 1936
Article 123. Equality of rights of citizens of the USSR irrespective of their nationality and race, in all spheres of economic, government, cultural, political and other public activity, is an indefeasible law.

West Germany, 1949
Article 1. The dignity of man is inviolable. To respect and protect it is the duty of all state authority. The German people therefore acknowledge inviolable and inalienable human rights as the basis of every community, of peace and of justice in the world.

Zaire (formerly Congo-Kinshasa), 1964
Article 3. All power emanates from the people who exercise it through their representatives or by means of referendum. No section of the people nor any individual may usurp the exercise of this right.

Venezuela, 1961
Everyone has the right to the free development of his personality, with no other limitations than those deriving from the rights of others and from the public and social order.

Poland, 1952
Article 4. The laws of the Polish People's Republic express the interests and the will of the working people.

Mauritania, 1961
Preamble. Confiding in the All-Powerful God, the Mauritanian People . . . proclaim their attachment to the Moslem religion and to the principles of democracy as defined in the Declaration of the Rights of Man of 1789 and the Universal Declaration of December 10, 1948.

Universal Declaration of Human Rights (approved by the U.N. General Assembly on December 10, 1948)
Preamble. Whereas recognition of the inherent dignity and of the equal and inalienable rights of all members of the human family is the foundation of freedom, justice and peace in the world,

Whereas disregard and contempt for human rights have resulted in barbarous acts which have outraged the conscience of mankind, and the advent of a world in which human beings shall enjoy freedom of speech and belief and freedom from fear and want has been proclaimed as the highest aspiration of the common people. . . .

The General Assembly proclaims this Universal Declaration of Human Rights as a common standard of achievement for all peoples and all nations, . . .

Article 1. All human beings are born free and equal in dignity and rights. They are endowed with reason and conscience and should act towards one another in a spirit of brotherhood.

---

cannot submit the future generations to its will." Future French constitutions were to return to the original, less revolutionary Declaration of 1789. Both the Fourth French Republic (1946) and de Gaulle's Fifth Republic (1958) made the Declaration of 1789 part of their constitutions by a simple statement of adherence. The preamble to the constitution of 1958 states:

> The French people hereby solemnly proclaims its attachment to the Rights of Man and the principles of national sovereignty as defined by the Declaration of 1789, reaffirmed and complemented by the Preamble of the Constitution of 1946.

Many of the newly independent African states that have remained associated with the French culture and economy have made the Declaration of 1789 part of their constitutions, usually combining it with a solemn acceptance of the principles of the United Nations Universal Declaration of Human Rights of 1948 (Chad, Dahomey, Gabon, Ivory Coast, Mauritania, Niger, Senegal, and Upper Volta); see Document A.5. Some constitutions refer only to the United Nations document (Algeria, Cameroon, Congo-Brazzaville, Madagascar, Mali, Somalia, and Togo).

The French and American lists of fundamental rights and liberties, echoing their English antecedents, have been circling in the constitutional orbit for nearly two centuries. The following chapters will examine their actual implementation or distortion and their modification in substance and style as well as their impressive increase in scope and length. All these changes have been made by political leaders—some honest and others less so—but all captives of different political cultures and all responding to changing times with their new challenges and unforseeable dilemmas.

NOTES

1   In a modified and abridged form this Introduction and chapter 1 were published in *Comparative Politics* 1:1 (October 1968), pp. 91–102 under the title "National Constitutions: A Functional Approach." Subsequently the article was reproduced in Roy C. Macridis and Bernard E. Brown, *Comparative Politics: Notes and Readings*, 4th ed. (Homewood, Ill.: The Dorsey Press, 1972), and in Louis J. Cantori, *Readings in Comparative Politics* (New York: Holbrook Press, subsidiary of Allyn & Bacon, 1972). Our comparative study does not include subnational constitutions such as those of the fifty American states, the fifteen Soviet republics composing the USSR, or the twenty-two cantons of Switzerland. Nor have we included constitutions of such semi-sovereign entities as Monaco, Andorra, San Marino, Liechtenstein, Sikkim, or Bhutan.

   English translations (both official and approved but unofficial) of constitutional texts quoted in this book were supplied by consulates, press and cultural attachés, and Permanent Missions to the United Nations of the respective nations in New York. The texts of Latin American constitutions were supplied by the Pan-American Union, General Secretariat of the Organization of American States in Washington, D.C. Constitutions and constitutional documents of Algeria, Chad, Guinea, Ivory Coast, Brazil, and Spain, were supplied to the author in their original languages by the respective embassies and were translated by him. Quotations from the North Vietnamese and Mongolian Constitutions are based on the texts in the encyclopedic collection of national constitutions, *Modern Constitutions*, Amos J. Peaslee, ed. (New York: Justice House, 1956–1967). The texts of the Communist constitutions may be also found in Jan F. Triska, ed., *Constitutions of the Communist Party-States* (Stanford: Stanford University Press, 1968).

   In the official or officially approved English versions, except when typographical errors were obvious, no attempt was made to correct grammatical and stylistic errors.

2   K. C. Wheare, *Modern Constitutions* (New York: Oxford University Press, 1965), p. 8.

3   Following the 1967 coup d'état in Greece, the military junta rejected the draft of a new Greek constitution prepared by a panel of constitutional experts since, in the view of the colonels, the lawyers had prepared merely a "rehash" of the old democratic constitution which, according to a government spokesman, "was responsible for so many of our difficulties." Subsequently, the Greek cabinet, composed of eighteen ministers, spent more than eighty hours in nine days to give the lawyers' draft political, that is authoritarian, finishing touches (*New York Times*, February 11, 1968).

4   *Literární Noviny* (Prague), October 8, 1966, p. 12.

5   Kwamena Bentsi-Enchill, "Problems in the Construction of Viable Constitutional Structures in Africa," a paper read before a conference on *The Next Twenty Years in African Research*, held at Lusaka, 1969, pp. 4–5.

6 The French Constitution of 1958 states in Article 2: "The national emblem is the tricolor flag, blue, white, and red. The national anthem is the *Marseillaise*. The motto of the Republic is Liberty, Equality, Fraternity." The constitution of Ivory Coast (1960) states in Article 1: "The national emblem is the tricolor flag, orange, white, and green in vertical stripes. The national anthem is the *Abidjanaise*. The motto of the Republic is: Union, Discipline, Work." The Constitution of Chad (1962) states in its preamble: "The national emblem is the tricolor flag, blue, gold, and red, in vertical stripes. The national anthem is the *Tchadienne*. The motto of the Republic is: Unity, Work, Progress."

7 The Communist party holds decisive power in fourteen countries as of 1972: Albania, Bulgaria, China, Cuba, Czechoslovakia, East Germany, Hungary, Mongolia, North Korea, North Vietnam, Poland, Rumania, the USSR, and Yugoslavia. It is claimed that the constitutions of some of them (e.g., the Soviet Union, Czechoslovakia, Rumania, and Yugoslavia) have elevated the system from an inferior level of people's democracy to socialism where the building of communism can begin. Extraconstitutionally the People's Republic of China is proclaimed, on the other hand, to have a more advanced revolutionary status than any other in the Communist orbit even though its constitution of 1954 still provides only a level of people's democracy in which different social classes still exist, while the state moves toward the ideal—a classless society. The plan for a new constitution to express the achievements of the cultural revolution was announced in 1971 (see also chapter 2).

8 The preamble of the Chinese Constitution of 1954 points to the first phase of transition from the lower form of socialism—people's democracy—to socialism as follows:

> This Constitution consolidates the gains of the Chinese people's revolution and the new victories won in the political and economic fields since the founding of the People's Republic of China; and, moreover, it reflects the basic needs of the state in the period of transition, as well as the common desire of the broad masses to build a socialist society.

9 Karl Marx's own words on this subject were quoted with emphasis and approval by V. I. Lenin in his pamphlet *State and Revolution* (Moscow: Collected Works, vol. 26, p. 140), prepared in Switzerland and completed as a guideline for the Russian and international Communist movement. Lenin's pamphlet rather than Marx himself is the source of inspiration for Communist constitutions. Lenin quotes Marx as follows:

> In a higher phase of Communist society, when the enslaving subordination of individuals in the division of labour has disappeared, and with it also the antagonism between mental and physical labour; when labour has become not only a means of living, but itself the first necessity of life; when, along with the all-round development of individuals, the productive forces too have grown, and all the springs of social wealth are flowing more freely—it is only at that stage that

it will be possible to pass completely beyond the narrow horizon of bourgeois rights, and for society to inscribe on its banners: "from each according to his ability; to each according to his needs!"

And Lenin adds a near-anarchic observation:

When the State exists, there can be no freedom. When there is freedom, there will be no State.

And we may perhaps add the obvious:

And there will be no constitution.

10 "If one would strike off the USSR Constitution (1936), chapters I and X, it would be next to impossible to realize that this is the model of a new social order." Karl Loewenstein, "The Value of Constitutions in Our Revolutionary Age," in Arnold J. Zurcher, ed., *Constitutions and Constitutional Trends Since World War II* (New York: New York University Press, 1955), p. 202. Chapters I and X referred to by Loewenstein deal with the "Social Structure" and "Fundamental Rights and Duties of Citizens," respectively. These two chapters, however, contain a heavy dose of Marxist-Leninist political and social concepts as well as terminology.

11 Robert E. Ward, "Origins of the Present Japanese Constitution," *American Political Science Review* 50:4 (December 1956), p. 1007. In an article entitled "Making the Japanese Constitution: A Further Look," (*American Political Science Review* 59:3 [September 1965], pp. 665–79) Justin Williams defends the constitution makers against the charge that they made a bad constitution and that they forced the text upon the Japanese in violation of Washington directives. The author has found the officers quite competent to produce a model constitution by following detailed directives (SWNCC 228) from Washington.

CHAPTER 1

Constitutional Fact & Fiction

When the term "national constitution"[1] is used by political leaders or scholars, it is generally understood to mean an official collection of major principles and rules which identify the sources, uses, purposes, and restraints of public power. Today such a collection of principles and rules is, in most cases, contained in a single written document—even though no meaningful study of a constitutional system can be limited to that central document. Such studies must examine constitutional practices, judicial interpretations (e.g., in the U.S.), general laws, and traditions and customs (e.g., in "constitutionless" England).

Most national constitutions contain four core ingredients:

(1) A *preamble* which functions as an emotional political manifesto;

(2) An *organizational chart,* or detailed description of the various governmental structures and agencies and the specific procedures to be followed by individuals and groups in achieving their goals in an orderly and legal fashion;

(3) *Amendatory articles* which provide for procedures to be followed when a revision of the supreme law of the land is desired; and

(4) A *Bill of Rights,* the implementation, or the violation, of which helps to determine whether a nation that has a constitution also enjoys, in fact, constitutionalism, i.e., limited, accountable, and responsive government. The distinction between merely having a constitution and having a constitutional government will be discussed in greater detail in the concluding portion of this chapter.

With the exception of England, Israel, Saudi Arabia and a few recently established mini-states all nation states have documents which are called national constitutions. Very few among them, however, have constitutional governments. On the other hand, England and Israel, two countries without written constitutions, seem to enjoy both responsible and limited governments.

In order to add a meaningful perspective to our comparative study of constitutional rights and liberties—the main subject of this book— the first three core components of national constitutions deserve a brief examination.

CONSTITUTIONS AS POLITICAL MANIFESTOES

Nearly all modern constitutions contain articles that describe national symbols and a preamble that often reiterates some of the major themes of the pre-constitutional declaration of independence or revolutionary ideological manifesto. These and other declamatory portions of national constitutions do not address themselves to the rational, organizational, or legal sense of men but to their collective memories, passions, and dreams.[2] Most modern preambles record with pride—and at length—the cost and glory of great common deeds in the past and the resolve to do more in the future. They are classical statements of nationalism.[3]

In several new constitutions national self-glorification is coupled with hostile expressions directed at foreign nations. The Algerian, Chinese, Czechoslovak, Polish, and North Vietnamese preambles name national enemies: France for the Algerians, the United States for the Communist Chinese; Nazi Germany for the Czechoslovaks; Prussia, Austria, and Czarist Russia for Poland (while the preamble dutifully glorifies the Soviet Union); and both France and the United States for the North Vietnamese. Other preambles contain polemics against internal enemies, especially against the systems which have been overturned by successful revolutions and replaced by new constitutional setups.

All preambles, whatever the past, express hope for a bright future. Thus, the main significance of constitutional preambles lies in their nonlegal, nationalist, political, and emotional messages. They are supposed to strengthen the people's identification with their nation's past, its present political, economic, and social system, and with the national future. Carl J. Friedrich's statement about constitutions in general applies to their declamatory portions in particular: "They are symbolic expressions of the unifying forces in a community and they are supposed to strengthen them further."[4] A constitution is evidently expected to play a role as one of the instruments of political socialization,[5] which, in our constitutional context, means the process by which citizens and officials of national systems acquire appropriate political attitudes and behavior described and prescribed in general terms by the supreme law of the land.

Constitutions with their emotional preambles are both a message and a framework for future messages about the political system, its commitment to particular goals, and the implementation of those goals. If, as Herbert Wiener has stated, communication is the cement that makes organization, a constitution then appears as one of many means to make the national community think together, see together, and act together. Through the instrumentality of the constitution the elite's messages are addressed to subordinate policymakers as well as the general public. Also in this way the audience learns about major rules, the institutional arrangements, and the ideological commitment of the political elite. Those who inspire or draft national constitutions expect that their charter will prove able at least partly or occasionally to affect and mold political attitudes and action and, in particular, to induce cooperative behavior and positive feelings toward the system.

To serve the purpose of political socialization, the nonlegal, declamatory portions of a constitution often play as important a role as its legal and organizational chapters. The power of emotional appeals should never be underestimated. Edward R. Murrow once said about Winston Churchill that he was the man who marshaled the English language and sent it to battle when he had little else. Similarly, many a leader of a newly born or reborn nation sends his constitution into domestic and international battle when he has little else to fight with. A newly adopted and propagandized constitution that glorifies its nation's immediately preceding revolutionary past and commits the community to a common program in the future is expected to quicken the pace of nation building. The national discussion concerning the new constitution may, and often does, represent a more powerful tool of political socialization than does the finished document. Through nationwide debate, the younger generation—and, in some countries, the potentially secessionist ethnic or tribal elites—may be inducted into national political roles. This certainly was in part the aim of China's nationwide discussion in 1954 when 150 million persons were officially reported to have taken part in the second grass-roots round of discussion on the definitive draft of the new constitution.[6] During the same period 1,180,420 proposals were allegedly transmitted to the drafting committee for consideration. In many new nations the proclamation and promotion of the new constitution is supposed to help the elite to reach down to the village level and to increase and regulate political participation as well as the relationship between officials and articulate citizens.[7] As Spiro puts it,

> Every self-respecting nation on the face of the earth *wants* to have a constitution if it does not have one. . . . Constitutionalism in this sense is one

of the dominant values of our time, all over the world. And no matter how often it seems to have been disproved by history, the belief persists that a deliberately constructed constitution is the best means available for assuring achievement of the common goals of a community.[8]

It is, of course, conceivable that a new constitution—produced, publicized, and launched into the political orbit—may develop its own momentum, independent of and beyond the expectation and design of the drafting elite. A constitution may be transformed from more than mere message into a root with a life of its own, thus becoming an autonomous fountain of political inspiration and a source of new goals, rather than a prescriptive yardstick of performance of the political system. So, for instance, the Soviet, Indian, Yugoslav, Czechoslovak, and Nigerian constitutions, which gave lingual and tribal nationalisms a federal accolade, might have energized those centrifugal forces that the drafters intended to weaken, regulate, control, or manipulate. The secession of Bangladesh from Pakistan in 1972 is a case in point.

The role that a constitution plays as a fountain of inspiration or a measuring rod naturally varies from country to country. We can surmise, for instance, that references to the constitution as a yardstick for the working of a political system may be more frequent, on account of the judicial review, in the United States than in France. In the older, established Western countries, the nationalistic and emotional preambles will probably be less frequently invoked than in those countries in the process of a febrile nation building.[9] In the Communist countries, on the other hand, we were able to witness a dramatic resurgence of references to long-forgotten bills of rights. In the era of liberalization, constitutions have been transformed from organizational charts, guideposts for governmental action, and instruments of mass deception into unintended standards of desired reforms and sources of inspiration for antigovernmental opposition.

In conclusion, it should be reemphasized that present-day expectations as to the planned or unplanned effects of national constitutions are exceedingly modest in comparison with the excessive hopes of the eighteenth and nineteenth centuries. At that earlier time, many people, assuming the perfectibility of man and society by means of constitutional texts, tended to view constitutions, in Eckstein's words, as "tickets to Utopia." The tragic fate of the Weimar Constitution, among others, demonstrates that a constitution, however well designed it may be, cannot protect a system against profound environmental changes or against usurpers. Constitutions today are no longer viewed as the centers of gravity of national political systems; they merely represent only one, though a useful one, of many elements that compose and characterize a political system. National constitutions are neither a starting nor a culminating point, only a midpoint, in the development of a political system. Along with many other instruments a national constitution may be expected, at best, to help to coordinate the people's activities and expectations. "Coordinated habits, rather than threats, keep things moving,"[10] Karl W. Deutsch has noted. Those who draft and proclaim national constitutions evidently do not want to overlook anything, including the traditional form and content of a national constitution, that might help to move events and men in the desired direction.

Thus every constitution and its preamble reflect, in capsule form, a view of the nation and the world which the national leaders wish to communicate to the people. Like all documents and manifestoes written by mere human beings (political leaders and their legal advisers are, indeed, only human) constitutions, as digests of the political autobiographies of national elites, may be expected to contain erroneous interpretations of past experience, false analyses of existing national and international realities, faulty estimates of future developments, and some deliberate deception. Constitutions also contain self-deceptions—in the form of their framers' wishful thinking about the nature of man and society and their ability to direct their mutual conflicts into nonviolent constitutional channels. Constitutions and especially their preambles are shorthand records of the memories and ambitions of drafting elites; therefore comparative studies of the tone and style of constitutional texts provide interesting insights into the motives and aims of the founding fathers. The verbal behavior of the drafters, their selection of historical references, ideological arguments, and national symbols (those reflected in the declamatory portions of a constitution) are as revealing as their concept of political power and its organization. It is symptomatic, for instance, that modern founding fathers, like their predecessors, tend to adopt fierce animals (lions, eagles, panthers, and tigers) as heraldic symbols of their nations; the study of "constitutional zoology" is often illuminating. When India, for example, adopted the peacock as a national symbol, the reason was not only tradition and the bird's gorgeous plumage, but also, and perhaps primarily, that the peacock is known to valiantly defend his territory.[11]

Communist constitutions typically include detailed descriptions that combine traditional national symbols with the proletarian hammer-and-sickle and the internationalist five-pointed star.[12] For example, the constitution of the People's Republic of Mongolia (1960), Article 90, depicts a coat of arms in which the center is formed by a circle enclosing

the symbolic figure of a workingman on horseback galloping toward the sun—communism—against the background of a landscape typical for the People's Republic of Mongolia. Where the ears of corn meet in the upper part of the circle, a red five-pointed star is depicted . . .

CONSTITUTIONS AS POWER MAPS

Every constitution combines a declaration of political intent with a blueprint for action expressed in legal terms. Usually well over one-half of the text deals with specific ways in which legal rules and political decisions will be made, applied, and adjudicated. Such descriptive organization charts, which are found in every constitution, may make for some dull reading, as is the case for all organizational charts issued by the management. In establishing specific agencies for the purpose of performing special, interconnected roles, nearly all national constitutions are divided into three parts: legislative, executive, and judicial. This is so not only in Western and democratic but also in non-Western and Communist constitutions; the Baron de Montesquieu would probably recognize some of his conclusions about the British system not only in the constitutions of India and Uganda, directly inspired by the British model, but also in those of de Gaulle's France, Salazar's Portugal, and Mao's China, and even in the newly adopted panchayat system of Hindu Nepal. Often he would find his model of a tripartite separation of powers grossly distorted in actual practice, but this would also have been so at the time of his somewhat inaccurate analysis of the working of the British system 200 years ago. Then as now, the British constitutional theory and practice divided *functions* within a system in which powers—and branches—of government were significantly linked rather than separated. In the majority of national constitutions today (the ratio is roughly six to five), the legislative branch of government enjoys, at least editorially, a preferential treatment; in the United States Constitution, for example, it is treated before the executive and judiciary. In reality, the former legislative monopoly of parliaments has been almost everywhere challenged and diluted by the legislative appetite of modern executives; nowhere in practice will we find today a real counterpart to the still important legislative and financial powers of the United States Congress. Everywhere else where legislators still play an important role, their dominant function is to check on the executive's performance and only to modify or reject, but not initiate, legislative proposals. The former constitutional terminology that differentiates between legislation and execution of laws has therefore long ceased to correspond to reality. This is why the newly coined, though not yet fully adopted, terminology—rule making, rule application, and rule adjudication—appears to us, too, to be often preferable to the traditional but outdated constitutional terms.[13]

To sum up: even autocratic systems need an organizational chart, or, in Herman Finer's words, an "autobiography of power distribution." There is a pragmatic need for a macroscopic map to facilitate political communication and the conversion of articulated demands or dictatorial decisions into enforceable rules. No modern political system—however revolutionary its origins or tyrannical its intentions, or however respectful of the people's will—can do without an established and official description of the various central, local, and functional agencies that make, implement, and adjudicate rules. The names, structures, and procedures of the most important governmental agencies are thus, by means of the constitutional text, communicated in a basic form to officials and citizens alike so that they can understand, use, and obey them.

Clearly, such communication is also expected to contribute to the process of political socialization.

CONSTITUTIONS AS THE SUPREME LAW

Whatever the legal theory of constitutions may be, political leaders have long realized that most people desire security and order and express that desire in the demand for a clear, precise, and enforceable rule of law. Some political elites profess, out of legal and political conviction, a belief in the rule of law—in particular, a hierarchical constitutional system. Others are less convinced but feign constitutional convictions for other reasons, e.g., to deliberately deceive the masses, or to provide the political system a gravitational point to be nominally treated as the supreme law for practical reasons.

When political will and power (either based on consensus or usurpation) are translated into legal terms and presented to the people as supreme law the constitutions thus proclaimed usually acquire three attributes, all eminently useful to a national leadership and each partly legal and partly political in nature:

First, there is an explicit or implicit message which is intended to legitimize enforceability of the constitution. The leaders hope that the propagandized sanctity of the constitution may make actual enforcement unnecessary and elicit positive support. The political leaders ordinarily know full well that no law, including the constitution, can be expected to be obeyed all the time by all of the people. A constitution cannot eliminate all unconstitutional behavior any more than a criminal statute can eliminate all criminal conduct. Consequently, there are but few illusions concerning the results of constitutional messages.

Second, constitutions provide a measuring rod for legislators and administrators, whose rule making and rule application are expected to conform to the fundamental principles spelled out in the constitution. A hierarchical legal system that subordinates ordinary laws, ordinances, and bureaucratic action to a superior law may be viewed as a construct of legal normative theory. It may also be seen, politically, as a useful means of promoting an image of consistency and order which contributes to the general stability and support of the system.

Third, the constitution's solemn legal superiority lends additional weight to the nonlegal, declamatory portions of the constitution, which, as we have already noted, seek to instill values and regulate political behavior through ideological appeals and emotional symbolism rather than by threats of legal enforcement. Many political leaders find it politically and ideologically useful to blur the distinction between constitutional rules and constitutional symbolism. In postrevolutionary situations in particular, when elaborate ideological and emotional declarations are made part of a new constitution, they are expected to justify and legitimize what was illegitimate before the revolution. Some revolutionary leaders hope, rather foolishly, that the proclaimed legal and ideological sanctity of their new constitutions will serve as a barrier against a new revolution which would sweep away their newly established regime. New leaders seize power in flagrant violation of existing laws. They then must legitimize themselves in a status quo group protected and shielded by their own new supreme law of the land.

CONSTITUTIONS AS MIRRORS OF CHANGE?

No drafter of a national constitution can claim that all the provisions of a new supreme law are meant to endure for eternity even though "some people are inclined to regret that institutions are far from immutable and are astonished when they become obsolete."[14] A constitution considered superior to all other contemporary rules and acts certainly cannot be deemed superior to future generational, ideological, political, and economic changes. The amendatory articles contained in most constitutions prescribe the appropriate and legitimate procedures to follow when a partial or total revision of the supreme law is desired by a substantial majority of the people or their legislators. The constitution of the French Jacobin Republic of 1793 (Article 28) proclaimed the "right to revise, reform, and change the Constitution since one generation cannot submit the future generations to its will." A similar view was held by Thomas Jefferson, the author of the American Declaration of Independence.

Communist constitutions deliberately give the impression that they are merely a brief stop (a people's democratic or socialist "mid-station") on a dialectical road to the Communist Utopia—when states, and presumably their constitutions, will wither away. Each new Communist constitution therefore marks the end of a phase before embarking on a second. Stalin addressed the extraordinary Eighth Congress of Soviets on November 25, 1936, on the subject of the new constitution and said the new charter was "a record and legislative enactment of what has already been achieved." In identical terms the Hungarian Communist leader, Mátyás Rákosi, noted ten years later that the new (1946) constitution of the People's Republic of Hungary "merely placed on record and consolidated in legal form what Hungary had in reality achieved and won." The constitutions of the Arab and some African states seem to imply that their nations are impermanent because of their commitments to an ultimate Arab or African unity.

In the West, systems much more conservative than those in the Communist and Third worlds also clearly anticipate the need to adapt their political systems to new circumstances. In Britain (often described as the permanent home of the "classic" cabinet system), "in each epoch of its history," as Harold J. Laski noted, "the character of parliamentary government has changed with the problems it has had to solve." And Laski concluded: "The 'classic' parliamentary system has never existed outside the imagination of the publicists."[15]

In the United States since 1789 about 5,000 proposals for amending the constitution have been made; by 1971, of the thirty-one amendments proposed by Congress, twenty-six had been made part of the constitution.

One question has often been raised: how many amendments of "fundamental importance" (itself a controversial term) can a constitution absorb and still be considered an original, though amended, document? Constitutions are often deemed new or old simply on the basis of their amenders' or drafters' claims.

To sum up: like any other documents recording man's hopes and plans for the future, no constitution is ever immune to the test of time, especially the changing concepts and values of new generations and their elites and the challenge of unexpected environmental and technological changes. Unanticipated realities invariably affect the constitutional plan and erode it beyond recognition. Like men, constitutions inevitably age. Many may be rejuvenated by timely amendment or judicial interpretation, some become senile and unusable, and some, like men, die in civil or international wars.

Several national constitutions attempt to differentiate between fundamental principles which cannot be amended and other provisions subject to amendment. Thus, in many long constitutions we find very short unamendable provisions. The United States, Turkish, Italian, French, and several Latin American constitutions, for instance, try to protect *republicanism* against any future changes (see Document 1.1). The French case is particularly understandable. In World War II, Marshal Pétain dismissed the constitution of the Third Republic[16] during the Nazi occupation. The first postwar constitution after France was

Document 1.1

UNAMENDABLE PRINCIPLES

Morocco, 1962
Article 108. Neither the monarchical system of the State nor provisions relating to the Moslem religion may be subject to constitutional revision.

Turkey, 1961
Article 1. The Turkish State is a Republic.
Article 2. The Turkish Republic is a nationalistic, democratic, secular and social State governed by the rule of law, based on human rights and the fundamental tenets set forth in the preamble.
Article 9. The provision of the Constitution establishing the form of the State as a republic shall not be amended nor shall any motion therefor be made.

Poland, 1952
Preamble.... the Regained Territories [a portion of East Germany] were restored to Poland forever.

China, 1931 (Provisional Constitution)
Article 3. The Republic of China shall be a unified Republic forever.

United States, 1789
Article 5. [Following the prescribed procedures] Amendments shall be valid to all Intents and Purposes, as Part of this Constitution ... Provided that no State, without its Consent, shall be deprived of its equal Suffrage in the Senate.

Brazil, 1891
Article 46. Bills having for their subject the abolition of the federal republican form of government or of equal representation of the states in the Senate, cannot be introduced for discussion into the Congress.

West Germany, 1949
Article 79. (1) The Basic Law can be amended only by a law which expressly amends or supplements the text thereof.
(3) An amendment of this Basic Law affecting the division of the Federation into Länder, the participation in principle of the Länder in legislation, or the basic principles laid down in Articles 1 and 20, is inadmissible.
Article 1. (1) The dignity of man is inviolable. To respect and protect it is the duty of all state authority.
(2) The German people therefore acknowledge inviolable and inalienable human rights as the basis of every community, of peace and of justice in the world ...
Article 20. (1) The Federal Republic of Germany is a democratic and social Federal state.

(2) All state authority emanates from the people. It is exercised by the people by means of elections and voting and by separate legislative, executive and judicial organs.

(3) Legislation is subject to the constitutional order; the executive and the judiciary are bound by the law.

---

liberated (Fourth Republic) proclaimed that the republican form of the French government was not amendable (Article 95) and stated (Article 94) that "in case of occupation of all or part of the metropolitan territory by foreign force, no procedure of amendment may be undertaken or continued." The French Constitution of 1958 (Article 89) forbids any amendment procedure "when the integrity of the territory is in jeopardy." The constitution of 1958 also proclaims the republican form of government unamendable. In other countries, drafters have ranked certain principles or values above constitutional provisions for any anticipated future transformation. In West Germany, for example, the *bill of rights* is above amendment, as are *national boundaries* in Poland, *monarchy* and *Islam* in Morocco, *national unity* in the provisional constitution of Nationalist China, 1931 (now on Taiwan), and the *federal bargain* in West Germany, Brazil, and the United States. In the latter two countries the principle of equal representation of unequal states is considered immune from amendment (see Document 1.1). The Communist constitutions, despite emphasis on constitutional impermanence, invariably indicate that commitment to socialism and the building of communism is immune to future change.

Some constitutions make amendment[17] difficult and are therefore called *rigid* constitutions; others are *flexible,* and a few extremely so. The British constitutional framework and some Commonwealth constitutions issuing directly from it are, in principle, the most flexible of all because parliaments are considered omnipotent. A simple Act of Parliament could transform democratic Britain into a Communist people's democracy and an ordinary law could change unitary New Zealand back to a federal monarchy, which she was between 1852 and 1876.

Constitutional rigidity or flexibility is, however, not indicative of actual practice. Many rigid constitutions (that of federal Switzerland, for example) have been frequently and significantly altered, whereas some relatively flexible constitutions (those of Norway and Denmark, for example) have rarely been amended.

All constitutions, whether flexible or rigid in a legal sense, are subject to constant change introduced by extraconstitutional forces such as political parties, technology, new power of technocrats and bureaucrats, generational succession, judicial interpretation, and, frequently through revolutionary or international violence which, in turn, create new elites and new constitutions in recurring cycles.

CONSTITUTIONS AS CHARTERS OF RIGHTS & LIBERTIES

Constitutional guarantees of individual freedom, civil liberties, and political, social, legal, and participatory rights represent the quintessence of constitutionalism in the sense of limited, responsive, and accountable government. A constitution without such guarantees would be only an organizational chart and a political manifesto. Bills of individual and collective rights are the most characteristic and appealing features of constitutional documents. For some authors those bills are the only part of national constitutions worth comparative examination as to content, frequency of violation, and observance. Giovanni Sartori's incisive essay on constitutionalism cited the French *garantisme* (in Italian: *garantismo*) as a particularly useful term to denote the sum total of constitutional guarantees of limits imposed on government. *Garantisme* is his measure of constitutional government as opposed to the mere existence of constitutions which practically all nations possess.[18]

Constitutional pledges of constitutionalism incorporate two basic concepts which clearly separate that pledge from the declamatory and organizational aspects of a constitution:

(1) The concept of *limited* government wherein the political authority accepts specific limits upon its exercise of power. In the past, constitutionalism began with a monarch's pledge of self-restraint. In a word, the political authority cannot exercise its monopoly of coercive power to accomplish all its ends without restraint.

(2) The concept of *responsive* and *accountable* government wherein institutionalized controls and the people's participation establish the general principle that the political authority must continue to respond and be accountable to the people. Specific constitutional provisions typically guarantee groups and individuals free expression of demands and grievances, access to decision-making processes, and controls over rulers and administrators whose tenure is, more or less, revocable. Some constitutions (e.g., those of France and the African states that had been French colonies) express the general principle of government responsiveness and accountability in ten words borrowed from the Gettysburg address—"government of the people, by the people, for the people." David Easton's analysis of political systems as mechanisms for convert-

ing inputs (demands and grievances) into outputs (authoritative decisions in the form of laws or policies),[19] suggests that a constitutional adoption of the Gettysburg formula could be perhaps called an "input-output model à la Lincoln."

Guarantees of governmental responsiveness and accountability are found in specific and editorially distinct bills of rights and also in other sections of the typical constitution. The organizational sections (i.e., the "organizational chart") for instance, establish and describe in detail the institutions of government to be consulted by the executive and those to which he is responsible. The sections and articles which deal with the judiciary and such matters as the rights of an accused are as important an aspect of constitutionalism as the bill of rights itself. Peter H. Merkl has succinctly stated:

> It is no accident that the protection afforded the accused in a criminal trial often forms the acid test of constitutional rule, considering that no other form of governmental action can so stringently interfere with the life and liberty of a person as can a criminal court.[20]

Other constitutional guarantees are found in amendatory articles and even in preambles. Clearly, evidence of constitutionalism must be sought in the whole body of a constitution and, above all, in the actual practice of government.[21]

No written constitution extant would dare proclaim an arbitrary exercise of unlimited and unrestrained power as bluntly as did the French absolute monarch, Louis XVI, on March 3, 1776:

> It is in my person alone that sovereign power resides. . . . It is from me alone that my courts derive their authority; and the plenitude of this authority, which they exercise in my name, remains always in me. . . . It is to me alone that the legislative power belongs. . . . The whole public order emanates from me, and the rights and interests of the nation . . . are necessarily joined with me and rest only in my hands.

The existence of such a constitution with an organizational chart formalizing a system of such exclusive and unlimited use of official power could only imply that a nation living under it was, in fact, denied constitutional government by its constitution.[22]

An opposite example can also be imagined in which a nation has no constitution in the usual sense, i.e., a written and formally proclaimed document, yet enjoys constitutional government in the sense of limited and accountable rule. This is the case in Great Britain and Israel where constitutionalism is practiced in each instance without a formal constitution. Many authors convincingly argue that some of the fundamental laws (to which we will refer later in more detail), in both Britain and

Israel, in conjunction with a basic national consensus, are, in fact, their "constitutions" and that these "constitutions" are more real and more frequently observed in practice than most of the written and solemnly codified ones. The supreme laws of Britain and Israel are perhaps, in Rousseau's words, "not graven on tablets or brass, but on the hearts of the citizen."

The blunt denial of constitutional restraints by a constitution à la Louis XVI and the existence of constitutional governments without constitutions occur so rarely that some authors regard the possibility of either to be mere theoretical constructs. In reality, all constitutional systems fall between those theoretical extremes. Most nations have formal constitutions that promise constitutional government, but only a few of them enjoy a constitutional government which restrains the use of public power through the institution of an independent judiciary, the people's right to oppose and criticize, and direct or indirect participation in the process of rule making and rule application.

EVOLUTION OF
CONSTITUTIONAL GUARANTEES

The concept of self-restraint, proclaimed and practiced by otherwise seemingly omnipotent rulers, may be the beginning of constitutionalism in the sense of limited and responsive government. It is probable that Stone Age cavemen acted in concert to restrain the rule of their chieftains. Unfortunately, the record of the "comparative constitutionalism of early cavemen" has not been preserved. We can only assume that prehistorical territorial chiefs displayed the same variety of "authoritarian" and "constitutional" tendencies as their latter-day progeny. Some certainly must have consulted their elders or their whole tribes as a matter of preference (should we say "enlightenment"?), as a result of experience or wisdom, or, simply, because of irresistible pressure from their subordinates. Similarly, in subsequent eras monarchic self-restraints sometimes reflected the wisdom or enlightenment of a king, more usually pressure from subordinate groups that were successively able to assert their power: barons, bishops, burghers, landowners, industrialists, and finally, the peasantry and the workers. Initially constitutional rights and liberties were presented to the people as a gracious gift of the sovereign, not as an inalienable right. These gifts eventually proved to be quite valuable: they were the starting point from which *institutionalized* checks and controls and enforceable rights and liberties developed. Institutionalized checks and controls should be distinguished from the *crisis-controls* to which even the most autocratic and self-confident rule has always been subject. The autocratic ruler necessarily fears that an organized group (e.g., feudal lords, the military, or a revolutionary party) may exploit popular discontent over his alleged injustice or incompetence. His fear of crisis is constant. That fear has always tended to attenuate, or limit, the seeming omnipotence of the autocrat. In imperial China the withdrawal of the "mandate of heaven" from a ruling emperor by insurrection was used to justify successful *coups d'état.* The anticipation of such an event, however, may be viewed as a potential corrective of official acts. As a matter of fact, the limit of the people's physical endurance in any type of system has always represented a limit on the exercise of power. The all-powerful modern dictator who can control a nation's economy, its propaganda media, and the police still cannot force his people to forego food and sleep for the sake of his grandiose plans. Those controls imposed on the political authority because violence is a potential response to extreme tyranny are labelled *crisis-controls* to distinguish them from the *continuing* controls of constitutional government.

Drawing by Chon Day; copyright 1968 Saturday Review, Inc.

"The queen is dying, the people are rebelling, the treasury is nearly empty . . . make me laugh."

It has been argued that constitutions that provide no continuing, institutionalized, controls or checks on the exercise of public power but instead pledge self-constraint and imply only crisis-control are constitutions in name only. Such constitutions are said to "organize but do not restrain the exercise of political power."[23] Nevertheless, such constitutions do set some limits, however minor, on the exercise of coercive power by establishing a definite and stable framework for autocratic rule making, and by assigning different functions to different institutions. Furthermore, all such constitutions pledge to respect the wishes and the rights of subjects and citizens. Even the most autocratic constitutions attempt to create the impression of a responsive, albeit not a responsible or accountable, rule. Such impressions, based on deceitful promises, may trigger a constitutional process. Some absolute monarchies in the nineteenth century and later began proclaiming their transformation into constitutional monarchies but their announced willingness to limit their autocratic power was evidently not meant seriously. The purpose of many constitutions (see the Russian Czarist Constitution in Document 1.2) was to offer the people constitutional hallucinogens in place of political concessions. Nevertheless such hypocrisies frequently accelerated the constitutional process by transforming an originally symbolic pledge of self-restraint into more meaningful checks and balances. Following the victory of the Western democracies in World War I over the German, Turkish, and Austro-Hungarian autocracies, Japan, which had a clearly autocratic constitution (see Document 1.2), became nearly a parliamentary democracy in the West European sense of the term for a brief period. The Japanese cabinet became increasingly responsible to the popularly elected lower house of the Diet, far beyond the point which the Meiji drafters of the constitution of 1889, inspired by the Prussian autocracy, had anticipated. Samples of three (past and present) autocratic grants yet "potential constitutions" are reproduced in Document 1.2.

SIX CATEGORIES OF
RIGHTS & LIBERTIES

Modern constitutional rights and liberties may be conveniently examined in six segments, bearing in mind their interlocked relationship and mutual dependence and reinforcement as well as their conflicts and mutual erosion:

(1) Guarantees of personal liberty, right to privacy, freedom of thought, right to equality, and minority and women's rights. They will be subject to comparative analysis in chapter 2.

Document 1.2

AUTOCRATIC "CONSTITUTIONS"

Russia, (Fundamental Laws of the Russian Empire), 1906
Article 4. The Emperor of all the Russias wields the supreme autocratic power. To obey his authority, not only through fear but for the sake of conscience, is ordered by God himself.
Article 5. The person of the Emperor is sacred. . . .

Japan (The Meiji Constitution), 1889
Preamble. Having, by virtue of the glories of Our Ancestors, ascended the Throne of a lineal succession unbroken for ages eternal; desiring to promote the welfare of, and to give development to the moral and intellectual faculties of Our beloved subjects, the very same that have been favored with the benevolent care and affectionate vigilance of Our Ancestors; and hoping to maintain the prosperity of the State, in concert with Our people and their support, We hereby promulgate, in pursuance of Our Imperial Rescript of the 12th day of the 10th month of the 14th year of Meiji, a fundamental law of State, to exhibit the principles, by which We are to be guided in Our conduct, and to point out to what Our descendants and Our subjects and their descendants are forever to conform. . . .

We now declare to respect and protect the security of the rights and of the property of Our people, and to secure to them the complete enjoyment of the same, within the extent of the provisions of the present Constitution and of the law. . . .*

Ethiopia, 1955
Preamble. [We] . . . Conquering Lion of the Tribe of Judah, Haile Selassie I. . . . Emperor of Ethiopia . . . do, on the occasion of the Twenty-Fifth Anniversary of our Coronation, hereby proclaim and place into force and effect as from to-day the revised Constitution of the Empire of Ethiopia for the benefit, welfare and progress of Our beloved people. . . .

Article 2. The Imperial Dignity shall remain perpetually attached to the line of Haile Selassie I, descendant of King Sahle Selassie, whose line descends without interruption from the dynasty of Menelik I, son of the Queen of Ethiopia, Queen of Sheba and King Solomon of Jerusalem.

Article 40. The supreme authority over all the affairs of the Empire is exercised by the Emperor as the Head of the State. . . . in the manner prescribed by the present Constitution.

Article 41. No one within the Empire may be deprived of life, liberty or property without due process of law. [Other articles "guarantee" freedom of speech and the press.]

---

*Text as in Ito Hirobumi, *Commentaries on the Constitution of the Empire of Japan* (Tokyo, 1889), translated by Ito Myoji.

(2) Right to social progress and happiness (chapter 3).

(3) Right to impartial justice (chapter 4).

(4) Freedom of expression and the right to be informed (chapter 5).

(5) Right of access to decision making through the intermediary of political parties and universal suffrage (chapter 6).

(6) Right to formulate specific group demands and form interest groups for this purpose (chapter 7).

Most of these rights and liberties reflect the traditional democratic concept according to which people create and simultaneously limit political authority by excluding in the constitution certain issues from the reach of governmental regulation while subjecting the decision-making process to people's influence and control.

All these freedoms and rights are precious in themselves. The knowledge and feeling of being free, the individual's right to use or not to use liberties and rights granted by a constitution can be psychologically rewarding. But, freedoms and rights are also eminently practical since they are *means* to other desirable ends. The right to assemble peaceably satisfies the human desire to belong and derive satisfaction from group membership and it is also a means of collectively defending beliefs and interests. The right to privacy is essential to the individual's desire to be alone and is also necessary to creative activity. The right to be educated is linked to our desire for knowledge and skill. If implemented, that right improves our chances of having better jobs, articulating our interests more clearly, and thus influencing rule making and rule enforcement more effectively.

The interdependence of rights and freedoms is particularly relevant in the economic and social sphere. Freedom of speech without social justice may become freedom to die from hunger. Material satisfaction without freedom of expression and creative innovation may result in spiritual starvation or death in a welfare prison. "If there is a shortage of bread, a shortage of butter and fats, a shortage of textiles and if housing conditions are bad," Stalin noted in 1935, "freedom will not carry you very far." True enough, but Stalin's words are also valid in reverse. Material satisfaction, if there is no freedom, also will not carry you very far. Under Stalin the following sardonic comment on "socialist realism," and the Kremlin-ordered and enforced form of art was born:

> What is expressionism in art? You paint as you feel. What is impressionism? You paint as you see. And what is socialist realism? You paint as you are told by the Central Committee.

All modern constitutions expand and amplify their bills of rights to include economic and social rights—or "welfare rights," as they are sometimes called. Such rights were inspired by socialist and Christian social doctrines. Eighteenth- and nineteenth-century bills of rights, linked historically to Saint Thomas Aquinas, John Locke, and Jean-Jacques Rousseau, incorporate the theory that natural rights are inalienable since they are granted to men by an extrapolitical power—God or nature. Many bills of rights imply that certain fundamental rights and liberties exist independently of authority and therefore need not action but restraint on the part of government. Nature-given rights have to be protected against the potentially arbitrary abuse of power by political authorities.

That assumption is frequently challenged in the argument that rights have no existence and no meaning apart from government. It is argued that laws identify these rights and guarantee they will not be violated by individuals, groups, or governments. This argument suggests that there are no rights unless there is a public coercive power which sanctions their existence and secures respect for them.

The controversy over the source of traditional rights and freedoms is interesting and inconclusive, but there is no doubt regarding the source of modern economic and social rights. The freedom *from* want, ill health, illiteracy, and economic exploitation is based on the expectation that the political authority will act as social worker, economic planner, mobilizer of national resources, investor, educator, and summer camp counselor. These twentieth-century freedoms imply a demand for *more* government. In contrast, the eighteenth- and nineteenth-century freedoms *of* speech and assembly, the freedom *of* expression, the freedom *of* the individual implied a desire for *less* government or for the restraint of political authority in those areas of social life where governmental action was needed.

The contrast between eighteenth- and nineteenth-century and twentieth-century concepts of rights and freedoms is well illustrated by comparing the First Amendment of the United States Constitution which, in a negative order, enjoins that the "Congress shall make *no* law . . . abridging the freedom of speech, etc.," with the demand for positive action found in the Indian Constitution of 1949:

> The State shall direct its policy toward securing that the ownership and control of material resources of the community are so distributed as best to subserve the common good (Article 39).
> The State shall . . . make effective provisions for securing the right to work, to education, and to public assistance in cases of undeserved want (Article 41).

In modern constitutions, the practice of adding economic and social rights, elaborating on traditional rights and liberties in greater detail and length, and the editorial preference of placing bills of rights after the preamble and ahead of other constitutional provisions should not lead to the conclusion that the rights of citizens and their participation in government have become more secure and more extensive than they were during the second half of the eighteenth century. In reality the gap between constitutional fiction and fact is bigger than ever before.

There are several reasons for this gap. Modern social rights are obviously limited by the economic and social resources that governments can mobilize to free their citizens from misery, sickness, and illiteracy. Article 41 of the Indian Constitution of 1949 stipulates that the state shall make effective provisions securing the right to work, *"within the limits of its economic capacity and development."* The traditional rights of speech and the press and the freedom of assembly produce a ubiquitous conflict between constitutionally guaranteed freedoms and other values (e.g., peace and progress) that governments and their citizens may consider more important under some circumstances. The Indian Constitution, for instance, values order, decency, morality, and friendly relations with other nations at least on the same level as freedom of speech and the press. It is worth noting that modern bills of rights make frequent references to future laws and ordinances which will subsequently stipulate how the great constitutional principles of liberty can be implemented in practice. Herein lies the danger of deliberate and sometimes unwitting distortion. Furthermore, several modern drafters have inserted paraphrased texts of the French Declaration of 1789 or other bills of rights into a draft constitution for the purpose of deceitful propaganda, not for implementation. Such bills of rights are, in fact, vicious invitations to take a psychedelic trip into a constitutional never-never land.

To estimate the width of the gap between constitutional promise and actual practice, two different measuring rods are usually employed. The first is supposed to distinguish between *constant* and only *occasional* violations, e.g., when partial and temporary suspension of a constitution is occasioned by transient emergencies or wars and that suspension is provided for in the constitution itself. Admittedly the difference between that which is constant and that which is only occasional is a matter of controversy. The second yardstick is supposed to differentiate between violations of *marginal* and violations of *essential* provisions of a national constitution. Here, again, the distinction is rarely clear. What appears to be a central issue in one historical context may appear quite peripheral in another and vice versa. For instance, the constitutional prohibition against quartering soldiers certainly evokes much less excitement in the 1970s than it did in the 1790s within the United States.

Nevertheless, in light of what has been said on the subject of *garantisme,* a nation may not enjoy constitutional government in practice if the organizational and heraldic sections of the constitution (i.e., those determining the composition of the national legislature and its periods and place of work[24] or those describing the design of the national flag and the manner of its display) are constantly and scrupulously observed while the constitutional guarantees of liberties and participatory and individual rights are constantly violated.

NOTES

1 See note 2 in Introduction.
2 What André Malraux said about political autobiographies—including his own *Antimémoires*—seems to apply to constitutional texts as well: "Face to face with the unknown, some of our dreams are no less significant than our memories." ("En face de l'inconnu, certains de nos rêves n'ont pas moins de signification que nos souvenirs,") André Malraux, *Antimémoires* (Paris: Gallimard, 1967), p. 17.
3 "Sacrifices in the past, as well as those one is prepared to make in the future," were identified by the French historian Ernest Renan as the two main ingredients of nationalism in his now classic statement on *What Is a Nation?* delivered at the Sorbonne in Paris in 1882.
4 Carl J. Friedrich in Arnold J. Zurcher, ed., *Constitutions and Constitutional Trends Since World War II,* 2nd ed. rev. (New York: New York University Press, 1955), p. 35.
5 Political socialization is the process by which individuals are inducted into the political culture and their orientations toward political objects and values are formed. A further discussion of this process may be found in Gabriel A. Almond and G. Bingham Powell, Jr., *Comparative Politics: A Developmental Approach* (Boston: Little, Brown, and Co., 1966), pp. 64–72. It is also the process "by which political cultures are maintained and changed." See also David Easton, *A Framework for Political Analysis* (Englewood Cliffs, N.J.: Prentice-Hall, 1965), p. 125, which states: "Sentiments of legitimacy, recognition of a general welfare, and a sense of political community are bred deeply into the maturing members of a system through the usual processes of political socialization." See also Peter H. Merkl, *Modern Comparative Politics* (New York: Holt, Rinehart and Winston, 1970), which deals with political culture and political socialization in chapters 2 and 3 (pp. 91–231).
6 Liu Shao-ch'i, *Report on the Draft Constitution of the People's Republic of China* (Peking: Foreign Languages Press, 1962), p. 3.
7 The study of the "crises of development" by Leonard Binder, James S. Coleman, Joseph LaPalombara, Myron Weiner, and Lucian W. Pye speaks of *penetration, participation,* and *integration* crises in this connection. See Lucian W. Pye, *Aspects of Political Development* (Boston: Little, Brown and Co., 1966), p. 65.

8   Herbert J. Spiro, *Government by Constitution: The Political Systems of Democracy* (New York: Random House, 1959), p. 11–12.
9   Only logical deduction points to these tentative conclusions. We have found no empirical data to indicate the frequency, intensity, and context of references to national constitutions in different political cultures.
10 Karl W. Deutsch, *The Nerves of Government* (New York: The Free Press, 1966), p. 123.
11 Zafar Futehally, "The National Bird of India," *India News*, May 2, 1969, p. 4. The author describes how two peacocks "jumped at each other with slashing feet" when the preceding intimidation tactics proved "an insufficient deterrent" in defense of their respective territorial domains.
12 A more detailed treatment of the role of constitutional preambles and national symbols will be found in Ivo D. Duchacek, *Power Maps: Comparative Politics of Constitutions* (Santa Barbara: Clio Press, 1973), chapter 1.
13 The traditional term "legislation" seems to connote "some specialized structure and explicit process whereas in many political systems the rule-making function is diffuse, difficult to untangle and specify," as Almond and Powell express it in their *Comparative Politics*, p. 132.
14 Robert Senelle, *The Revision of the Belgian Constitution and the Adaptation of its Institutions to fit Contemporary Realities* (Brussels: Ministry of Foreign Affairs and Foreign Trade, 1965), p. 2.
15 Harold J. Laski, "The Parliamentary and Presidential System," *Public Administration Review* 4:2 (Autumn 1944), p. 347.
16 Constitutional Act Number 1 of July 11, 1940, proclaimed in Vichy, stated: "We, Philippe Pétain, Marshal of France, by authority of the Constitutional Law of July 10, 1940, declare that we assume the functions of Head of the French State. Therefore we decree: Article 2 of the Constitutional Law, 1875 shall be repealed." This was a part of the Constitution of the French Third Republic that provided for the election of the president by the two houses of the National Assembly. Constitutional Act Number 2 transferred plenary governmental powers to the head of the French state. Ministers were made responsible to him; he was also made the source of legislative powers. All constitutional laws that had established the Third Republic were annulled.
17 When a constitution is revised, the term "amendment" is usually employed to describe both the process and the result. Derived from the Latin verb *emendare* (to correct a defect), amendment literally means: modification for the better. It should be recognized that many constitutional amendments, in fact, mean modification for the worse.
18 Giovanni Sartori, "Constitutionalism: A Preliminary Discussion," *American Political Science Review* 56:4 (December 1962), p. 853.
19 David Easton, *A Systems Analysis of Political Life* (New York: Wiley, 1965), pp. 278–343.
20 Peter H. Merkl, *Political Continuity and Change* (New York: Harper and Row, 1967), p. 164.
21 Compare the French Declaration of the Rights of Man and Citizen, 1789, which states: "Any society in which the guarantee of rights is not secured,

or the separation of powers not determined has no constitution at all." The French Declaration optimistically assumed that having a constitution guaranteed enjoyment of constitutional government.

22 Such a case is perhaps Saudi Arabia whose "constitution" is composed of only a few decrees. One (Decree 2716) established the Kingdom of Saudi Arabia on September 18, 1932, composed of the former Kingdom of Hejaz, Nejd, and their Dependencies. Other decrees concern the organization and power of the Council of Ministers. There is neither a bill of rights nor articles on the legislative and judiciary organization and powers. It can be argued, of course, that even in this case there are some restraints since the contents of any rule cannot contradict the supreme law of the land, namely Koran and Sunna (Muslim law). For example, it may be suggested somewhat facetiously that an Arabian king, however absolute his rule may be, would certainly feel restrained from decreeing Yom Kippur an Arab national holiday.

23 Giovanni Sartori, "Constitutionalism: A Preliminary Discussion," p. 861.

24 Article 30 of the Soviet Constitution states: "The highest organ of State power in the USSR is the Supreme Soviet of the USSR." Article 21 of the Chinese Constitution states: "The National People's Congress of the People's Republic of China is the highest organ of state power." The Soviet and Chinese central legislatures exist as prescribed by their respective constitutions. When those legislatures occasionally meet, they never legislate and never really debate political issues. They only nod and praise the legislative and political decisions made by the party, the real "house of first jurisdiction." It may be said that the Supreme Soviet and the Chinese People's Congress have never done anything in particular but they have done so with all possible pomp and circumstance.

CHAPTER 2

Personal Liberty & Equality

Five intimately related liberties and rights will be successively examined in this chapter: personal liberty, the right to privacy, freedom of thought, freedom of religious belief, and equality—a very broad category that also includes minority rights, the right to one's own language, and the status of women.

In a different form and order of priorities these five freedoms and rights, and their subcategories, were expressed in the bills of rights of the nineteenth century. They are now part of most modern constitutions, with a new emphasis on egalitarianism and the right of privacy. Liberty and equality have always needed protection; they have never been as self-evident as the American Declaration of Independence of 1776 and the French Declaration of the Rights of Man and Citizen of 1789 seemed to assume (see Document A.4, Introduction).

At the dawn of the era of constitutional bills of rights personal liberty had to be first asserted against the practice of slavery and serfdom, and later against different forms of forced labor. The definitional line between slavery, serfdom, and forced labor is frequently blurred. *Slavery* is usually defined as a "status or condition of a person over whom any or all the powers attached to the right of ownership are exercised." *Serfdom* may be defined as "a condition of a person adscript to the soil and more or less subject to the will of the owner of the land." And *forced labor* means "all work or service which is exacted from any person under the menace of penalty and for which the said person has not offered himself voluntarily."[1]

It is interesting to note that some of the countries that had already established constitutional government and proclaimed their bills of rights (America, England, and France) had simultaneously engaged in either practice of slavery or slave trade. After all, the often-quoted sentence "all men are created equal" was written by a slaveowner—

Thomas Jefferson. On the other hand, some countries which were still far from the concept of constitutional government or a bill of rights (e.g., Russia, Portugal, and Spain) considered it useful and wise to be concerned with the issue of slavery on the international level. Thus, in 1815 at the Congress of Vienna (which concluded the period of Napoleonic wars in Europe), eight European powers (Austria, France, Great Britain, Portugal, Prussia, Russia, Spain, and Sweden) signed a declaration (February 4, 1815) that stated:

> that the commerce known by the name of the "Slave Trade" (Traité des Nègres d'Afrique) has been considered, by just and enlightened men in all ages, as repugnant to the principles of humanity and universal morality; . . . that, at length, the public voice, in all civilized countries, call aloud for its prompt suppression; that since the character and details of the traffic have been better known, and the evils of every kind that attend it completely developed, several European Governments have virtually come to the resolution of putting a stop to it; and that successively all the Powers possessing Colonies in different parts of the world have acknowledged, either by Legislative Acts, or by Treaties, or other formal engagements, the duty and necessity of abolishing it.[2]

It should be noted that West European countries began to deal with the international aspects of human rights and liberty—the slave trade—earlier than the domestic practice of it. Slavery and serfdom were ended by domestic acts rather than international treaties.

BORN FREE?

The French Declaration of 1789 placed the right to personal liberty at the head of seventeen major themes: "Men are born and remain free." In the United States, slavery, on which the Southern economy had been partly built, delayed including the fundamental right of personal liberty for 74 years. In 1865 the Civil War and the resulting Thirteenth Amendment brought the United States Bill of Rights into step with the French Declaration of 1789. Liberia, the African state formed by freed slaves, made the prohibition of slavery the subject of Article 1 of her constitution two decades before the Thirteenth Amendment:

> There shall be no slavery within the Republic. Nor shall any citizen of this republic, or any person residing therein, deal in slaves, either within or without this Republic, directly or indirectly.

The constitutions of Latin American countries—former importers of slaves from Africa—have also prohibited slavery and the slave trade.

Some have provided that any slave who reaches the national soil may be liberated. The Argentine Constitution of 1853 (promulgated nearly a decade before the outbreak of the Civil War in the United States), for instance, stated:

> In the Argentine nation there are no slaves; the few that exist today are free from the promulgation of this Constitution; and a special law shall regulate whatever indemnifications this declaration may give rise to. Any contract for the purchase or sale of persons is a crime for which those committing it, and the notary or official authorizing it, shall be responsible. And slaves, by whatever manner they may be introduced, shall be free by the mere act of setting foot in the territory of the Republic.

Slavery and serfdom in the nineteenth-century meaning of the terms have ceased to be a major preoccupation of the drafters of constitutions in the twentieth century. More subtle forms of involuntary servitude are now the subject of concern. Modern constitutions try to define situations in which involuntary service or work does not violate positive constitutional commitments to personal liberty. Generally speaking, forced labor as punishment for crimes, compulsory work in national emergencies and military service (conscription or draft)[3] are not categorized as slavery. Many constitutions promote the concept of personal liberty yet proclaim military service to be a constitutional obligation, a sacred duty, or even a precondition for a public service career.[4]

Many constitutions stipulate the obligation to work and simultaneously proclaim the principle of personal freedom which, in the opinion of many men, includes the right of choice in using one's muscles or mind. Communist constitutions bluntly provide that he who does not work does not eat. A number of constitutions authorize compulsory work in national emergencies, raising an obvious problem in determining who can proclaim national emergencies and how long the emergencies shall legitimately last. In some developing countries modernization and industrialization may result in national emergencies that will last for several generations. Shall the conscription of labor then be permitted under the constitution? The Indian Constitution, which forbids traffic in human beings and all forms of forced labor (Article 23), authorizes labor conscription but forbids its use for discriminatory purposes:

> Nothing in this article shall prevent the State from imposing compulsory service for public purposes, and in imposing such service the State shall not make any discrimination on the grounds only of religion, race, caste, or class or any of them.

Modern slavery becomes a more acute issue in countries where elites are dedicated to the idea of total and totalitarian planning. National emergencies in those countries may extend over several five-year plans.

Logically, five-year plans require labor to be available in quantity and quality at given times and in given areas; consequently college students may be committed to predetermined jobs and regions in exchange for tuition-free educations. The fulfillment of national plans for progress and advancement may thus become more important than the free choice of work and residence. Conceivably, whole nations could be transformed into forced labor camps in the interest of a five-year plan—or in response to a national emergency. The political abuse of criminal procedures joined with an ambitious economic plan and an omnipotent political party might develop a truly monstrous situation in which personal liberty could be replaced by a modern form of slavery. Forced labor could become institutionalized as an integral part of the cost and expenditure calculations of a five-year plan. This occurred in Stalin's Russia, where the secret police (GULAG, or Chief Administration of Corrective Labor Camps and Labor Settlements) became the most important employer of all Soviet agencies. GULAG was fully associated with the national drive to meet and overfulfill production quotas. Unlike the Nazi death camps, the Soviet camps were designed to exploit, not eliminate, particular groups of people. In 1929 a new Soviet law prescribed that those "sentenced to deprivation of liberty for a period of more than three years must be exiled into Corrective Labor Camps." Subsequently, the number of hard labor sentences passed by the Soviet courts increased dramatically (from 18.6 percent in 1927 to 56.5 percent in 1930). The White Sea-Baltic and the Moscow-Volga canals and other projects were built mostly by forced labor under the direction of the secret police—a strangely integral part of the five-year plan of building of socialism.

The Asian and African institution of prearranged marriages is a special kind of "involuntary servitude," in which the participants are not consulted (e.g., child marriages in India). The Japanese Constitution of 1949 (Article 22) was an attempt to eliminate this tradition and its bill of rights specifies a marital right which might appear unworthy of a constitutional article in the United States:

> Marriage shall be based only on the mutual consent of both sexes and it shall be maintained through mutual cooperation with the equal rights of husband and wife as the basis. With regard to choice of spouse, property rights, inheritance, choice of domicile, divorce[5] and other matters pertaining to marriage and the family, laws shall be enacted from the standpoint of individual dignity and the essential equality of the sexes.

In modern Japan, many families even today disregard the constitutional prohibition of pre-arranged marriages because public authorities are neither willing nor equipped to invoke sanctions against traditional and solemn inter-family arrangements.

Another personal freedom, the right to move within and out of one's country, is specified in several constitutions. However, this right is so "natural" in most West European countries that it has become sacrosanct and needs no constitutional guarantee. The Mexican Constitution of 1917 (Article 11) specifically prohibits the "internal" passports that have been used by many autocratic regimes (including Stalin's Russia) to prevent the movement of persons without surveillance. Morocco places "freedom of movement and the right to settle in all parts of the Kingdom" (Article 9) ahead of freedom of opinion, speech, and assembly. The American-inspired Japanese Constitution (Article 22) couples "freedom of all persons to move to a foreign country" with the right "to divest themselves of their nationality." This provision clearly reflects the American drafters' reaction to the thesis promoted in Japan during World War II, i.e., that American citizens of Japanese descent, those naturalized or born in the United States, owed a primary loyalty to Japan as their country of origin.

THE PREROGATIVE OF PRIVACY

"The right to be let alone," said Justice Brandeis, is "the right most valued by civilized men."[6] The modern French writer, Bertrand de Jouvenel, identified the right to defend the prerogative of privacy and political participation in government as two fundamentals of democracy. The individual's right to prevent officials from intruding into his home, correspondence, or thoughts—his right to protect his abode, communications, even his free time from unauthorized intrusion—are essential elements of personal liberty. During the Stalinist fifties many refugees from East European Communist countries indicated that the constitutional freedom or right they missed most was not freedom of expression, rather it was the right to be alone, "the right to a free evening to think" without party indoctrination. Oscar Wilde's candid observation that socialism would take too many evenings away was close to the mark.

Many modern constitutions grant citizens an *absolute* freedom of thought and belief and make the freedom to manifest, express, or disseminate thoughts *relative* to competing values such as public order, decency, morality, religion, health, interests of socialism, peace, and friendly relations among nations. Generally, modern constitutions follow the distinction between opinion and its expression made in the French Declaration of the Rights of Man and Citizen in 1789:

No one should be disturbed on account of his opinion, even religious, provided their *manifestation* does not derange the public order (italics added).

The constitutional and extraconstitutional limits on the freedom of expression will be discussed in chapter 5 in more detail. Here we are concerned with two other problems.

First, at what point is a private view on public affairs to be considered "manifested" or "disseminated?" Are an individual's beliefs disseminated when they are shared with a priest, a mistress, a friend, one's family, a group of classmates, or his co-workers? In the period of Stalinist and Maoist socialism, authors were prosecuted for noting their inner thoughts on private papers buried in the bottom drawers of their desks. The socialist totalitarian police argued that such actions were evidence of an intention to publish such thoughts abroad or at a later date. Boris Pasternak's *Doctor Zhivago* (Nobel Prize for Literature in 1958, unpublished in the Soviet Union), Aleksandr I. Solzhenitsyn's *The Cancer Ward* and *The First Circle* (Nobel Prize, 1970, best-sellers in the West but not published in the Soviet Union),[7] memoirs of Svetlana Aliluyeva (Stalin's daughter), and novels by Andrei D. Sinyavsky (Abram Tertz) and Yuli M. Daniel are examples of modern Russian writing which originated as "drawer" literature. In the sixties Spanish authority did not censor moderate criticism of the Spanish reality as long as it was not printed. However if such critical essays were typed, five carbon copies allegedly constituted private circulation; a sixth copy apparently made the difference between private thought and punishable public dissemination.

The second problem is concerned with the actual difficulty of *having* private thoughts at all in the modern society. There is a fear of the criminal and economic consequences of nonconformity in all societies; everywhere the mass media tend to generate similar outlooks in the citizenry.

Several modern constitutions address themselves to the question of subliminal, anonymous invasions of privacy. The Venezuelan Constitution of 1961 pathetically asserts that "everyone has the right to free development of his personality." Similarly, the Turkish Constitution, also enacted in 1961, assures every Turkish citizen (Article 20) of his right "to have his own opinions and think freely." It would be interesting to explore how the right of "free personality" and "independent thinking" could be guaranteed in a modern mass society where everybody conforms to an invisible rule. "The rule by nobody is not necessarily no-rule; it may indeed, under certain circumstances, even turn out to be one of its cruelest and most tyrannical versions. . . . [a rule] by an 'invisible hand,' namely, a rule by nobody."[8] The result may be "compulsive conforming."[9]

The constitutional right to express very personal thoughts or beliefs may become secondary to the possibility of *having* a personal view at all. In matters of personal privacy we may be nearer to Orwell's *1984* than it is comfortable to believe.[10]

CITIZENS' PRIVACY & CRIMINAL PROSECUTION

Even those governments sincerely dedicated to the protection of the individual's right to privacy are faced with a difficulty in maintaining a reasonable balance between the citizens' right to be let alone and its duty to protect citizens from kidnappers, robbers, blackmailers, murderers, arsonists, and terrorists (see Document 2.1). The reconciliation of the need to respect the privacy of the individual on one hand, and to prevent abuses of that right, on the other, has always been difficult. The right of privacy, if it is interpreted as absolute, could render criminal prosecution impossible or protect the "privacy" of criminal conspiracies. In our era, called "Technectronic" by Professor Brzezinski, privacy is even more vulnerable to official and private invasion because of fantastic advances in the techniques of surveillance,[11] such as wire-taps, microminiaturized "bugs," telescopic lenses, infrared cameras, devices that record vibration of window panes to listen to private conversations, closed-circuit TV, and data computing.

National constitutions either spell out the right to privacy in positive terms or imply the privilege of privacy by prohibiting acts that would constitute an unlawful invasion of privacy. Yet, they all qualify the concern for privacy by including such words as "except," "save for," "with appropriate warrant," and other formulas.[12]

In authoritarian systems there is an additional problem. Expressions of political dissent in those countries usually fall into the category of crimes of treason or sedition whose investigation permits a departure from the constitutional pledge to respect the citizens' privacy. The provisions of the Yugoslav Constitution, quoted in Document 2.1, for instance, seem to be as balanced as any other similar constitutional provision. Yet, in the Communist context those provisions did not inhibit the Yugoslav political police from entering the home of Milovan Djilas and seizing him and all his papers. Djilas was a Communist leader and former guerrilla revolutionary whose interpretation of Marx and Lenin differed from that of President Tito and the Soviet leaders. He spent nine years in prison as punishment for his books *The New Class* and *Conversations with Stalin*—the latter was allegedly a crime against Yugoslavia's friendly relations with the Soviet Union.

The United States Supreme Court held in 1968 that Federal agents violated the rights of Los Angeles gambler Charles Katz when they

Document 2.1

INVIOLABILITY OF ABODE

United States, 1789

Fourth Amendment, 1791. The right of the people to be secure in their persons, houses, papers, and effects against unreasonable searches and seizures, shall not be violated, and no Warrants shall issue, but upon probable cause, supported by Oath, or affirmation, and particularly describing the place to be searched, and the persons or things to be seized.*

Hugo Black (U.S. Supreme Court Justice, 1967): Crimes, unspeakably horrid crimes, are with us in this country and we cannot afford to dispense with any known method of detecting and correcting them, unless it is forbidden by the Constitution or deemed inadvisable by legislative policy—neither of which I believe to be true about eavesdropping.

Yugoslavia, 1963

Article 52. The dwelling shall be inviolable. . . . A search may be carried out only in the presence of two witnesses. Subject to the conditions to be determined by law, a person in an official capacity may enter a dwelling or premises without a warrant from the competent authority and carry out a search in the absence of witnesses if this is indispensable for the direct apprehension of a criminal offender, or for the safety of life and property, or if it is beyond doubt that evidence in criminal proceedings cannot be secured otherwise. Illegal entry and search of a dwelling or premises are prohibited and shall be punishable.

Article 53. The privacy of letters and of other means of communication shall be inviolable.

Provision may be made only by federal law to depart, in accordance with the decision of a competent authority, from the principle of inviolability of privacy of letters and of other means of communication, if this is indispensable for the execution of criminal proceedings, or for the security of the country.

---

*The key terms—both highly controversial—are obviously "unreasonable" searches and "probable" cause.

---

bugged the telephone booth where he conducted his business. The eavesdropping device used was taped to the top of the booth and did not penetrate inside (the booth obviously could not be claimed to be Mr. Katz's home), yet the court ruled that his conversations could not be used as evidence. According to the court, the Fourth Amendment "protects people, not places." The court, however added a postscript: "If the federal agents had obtained a search warrant from a judge, their eavesdropping on Katz would have been constitutional and the evidence could have been used against him."

Unless the Supreme Court changes its mind, electronic eavesdropping (which indeed is a modern form of search and seizure) is constitutional if pursuant to judicial warrants, i.e., if a judge and his opinion are placed between the police and a suspect. This is how the Crime Control Act of 1968 (Title III, entitled the "Omnibus Crime Control and Safe Streets Act" permits electronic searches and seizures) is expected to be implemented in the future without violating the Fourth Amendment. The police may also eavesdrop for forty-eight hours *without* a warrant when investigating organized crime or national security (espionage) cases. Domestic radicals *who have no foreign ties* cannot be subject to wiretapping without a court warrant according to a unanimous Supreme Court decision (June 19, 1972). Accordingly, radical groups considered dangerous to the national security cannot be subjected to wiretapping without first obtaining court approval.

DOSSIER DICTATORSHIP[13]

Computer technology introduces another dimension of "electronic search and seizure" unforeseen by the Fourth Amendment or in any other constitution. The computer can now store all types of information and hearsay, and it permits total recall and instantaneous retrieval. Several agencies of the federal government, for example, have compiled magnetic tape and microfilm files on hundreds of thousands of "persons of interest," i.e., persons capable of subversion, inciting to riot, and threatening national leaders. In 1970, the U.S. Secret Service, charged with the president's security, had an advanced computer capable of instantly sorting and identifying individuals by name, alias, locale, method of operation, affiliation, and physical appearance. According to the *New York Times* (June 28, 1970) the computer contained in its data bank:

> the names and dossiers of activists, malcontents, persistent seekers of redress of "imaginary" grievances, and those who would "embarrass" the President or other Government leaders . . . filed with those of potential assassins and persons convicted of "threats against the President."

The persons responsible, and the method used to encode the records of non-criminals recorded as potential lawbreakers are crucial. The guidelines distributed by the Secret Service in August 1969 seem broad (see Document 2.2).

Other data banks are maintained by the Department of Justice, with a focus on civil disturbance, by the Federal Bureau of Investigation's National Crime Information Center, and by the Army's Counter-Intelligence Analysis Division in Alexandria, Virginia, the National

Science Foundation (data on scientists), Customs Bureau, the Department of Housing and Urban Development (loan applicants) and the Department of Health, Education and Welfare, whose cumulative file on 300,000 children of migrant farm workers is expected to speed the distribution of their scholastic records, including often quite subjective teachers' judgments on their pupils' attitudes. In addition to governmental agencies numerous private institutions collect, store, and evaluate information on citizens for the purpose of verifying loan applications, installment payments, insurance, and credit cards (see Ralph Nader on this point in Document 2.3). Their files are often accessible to government agencies.

The above list indicates that law-enforcing and governmental investigating agencies are not the only invaders of the individual's privacy. The imperatives of modern economic, social, and welfare planning force authorities everywhere to collect reliable and retrievable information on the real needs of citizens requiring aid and assistance. There is little doubt that men may indeed fare better if their government is reliably informed concerning real welfare needs. However, is improved welfare administration worth a possible loss of privacy? The pros and cons of this question were discussed in a proposal to establish a national data bank in the United States. The case for the bank was made by Carl Kaysen, director of the Institute for Advanced Studies at Princeton:

> It is becoming increasingly difficult to make informed and intelligent policy decisions on such questions in the area of poverty and welfare payments . . . simply because we lack sufficient "dis-aggregated" information—breakdowns by the many relevant social and economic variables—that is both wide in coverage and readily usable. The information the government does have is scattered among a dozen agencies, collected on a variety of not necessarily consistent bases, and not really accessible to any single group of policy-makers. . . .[14]

Who would really dare oppose a computer center that could double-check and store reliable information on the health, work, skills, education, and needs of all citizens and help to free them from want? But the other side must be heard as well. Lawrence Speiser, director of the Washington office of the American Civil Liberties Union, testifying at a Senate committee hearing on a federal data center, emphasized that "efficiency is not the only hallmark of a good government." He added:

> The establishment of a federal data center could create a machinery for the maintenance of personal dossiers on a great many Americans—a concept odious to a free society. . . . Not all the danger relates to abuse of a malicious nature by one seeking political power . . . [the data center] may be a cause of harm even in high-principled hands. . . . [The] great bulk of information is not gathered as the result of inquiries by skilled government

Document 2.2

TOWARD "1984"?

Protective Information . . . U.S. Secret Service guidelines on the types of information solicited for insertion in the computer, August 1969 . . .

(A) Information pertaining to a threat, plan or attempt by an individual, a group, or an organization to physically harm or embarrass the persons protected by the U.S. Secret Service, or any other high U.S. Government official at home or abroad.

(B) Information pertaining to individuals, groups, or organizations who have plotted, attempted, or carried out assassinations of senior officials of domestic or foreign governments.

(C) Information concerning the use of bodily harm or assassination as a political weapon. This should include training and techniques used to carry out the act.

(D) Information on persons who insist upon personally contacting high Government officials for the purpose of redress of imaginary grievances, etc.

(E) Information on any person who makes oral or written statements about high Government officials in the following categories: (1) threatening statements; (2) irrational statements, and (3) abusive statements.

(F) Information on professional gate crashers.

(G) Information pertaining to "terrorist" bombings.

(H) Information pertaining to the ownership or concealment by individuals or groups of caches of firearms, explosives, or other implements of war.

(I) Information regarding anti-American or anti-U.S. Government demonstrations in the United States or overseas.

(J) Information regarding civil disturbances.

Peter Schrag, "Dossier Dictatorship," *Saturday Review,* April 17, 1971, p. 24–25:

It does not take a long memory to recall the days when that segment of the Orwellian universe that dealt with government surveillance of private citizens and the collection of "dossiers" was largely the concern of fiction writers, students of Stalinist Russia and Nazi Germany, and a small number of others who were generally regarded as paranoids. . . .

We now know . . . that during the last generation (and more precipitously in the past three or four years) agencies of the government have created an extensive apparatus for the collection, storage, and exchange of what we once regarded as privileged information about the most intimate details of our private lives. . . .

Privacy, like clean air and water, can be polluted until none is left. Then we will have Big Brother.

THE INVASION OF PRIVACY

Ralph Nader, "The Dossier Invades the Home," *Saturday Review*, April 17, 1971, p. 18:

Hundreds of bits of information filed in dossiers on millions of individual Americans today constitute a massive assault on privacy whose ramifications are just beginning to be realized.

When you seek to borrow money, your creditor receives a file from the credit bureau to establish your "credit rating." This dossier contains all the personal facts the credit bureau can assemble—your job, salary, length of time on the present job, marital status, a list of present and past debts, and their payment history, any criminal record, any lawsuits of any kind, and any real estate you may own. The dossier may include your employer's opinion on your job performance or even your IQ rating from a high school test. By the time the creditor has finished talking to the credit bureau, he is likely to know more about your personal life than your mother-in-law does.

Arthur R. Miller, *The Assault on Privacy: Computers, Data Banks, and Dossiers* (Ann Arbor: University of Michigan Press, 1971), p. 333:

Of late lawyers and social scientists have been reaching the conclusion that the basic attribute of an effective right of privacy is the individual's ability to control the circulation of information relating to him—a power that often is essential to maintaining social relationships and personal freedom. Correlatively, when an individual is deprived of control over the spigot that governs the flow of information pertaining to him, in some measure he becomes subservient to those people and institutions that are able to manipulate it.

Carl Cohen, "The Poisonous Tree," *The Nation*, February 22, 1971:

The Omnibus Crime Control and Safe Street Act of 1968. . . . . does not "limit the constitutional power of the President to take such measures as he deems necessary to protect the Nation against actual or potential attack or other hostile acts of a foreign power, or to obtain foreign intelligence information deemed essential to the security of the United States, or to protect national security information against foreign intelligence activities. Nor shall anything contained in this chapter be deemed to limit the constitutional power of the President to take such measures as he deems necessary to protect the United States against the overthrow of the Government by force or other unlawful means, or against any other clear and present danger to the structure or existence of the Government. . . ."

Through this hole in the dike the Attorney General of the United States and his subordinates have surged, and the federal courts now face the difficult problem of restraining the zeal of law enforcers eager to tap the wires of anyone who might, by their lights, be deemed a threat to "national security." The threat, more deeply understood, is *from* the government—and the privacy of citizens is its victim.

The rub lies here. Who decides what is necessary for "national security"?

investigators. Rather, it is often acquired by government employees of poor judgment, by private agencies, credit unions, insurance companies and businesses. . . . The individual who is denied the chance of employment or some other opportunity on the basis of such information is given no chance to rebut or disprove it. . . . Once an unreliable bit of information makes its way into a file it forms an indelible mark on a person's record. . . . The computerization of such information . . . only compounds the basic abuse.[15]

The most advanced countries of Western Europe (admittedly three to five years behind the use of computerized personal data in the United States) witnessed an identical worry about the computer invasion of privacy during the seventies. All police files were computerized in socialist Sweden in 1972. In Sweden every citizen has a six-digit registration number given to him at birth and it appears on his social security, military, medical, police, tax, and motor-vehicle records. The number permits the records of different governmental agencies to be easily combined. This system is almost an invitation for abuse. The welfare state's separate files on health, family, finances and personal life can be combined to create a complete dossier on an individual from the cradle to the grave—including his hotel registrations and frequency of sexual intercourse. Sweden, Denmark and Britain have established committees to explore the problem of privacy in the computer age. Legislation was passed in France and West Germany to strengthen the citizens' rights to privacy. French doctors, for instance, noted that their patients may feel inhibited in discussing their ailments knowing that the data might be fed into computers; many patients with venereal or psychiatric diseases may avoid treatment to keep that information out of their medical records. In France laws on privacy were sharply strengthened in 1970 to protect citizens from unauthorized eavesdropping, recordings, and photographs in private places. A new bill proposed in 1972 was supposed to create an "ombudsman" of privacy (*haut-commissionaire défenseur*) to deal with complaints of citizens against invasion of privacy by computers and data banks. In West Germany a high degree of sensitivity to the "dossier-dictatorship" was acknowledged by a British civil libertarian, Andrew Martin, who addressed the Council of Europe on this subject (the *New York Times,* April 17, 1971, p. 10). He said:

> As a reaction to the whole system of Fascism, the West Germans are extremely jealous of what they call the *right of personality.* . . . In their treatment of bugging, spying, and industrial espionage, the West Germans have gone out of their way to protect privacy.

In Communist states, in addition to the ubiquitous secret police, the Communist party and mass organizations under party supervision maintain personal files on citizens from kindergarten to the grave. These profile dossiers contain hearsay reports as well as valid information about the citizen: his class background; the attitudes he has demonstrated toward communism in school and youth organizations; his record of attendance and reaction to ideological indoctrination and Russian language courses; and reports of classmates, co-workers, personal enemies and friends, and, of course, *concierges* or janitors, without whom few police establishments in the world can successfully operate. The ruling party bureaucrats in the Communist states use the contents of party dossiers to determine the career, and even the survival, of their citizens. During the short period of liberalized communism in Czechoslovakia (1967–1968) the first two instruments of socialist oppression to be eliminated were the use of party dossiers and press censorship. Both have been restored since the Soviet invasion of Czechoslovakia in August 1968.

When the Communist and Fascist systems become as computerized as the United States, totalitarian control over their subject populations will take a giant step "forward"—far beyond the present system of party files. In 1971 it was estimated that there were 5,500 to 6,000 computers in the Soviet Union, 63,000 in the United States and 24,000 in Western Europe. One American expert, Dr. Barry W. Boehm of the Rand Corporation, estimated that despite the current Soviet lag in the production and use of computers they had "the raw potential to achieve something near parity" with the United States within ten years (*New York Times*, March 14, 1971, L–4). It is worth noting that date is close to 1984.

FREEDOM OF RELIGION

Constitutions are about evenly divided between countries which have established a national church interlocked with the national government, and secular countries which constitutionally separate church and state. The countries having an established church include Protestant England[16] and the Scandinavian countries,[17] Catholic Ireland (until 1972), Spain, Portugal and most Latin American republics,[18] Orthodox Greece, Buddhist Burma,[19] Cambodia, Laos, and Ceylon (since 1972), Hindu Nepal[20] and Muslim countries from the Arab North and West Africa and the Middle East to Afghanistan,[21] Malaysia, and Pakistan in South Asia. The secular countries include the United States, France, India, and, of course, all Communist countries.

In reality the difference between religious and secular countries is less dramatic than the constitutional contrast between an established national church and separation of state and church might suggest. No national state is completely homogeneous in religion; therefore, constitutions for countries with an established church tend to pledge tolerance toward religious minorities.[22] By contrast, secular constitutions abstain from favoring any religion but pledge equal respect for all religions as well as freedom for atheist belief and action (this is so in Communist constitutions).

In the constitutional wall separating state and religion, however, many holes have been made in practice and by subsequent judicial interpretations. Churches receive official support for charitable or educational activities and religious symbols are allowed to penetrate the state's domain. In the United States, which is constitutionally secular, the sessions of the Congress which, according to the First Amendment, "shall make no law respecting an establishment of religion," open with religious invocations; actually,

> on the same day that the First Congress resolved to submit the First Amendment to the states it also adopted a resolution requesting the President to recommend to the people "a day of public thanksgiving and prayer, to be observed by acknowledging, with grateful hearts, the many signal favors of Almighty God."[23]

American coins bear the motto "In God We Trust," and the taxpayers' money is used to support directly or indirectly, religious education (e.g., transportation of children to parochial schools, use of classrooms for prayers or religious education, "secular" study of the Bible, free meals and textbooks, and released time programs that permit public school children to attend religious classes). The United States also has maintained periodic semi-diplomatic representation at the Vatican, and the armed forces have always employed and paid chaplains of major faiths.[24]

The secular Philippine Constitution authorizes service by chaplains in penal institutions, orphanages, and leprosaria. Several provisions in the secular constitution of India reflect a tender interest in Hinduism, the religion of the majority; Article 48 prohibits "the slaughter of cows and calves and other milch and draught cattle," a provision which may be considered nonneutral by the 50 million beef-eating, but not pork-eating, Muslims of India.[25]

In Italy, where the national capital is also the world center of Roman Catholicism, the delicate problem of the relationship between the Italian state and the Holy See was subject to formal agreement, the Lateran Treaty and Concordate of 1929. The treaty negotiated between Fascist Italy and the Holy See gave sovereignty to the Pope over Vatican City and its international diplomatic contacts. It also recognized ten religious festivals as national Italian holidays, gave official effect to marriages sanctioned by Catholic priests,[26] returned religious education and symbols to Italian state schools and reaffirmed the Italian Constitution of March 4, 1848, which established "the Catholic Apostolic Roman religion is the only State religion," (Article 1 of the Lateran Treaty of 1929). The new Italian Constitution of 1947 expresses the idea of mutual dependence and independence in a somewhat ambiguous way (Article 7): "The State and the Catholic Church are, each within its own orbit, independent and sovereign. Their relations are regulated by the Lateran Pacts" [whose Article 1, quoted above, makes Catholicism the state religion of Italy].

Secular constitutions of the Communist world provide interesting similarities and contrasts with the secular as well as religiously committed constitutions of the Western world. The Communist systems are committed to atheism and the ultimate elimination of religion. Similar to the practice of countries with established churches which use public funds to support those churches, atheist Communists use public funds to promote antireligion, especially within the youth movement. Religious groups are left largely to their own devices for survival and growth. Superficially this practice resembles that of countries with established Muslim, Roman Catholic, and Protestant churches where atheists and nonconformists are left to their own devices. Atheism seems to be the established church in Communist countries. In practice, of course, there is a great difference. In a free society private religious bodies may achieve reasonable independence and growth through their own private efforts. Their financing has been done by Catholics and Jews in Protestant countries, Protestants and Jews in Catholic countries, and Christians in Muslim countries. In Communist countries, however, private groups are severely handicapped not only by the general lack of freedom and by abuses of political power but also because controlled economies are inimical to private sources of funds and income. Although all Communist constitutions proclaim the separation of state and church and contain guarantees of freedom for antireligious propaganda (financed by the state) along with guarantees of religious freedom (marked for extinction), a paradox has developed. In practice, nearly all Communist systems assign modest sums from public funds to religious bodies and make their ministers and priests dependent on the Communist treasury for salaries and other organizational needs. Some newer Communist constitutions actually authorize state aid to religion. The Yugoslav Constitution (Article 46) states, for instance, that "the social community may give material assistance to the religious communities" which also have the right "to ownership to real estate within the limits determined by federal law."

BELIEF & PRACTICE

So long as religious beliefs remain a matter of private thought and feeling no constitutional problems seem to arise. But when a creed requires, as most do, action on the part of its adherents, the citizen finds himself torn between his duty to obey the dictates of his religion and conscience, on one hand, and the duty to obey public law, on the other. His dilemma can rarely be solved by following the Biblical fiat: render therefore unto Caesar the things which are Caesar's; and unto God the things that are God's. For instance, should a Muslim work without interruption as required by the National Modernization Plan or should he stop working during the feast of Ramadan, as required by the Koran? If he does the latter he would jeopardize the plan's timetable and targets. This was an acute problem in Tunisia. The issue of religious holidays versus modern life divides secular modernizers and orthodox Jews in Israel over such questions as: should businesses be operated on the Sabbath?

In Zaire a similar conflict affected African Catholics in 1972. There the secular constitution was interpreted by the ruling People's Revolutionary Movement under President Mobutu to be an authorization for eliminating those Roman Catholic practices in conflict with the government's campaign to restore an African identity. The movement had already changed the name of the Congo, a former Belgian colony, to the ancient African name of Zaire and President Mobutu abandoned his Christian name Joseph Désiré in favor of Mobutu Sese Seko. Under a new law the movement made Catholic priests liable to criminal prosecution if they refused to give authentic Zairian names to children at baptism and instead insisted on giving children names of Roman Catholic saints. Those Zairians who found their Catholic faith compatible with negritude were left with no freedom of religious choice.

Practically all constitutions that guarantee freedom of faith and creed differentiate between *belief* (which is considered absolute), and *practice* (which is considered subordinate to other societal values). Typically, the Egyptian Constitution proclaims (Article 34) that "freedom of belief is absolute," but holds that the practice of religion is quite relative. Religion is protected "provided that it does not infringe upon public order or conflict with morality." The Swiss Constitution of 1848 similarly guarantees "the freedom of worship within the limits compatible with public order and morality," but proscribes kosher killing,[27] the Order of the Jesuits,[28] and the founding or reestablishment of any Catholic orders in Switzerland. Here, as in Zaire, the issue seems to be the protection of national sovereignty and unity against possible interference by internationally organized religious bodies.

Public order, public health, and morality, broadly interpreted, are usually invoked by constitutions and subsequent constitutional practices to limit the guaranteed freedom of worship. Thus, members of religious groups are nowhere permitted to refuse to pay taxes, no matter how strong their invocations of an Anti-Tax Divinity. No religious group is allowed to praise God by human sacrifice, or impose suicide on widows as used to be done in India, or practice polygamy in non-Muslim countries, or, in the words of the Swiss Constitution, to "bleed slaughter animals which have not been previously stunned."

The First Amendment to the United States Constitution states: "Congress shall make no law prohibiting the free exercise" of religion. There seems to be no qualification, yet, in practice, controversies and conflicts between the constitutional guarantee of the free exercise of religion and other societal values have been quite numerous. They have arisen over the Mormon practice of polygamy in the territory of Utah, the Jehovah's Witnesses' refusal to salute the American flag (a symbol of the Evil One to that religious sect), the Christian Scientists' refusal to have their children vaccinated, and Sunday closing laws passed to provide a common day of rest even though Sunday is not observed as the sabbath day by several religious groups.

In 1972 the United States Supreme Court ruled seven to zero (*Wisconsin* v. *Yoder,* May 15, 1972) that the free exercise of the Amish religion (a strict sect of followers of the Swiss Mennonite bishop Amman that settled in America) included the right of the parents to disobey the state compulsory laws that required all children to attend school beyond the eighth grade. The Amish parents in Wisconsin objected to public education beyond the eighth grade since they believed public schools taught the theory of evolution and conditioned children for highly competitive participation in a modern industrial society. These teachings were at odds with the God-fearing traditions and Spartan pattern of rural life of the Amish community. Parents also objected strongly to the public school requirement that shorts be worn in physical education classes. One of the seven judges, Justice William O. Douglas, raised the issue that the children's own preferences and aspirations should have been probed in addition to their parents' belief in the Amish basic dogma: "Be not conformed to this world." Tyranny exercised by parental authority may be as stultifying as that exercised by principals and teachers in public schools.

The citizen's deep-felt obligation to follow the religious commandment "Thou Shalt Not Kill," and a military command to kill the enemies of the nation results in a soul-devastating conflict between religious conviction and patriotic duty. Most national constitutions answer the question of "God or Caesar?" with no reservation: Caesar is invariably endowed with a divine halo. For example, Catholic Italy's Constitution of 1947 (Article 42), the United Arab Republic's Constitution of 1964 (Article 43), and the Soviet Constitution of 1936 (Article 133) and many other Communist constitutions proclaim in identical "constitutionalese" that: "To defend the motherland is the *sacred* duty of every citizen." (Italics added.) The term "sacred" is readily explained and understood when used in Christian and Muslim constitutions in reference to national defense. It is more difficult to explain the consistent use of the identical adjective, sacred, (*svyashchennyi* in Russian) in nearly all Communist constitutions. A pacifist, a Gandhian conscientious objector, or a person who truly believes in the Sermon on the Mount all experience great difficulty in rendering unto God what is God's—whenever the national constitution declares that the duty to fight is a sacred obligation.

Only West Germany among major nations has a specific constitutional provision protecting conscientious objectors (Article 4/3): "No one may be compelled against his conscience to render war service as an armed combatant." This unique constitutional assumption of individual responsibility reflects the liberal traditions of Weimar Germany (established after World War I), and the philosophy of the Nuremberg War Crimes Trial after World War II, which held that international crimes are committed by men and not by states as abstract entities, and that individuals should be held responsible for violations of international norms even when they obey their own national law.

It was not anticipated that relatives of prominent Nazi war criminals might invoke Article 4 to refuse service in the West German contingent of the Allied Armies. In 1959, Wolf Rudiger Hess, the son of Hitler's aide, Rudolf Hess, who was condemned by the Allies to life imprisonment, objected to being drafted:

> My conscience forbids me to serve in the West German Army and so serve those [Americans, English, and French] who judged and condemned my father at Nuremberg. Moreover, in performing military service which might be construed as aiding in the preparation for a next war, I might some day suffer the same unpleasant consequences that my father did.[29]

In contrast to the West German Constitution there is no explicit provision for conscientious objectors in the United States Constitution, which was enacted only thirteen years after a successful war of independence. There are several very clear constitutional provisions which subordinate individual freedom to the national security:

> to provide for the common defense (preamble)
> to declare War, . . . raise and support Armies, . . . provide and maintain a Navy, . . . provide for calling the Militia to execute the Laws of the Union,

suppress insurrections and repel Invasions (Congressional powers, Article I/8)

The President shall be the Commander in Chief of the Army and the Navy of the United States, and of the Militia (i.e., the national guard) of the several States (Presidential powers, Article II/2)

Nevertheless, in colonial times the states made provisions for exempting objectors from service in the militia. Congress followed the state practice and, within narrow limits, exempted persons from military duty who by reasons of religious belief were opposed to participation in wars in any form (54 *Stat.* 885, 1940). After World War II, another act of Congress (62 *Stat.* 613, 1948) interpreted the free exercise of religion in conflict with military duties to include "an individual's belief in a relationship to a Supreme Being involving duties superior to those arising from any human relation, but does not include essentially political, sociological, or philosophical views or a merely personal code." Subsequent interpretations by the courts (including the Supreme Court) confirmed the constitutionality of such exemptions. During the United States military involvement in Vietnam there has been a significant increase in the number of young men who claimed exemption on the basis of strong antiwar convictions. In 1965 the Supreme Court extended the concept of "religious objection" to include "belief in and devotion to goodness and virtue for their own sakes, and a religious [?] faith in a purely ethical creed" (380 U.S. 163). The Supreme Court sided with the objectors and tried to clarify two tests to be applied in each case. First, does the claimed ethical and nonreligious belief occupy the same place in the life of the objector as a more traditional belief in God holds in the life of one clearly qualified for exemption (such as a Quaker)? Second, does the objector sincerely believe in the pacifist doctrine he proclaims or does he simply want to evade military duty out of concern for his personal safety or comfort?

Evidently, both yardsticks pose some problems when applied to concrete cases. They are designed to solve controversies, but they may prove controversial in themselves. But, of course, that could be said about all criteria of complex human motivations and behavior.

EQUALITY[30]

The right to equality asserted in the French Declaration of 1789, (see Document A.4, point 1), is mentioned in nearly all constitutions. The emphasis is on equal *rights,* since men obviously are not equal in intelligence, skill, and background. Men also readily accept inequality in hierarchially organized institutions such as political parties, the armed forces, bureaucracies, industry, and educational establishments. The right to an equal share in economic and social progress will be analyzed in greater detail in chapter 3. This chapter is primarily concerned with equality defined as freedom from inferior-superior relationships not based on consent. Such relationships may be sanctioned by constitutional texts or they may exist extraconstitutionally.

A very few constitutions openly deny the validity of the egalitarian claim of 1789. Examples of that denial are found in many hereditary monarchical systems (hereditary privilege denies equality by definition) in which a hereditary aristocracy is combined with imperial (e.g., Ethiopia), royal, or ducal (e.g., Luxembourg) institutions. Japan is an exception wherein there is a monarchy without an aristocracy—the

Drawing by Weber; © 1968 The New Yorker Magazine, Inc.

"If you hold those truths to be so self-evident, how come you keep harping on them?"

hereditary imperial dynasty was retained but the peerage was eliminated by the United States occupational authority after World War II.
The Japanese Constitution of 1949 states:

> The Emperor shall be the symbol of the State and of the unity of the
> people, deriving his position from the will of the people with whom resides
> sovereign power (Article 1).
> The Imperial Throne shall be dynastic and succeeded to in accordance
> with the Imperial House Law passed by the Diet (Article 2).
> Peers and peerage shall not be recognized. No privilege shall accompany
> any award of honor, decoration, nor shall any such award be valid beyond
> the lifetime of the individual who now holds or hereafter may receive it
> (Article 14).

In Great Britain the old aristocracy is still an important status group.
Every year new lords, or at least knighted or bemedaled individuals, are
added to an aristocratic list dating back to Saxon and Norman times. In
June 1965, the Queen's Birthday Honors List contained the names of
George Harrison, Paul McCartney, Ringo Starr, and John Lennon—the
Beatles. They were honored by being made Members of the British
Empire (the Empire is non-existent) as a public reward for their rock
singing which produced a hard-currency-earning international tri-
umph.[31] Britain thus flexibly combines the old aristocracy with honors
"based upon public utility" (in the words of the French Declaration of
1789). The Communist countries similarly bestow annual honors, titles,
and medals on Lenin Prize winners, Artists of the Nation, Actors, Writers, Poets Laureate, and Socialist Heroes of Labor. It is too early to
determine whether the progeny of this new socialist nobility will benefit
from the status of their parents.

MINORITY RIGHTS

The recognition of superiority and privilege based on aristocratic birth or socialist award is matched, all too frequently, by the
imposition of inferiority in law and in practice because of birthplace,
ethnic origin, race, religion, and caste (in India and Pakistan). National
constitutions usually prohibit discriminatory practices based on these
criteria. In addition, the drafters of modern national constitutions have
tried to remove the many legal and economic discriminations against
women. The purpose of such constitutional interdictions is not to obliterate different skin colors, differences between sexes, or differences in
religious belief and ethnic origin—that would be impossible. Rather, the
purpose is to eliminate discrimination based on those differences.

The Indian Constitution did not abolish the hierarchical caste system which divides Hindus into groups distinctly classified in terms of prestige, severity of rituals, degree of self-government, occupational specializations, and, above all, into groups distinguished by their assumed proximity to the gods. The Indian Constitution does ban political, economic and legal privileges or disadvantages arising from a citizen's birth into a particular caste. Only those 65 million untouchables held at the bottom of Hindu society by religious rules were freed by the constitution from the extreme inequalities of the caste system. The constitution (Article 17) proclaims the "enforcement of any disability arising out of untouchability a criminal offense." Article 15 further stipulates:

> No citizen shall, on grounds only of religion, race, caste, sex, place of birth or any of them, be subject to any disability, liability, restriction or condition with regard to—
> (a) access to shops, public restaurants, hotels and places of public entertainment; or
> (b) the use of wells, tanks, bathing ghats, roads and places of public resort maintained wholly or partly out of State funds dedicated to the use of the general public.

In the United States the Civil War Amendments (13, 14, and 15) were supposed to abolish discriminatory practices based on race and skin color. The Fourteenth Amendment (1868) stipulated that no state can "deprive any person of life, liberty, or property, without due process of law, nor deny to any person within its jurisdiction the equal protection of the laws." The Fifteenth Amendment (1870) promised that the right to vote "shall not be denied or abridged by the United States or by any State on account of race, color, or previous condition of servitude."

These amendments remained unimplemented in several sectors of the country for too many years. In 1896, the Supreme Court held *(Plessy* v. *Ferguson)* that state-imposed segregation was not discrimination if Negroes were provided with separate but equal facilities. It wasn't until 1954 that a Supreme Court ruling *(Brown* v. *Board of Education of Topeka)* reversed the "separate but equal" doctrine and proclaimed segregation of the races to be inherently discriminatory. The Fifteenth Amendment (which gave Negroes the vote) was not fully implemented until 1965, when Congress passed the Voting Rights Act, which permits the federal government to send agents to enroll voters and supervise the regularity of electoral processes if a state or local situation warrants it.

Today, most national constitutions prohibit discriminatory practices based on race,[32] ethnic origin, religion, and sex (the concluding section on "Status of Women" in this chapter will return to the problem of women's equality in greater detail). A prohibition of discrimination is only one of several possible legal devices to assure citizens of their right to equality. Another device is a constitutional pledge of special favors to underprivileged groups. The purpose of these special advantages is either to permit those groups to catch up with the rest and become undistinguishable from the whole or, on the contrary, to become equal by preserving, with official help, their cherished religious, ethnic, linguistic, and racial differences.

INDIVIDUAL OR COLLECTIVE RIGHTS?

When a constitution contains a bill of rights that guarantees freedom and equality to the individual, is it necessary to add pledges of collective group rights? It is for two reasons: first, the concept of liberty and equality includes the right to be *collectively free and equal.* The individual satisfaction derived from a feeling of belonging to a respected group and identifying with its collective sense of dignity may be viewed as part of the "pursuit of happiness." Second, the guarantee of collective rights is additional protection against the splitting of a society into a permanent majority aligned against a selected minority to make it collectively and individually unfree and unequal.

In summary: the right to be equal and free includes the right to assimilate and integrate as well as the right to be equal *and* separate. The status of being equal and separate is discriminatory when that status is imposed by a ruling group, but that status is not discriminatory if it is desired by a minority—self-segregation is also a basic right. Evidently the American motto "separate but equal" has changed. It is no longer a rallying cry for the advocates of discrimination. It is now often invoked by the critics of past discrimination and proponents of black and Hispanic separatism.

When discrimination and injustice are applied collectively to self-sustaining groups living in compact areas it necessarily evokes strong collective responses. Deep feelings of unity, whether racial, ethnic, or religious in origin, are usually coupled with a desire to translate the group's alienation and despair into territorial secession and independent statehood or, at least, into territorial self-government in a federal or confederal framework.

Alienated groups have always tended to exercise the right of national self-determination by secession from *foreign* governments, i.e., governments that are either ethnically foreign and therefore unjust, or unjust and therefore foreign. Thomas Jefferson's succinct and elegant Declaration of Independence (Document 2.4) transmitted precisely that message to England.[33] The arguments used by English colonists against

England were later invoked by the Southern Confederacy against the North when the South determined "it became necessary to dissolve the political bonds which connected them with another." The words of the Declaration of 1776 were repeated almost *verbatim* in a different context in 1847 in the Liberian Declaration of Independence (Document 2.5). The American Declaration of Independence is still the model and the document most often quoted by groups in Europe, Asia, Africa, and Latin America fighting inequality by seeking separation from existing territorial and constitutional frameworks, i.e., by invoking their right to be politically and territorially independent.

The desire of a territorial-ethnic group for recognition of a separate identity and destiny is also frequently sought through constitutional grants of territorial self-rule to various ethnic, racial, or lingual components within federal systems, i.e., through a federal polyethnic formula.[34] Federal India, Switzerland, Yugoslavia, Pakistan (before the secession of Bangladesh in 1972) and Czechoslovakia (since 1968) have all experienced this approach. The federal Soviet Constitution of 1936, as amended in 1944, grants the major territorial-ethnic components of the Union—the fifteen union republics—the right of secession (on paper only, of course); the right to establish their own military formations (on paper only); and the right to conduct their own foreign relations. Two of the fifteen republics of the Soviet Union (Ukraine and Byelorussia) have acquired, at least symbolically, a partial international status on this basis by becoming members of the United Nations in 1945. The Soviet Union is, of course, also a member. Thus the Soviet Union has become the only nation with three votes in the world organization: as a great power the Soviet Union has the right to veto in the Security Council, while its two component republics, the Soviet Ukraine and Soviet Byelorussia, have the status of all the other members of the United Nations which are not great powers.

Federal polyethnic solutions evidently presuppose that ethnic, racial, and lingual groups claiming constitutional recognition and territorial autonomy constitute *territorial communities*, i.e., they are compact groups living within geographically delineated areas.

In the case of oppressed minorities living in *dispersed* areas with no realistic claim that their widely separated living spaces are independent or autonomous national territories, two remedies have been tried. The first remedy is *migration* to new, more politically hospitable territories which are then transformed into territorial nation-states. Migration is a "secession" of sorts in which the people, but not a territory, secede from the existing framework. Liberia and Israel are examples.

The second remedy is *coexistence* based on a promise and the eventual realization of equality. Coexistence is a non-territorial solution which requires difficult and substantial concessions on the part of ruling groups which have caused inequality and oppression in the first place. Such concessions are infrequently obtained by appeals to the good will and self-interest of the ruling groups. More often they are obtained through reasoned persuasion coupled with intimidation or violence—the latter have often proved most effective on a short-term basis.

ISRAEL & LIBERIA

The cases of Liberia (founded in 1847) and of Israel (founded in 1947) provide an interesting comparison of the efforts made by two dispersed minorities (black Americans and the Jews) in seeking to remedy discrimination and inequality. The comparison reveals certain striking parallels and significant differences. All three major solutions were tried: assimilation (integration), coexistence and equality on the basis of separation (self-segregation) and migration to a "new" territory. Actually, the "new" territory was the home of origin for each, Canaan in the case of the Jews, and the African continent in the case of the American blacks. None of the three remedies elicited total support from either of the two dispersed minority groups. The leaders and members of both groups have continued a controversy over the choice of one of the three variants to the present day.

The response of the Jews, who had been dispersed all over the world, to discrimination and injustice resulted in a strong sense of group identity and unity, especially when assimilation proved unacceptable to many Jews as well as gentiles in many parts of the world. After World War I, the Zionist dream of a national state, i.e., a return *en masse* to the former home territory, and the Nazi program of mass extermination of all Jews combined to transform the dispersed Jewish minority into a unified modern nation, the state of Israel. Nevertheless, a majority of Jews refused physically to join the new nation. Some preferred assimilation in other states, others adhered to their orthodox religious beliefs in dispersion and opposed Zionism. A great many supported Israel emotionally, financially, and politically, but continued lives and careers in relatively tolerant countries. The United States is still the home of the largest Jewish community in the world (6 million, double the population of Israel). In 1972 Rabbi Meir Kahane, representative of an extremist minority, and chairman of the Jewish Defense League, called for an "immediate mass migration to Israel." His article in the *New York Times*

Document 2.4

THE AMERICAN DECLARATION OF INDEPENDENCE,
July 4, 1776

When in the Course of human events, it becomes necessary for one people to dissolve the political bands which have connected them with another, and to assume among the Powers of the earth, the separate and equal station to which the Laws of Nature and Nature's God entitle them, a decent respect to the opinions of mankind requires that they should declare the causes which impel them to the separation.

We hold these truths to be self-evident, that all men are created equal, that they are endowed by their Creator with certain unalienable Rights, that among these are Life, Liberty and the pursuit of Happiness. That to secure these rights, Governments are instituted among Men, deriving their just powers from the consent of the governed, That whenever any Form of Government becomes destructive of these ends, it is the Right of the People to alter or to abolish it, and to institute new Government, laying its foundation on such principles and organizing its powers in such form, as to them shall seem most likely to effect their Safety and Happiness. . . . when a long train of abuses and usurpations, pursuing invariably the same Object evinces a design to reduce them under absolute Despotism, it is their right, it is their duty, to throw off such Government, and to provide new Guards for their future security.—Such has been the patient sufferance of these Colonies; and such is now the necessity which constrains them to alter their former Systems of Government. The history of the present King of Great Britain is a history of repeated injuries and usurpations, all having in direct object the establishment of an absolute Tyranny over these States. To prove this, let Facts be submitted to a candid world. . . .

[The King] has combined with others to subject us to a jurisdiction foreign to our constitution, and unacknowledged by our laws; giving his Assent to their Acts of pretended Legislation. . . .

For imposing taxes on us without our Consent. . . .

In every stage of these Oppressions We have Petitioned for Redress in the most humble terms: Our repeated Petitions have been answered only by repeated injury. A Prince, whose character is thus marked by every act which may define a Tyrant, is unfit to be the ruler of a free People. . . .

(May 26, 1972) argued that there was a latent anti-Semitism in the United States which could be awakened by an economic and social crisis that was shaking the foundations of American society. He said:

For the first time in a quarter century large numbers of people face the loss of the good life they have known for so long. Such people are dangerous for they will not come to terms with poverty after having tasted the good life for decades. They will sooner turn to demagogues and racists who will

Document 2.5

THE LIBERIAN DECLARATION OF INDEPENDENCE,
July 26, 1847

While announcing to the nations of the world the new position which the people of this Republic have felt themselves called upon to assume, courtesy to their opinion seems to demand a brief accompanying statement of the causes which induced them, first to expatriate themselves from the land of their nativity and to form settlements on this barbarous coast, and now to organize their government by the assumption of a sovereign and independent character. Therefore we respectfully ask their attention to the following facts.

We recognize in all men, certain natural and inalienable rights: among these are life, liberty, and the right to acquire, possess, enjoy and defend property. By practice and consent of men in all ages, some system or form of government is proven to be necessary to exercise, enjoy and secure those rights; and every people have the right to institute a government, and to choose and adopt that system or form of it, which in their opinion will most effectually accomplish these objects, and secure their happiness, which does not interfere with the just rights of others. The right therefore to institute government and all the powers necessary to conduct it, is an inalienable right, and cannot be resisted without the grossest injustice. . . .

In assuming the momentous responsibilities of the position they have taken, the people of the Republic feel justified by the necessities of the case, and with this conviction they throw themselves with confidence upon the candid consideration of the civilized world.

We the people of the Republic of Liberia were originally the inhabitants of the United States of America. In some parts of that country, we were debarred by law from all the rights and privileges of men—in other parts, public sentiment, more powerful than law, frowned us down. We were everywhere shut out from all civil office. We were excluded from all participation in the government. We were taxed without our consent. We were compelled to contribute to the resources of a country which gave us no protection.

We were made a separate and distinct class, and against us every avenue to improvement was effectually closed. Strangers from all lands of a color different from ours, were preferred before us. We uttered our complaints, but they were unattended to, or only met by alleging the peculiar institutions of the country. . . .

---

promise them the good life in return for their liberties, and at the price of the scapegoat—the Jew. . . . Today, not tomorrow, is the time to call for an emergency conference of American Jewish communities and organizations to plan a massive organized propaganda campaign to explain the threat to the American Jewish future, and to plan for a practical mass aliyah to the land of Israel.

Rabbi Kahane's controversial appeal led to a situation similar to the dilemma which confronted American blacks in choosing between integration, a separate existence within the United States, or emigration as a solution to discrimination and inequality.

In the first half of the nineteenth century, for instance, several black leaders in the United States advocated return to Africa and the creation of a free black state. Although their efforts did not lead to a mass exodus, a sufficient number of freed slaves were anxious to return to Africa and the result was the Republic of Liberia. The Liberian Declaration of Independence (i.e. the liberation from inequality and discrimination in the United States by migration) was proclaimed in Monrovia on July 26, 1847 (see Document 2.5).

The obvious similarity between the American and Liberian Declarations of Independence was deliberate, understandable—and ironic. (The Liberian Declaration of Independence is followed by Document 2.6 which reproduces portions of the Black Declaration of Independence of July 4, 1970, prepared and publicized by the National Committee of Black Churchmen. Since the black aspirations in the United States lack a *clear* territorial dimension, the declaration calls for freedom and independence "from the injustice, exploitative control, institutionalized violence and racism of white America.") There are, of course, significant differences. The American document of 1776 charged George III as the main villain. In the Liberian document the gap between the promise of the American Declaration of Independence and the constitution, on the one hand, and the realities of slavery and discrimination, on the other, was the target. (Jefferson's first draft of the Declaration of Independence contained an attack on slavery which was omitted from the final draft.) According to the Liberian Declaration "The anti-Negro political sentiment" proved "more powerful than law," and all hope for a favorable change in America was "wholly extinguished in our bosoms." The disillusionment of the freed slaves with the American reality did not prevent Liberian leaders, helped by American white philanthropy, from naming their nation's capital after the American President Monroe—Monrovia.

Free Negroes decided to purchase a new country from native tribes on the west coast of Africa as an asylum from "deep degradation." The native tribes realized too late the full implication of the sale of their lands to the Americo-Liberians. The early record of the Liberian Republic unfortunately shows that oppression and discrimination are indeed color-blind. American black settlers and their descendants openly discriminated against the backward native tribes in government, employment, and social relations for a long time. As a consequence, "The tribal

Document 2.6

DECLARATION OF BLACK INDEPENDENCE,
July 4, 1970

When in the course of Human Events, it becomes necessary for a People who were stolen from the lands of their Fathers, transported under the most ruthless and brutal circumstances 5,000 miles to a strange land, sold into dehumanizing slavery, emasculated, subjugated, exploited and discriminated against for 351 years, to call, with finality, a halt to such indignities and genocidal practices—by virtue of the Laws of Nations and of Nature's God, a decent respect to the Opinions of Mankind requires that they should declare their just grievances and the urgent and necessary redress thereof.

We hold these truths to be self-evident, that all Men are not *only* created equal and endowed by their Creator with certain unalienable rights among which are Life, Liberty, and the Pursuit of Happiness, but that when this equality and these rights are deliberately and consistently refused, withheld or abnegated, men are bound by self-respect and honor to rise up in righteous indignation to secure them. Whenever any Form of Government, or any variety of established traditions and systems of Majority becomes destructive of Freedom and of legitimate Human Rights, it is the Right of the Minorities to use every necessary and accessible means to protest and to disrupt the machinery of Oppression, and so to bring such general distress and discomfort upon the oppressor as to the offended Minorities shall seem most appropriate and most likely to effect a proper adjustment of the society.

Prudence, indeed, will dictate that such bold tactics should not be initiated for light and transient Causes; and, accordingly, the Experience of White America has been that the descendants of the African citizens transported to the shores of the Caribbean Islands, as slaves, have been patient long past what can be expected of any human beings so affronted. But when a long train of Abuses and Violence, pursuing invariably the same Object, manifests a Design to reduce them under Absolute Racist Domination and Injustice, it is their Duty radically to confront such Government or system of traditions, and to provide, under the aegis of Legitimate Minority Power and Self Determination, for their present Relief and future Security. . . .

We, therefore, the Black People of the United States of America, in all parts of this Nation, . . . Solemnly Publish and Declare that we shall be, and of Right ought to be, FREE AND INDEPENDENT FROM THE INJUSTICE, EXPLOITATIVE CONTROL, INSTITUTIONALIZED VIOLENCE AND RACISM OF WHITE AMERICA, that unless we receive full Redress and Relief from these Inhumanities we will move to renounce all Allegiance to this Nation, and will refuse, in every way, to cooperate with the Evil which is perpetrated upon ourselves and our Communities. And for the support of this Declaration, with a firm Reliance on the Protection of divine Providence, we mutually pledge to each other our Lives, our Fortunes, and our sacred Honor.

people regard themselves as Bassa or Kpelle rather than Liberians."[35] All twenty presidents of Liberia have been Americo-Liberians. The Liberian theme of integration and unification became policy after World War II. That policy was reflected in the speeches of the two last presidents, William V. S. Tubman (who died in 1971 after 27 years in office) and his successor, William R. Tolbert Jr. Incidentally, Tolbert is the first president of Liberia who speaks a tribal language (Kpelle) in addition to his mother tongue, English. One of his early statements on the subject of unification between the Americo-Liberians and the aborigines clearly indicated that unification was meant as a process by which the tribes were to absorb Americo-Liberian values and way of life: "The masses of our people must be raised from the mats on the floor to a mattress on every bed."

Some of the internal conflicts and friction experienced in Liberia recall similar problems in Israel that have divided European Jews from the Jewish groups of Asia and Africa. A symptomatic complaint against an alleged concentration of power in the hands of East European Jews (Ashkenazim) and a demand for a better representation of Sephardic-Oriental Jews was voiced in a letter to the *New York Times* (August 16, 1972). The letter written by Dr. Joseph A. Hasson argued, for instance, that

> Ninety percent of important positions in government, the military, the Histadruth [Israel's major labor union], the Jewish Agency, and industry are filled by Ashkenazim, or children of parents born within a 600-mile radius of the Minsk-Pinsk area of East Europe. . . . In education, the drop-out rate among Sephardim is high; while they constitute 67 percent of the primary school population, they represent only 4 percent of university graduates. The consequence is the evolution in Israel of a caste-class-social order with Sephardim relegated to the unskilled, menial tasks.

Despite the obvious parallels there are additional differences that distinguish the rise and growth of Jewish from black nationalism. The Afro-Americans lacked the dynamic messianic religion of the Jewish people with its clear territorial focus on a promised land. A relatively small number of twentieth-century American blacks seem thrilled by the prospect of returning to Africa to build another Liberia, or a black "Israel." Other territorial alternatives, i.e., migrations to Canada, Mexico, Haiti, or other Caribbean territories appear even less attractive. To many observers these solutions are unrealistic since no country appears willing to open its doors to millions of immigrants. Besides, the blacks who have the skills and resources most needed to build a new nation have generally been those least attracted to such a program.[36]

A somewhat more attractive alternative to some groups is the creation of a uniracial black state to be carved from the territorial area of the United States. One such plan would combine Mississippi, Louisiana, Alabama, Georgia and South Carolina into a black American nation. Others would prefer the territory of California and Oregon. The idea of a black American State was once backed by the Communist party and the Black Muslims and later by the movement called the Republic of New Africa.[37] This plan does not consider the problems involved in inducing the United States government to provide financial support and, in a sense, pay for its own destruction. These plans also leave unclear the proposed status of whites in the black territory or that of blacks who might choose to remain in white territories.

DISPERSED GROUPS & QUOTA SYSTEMS

There is a wide range of constitutional answers to the problem of recognizing the rights of dispersed minorities. They range from the simple verbal recognition of the existence of separate though dispersed ethnic, racial, or religious groups to specific promises and privileges which may include: use of a minority language in schools, courts, and mass media (see below); grants of land (e.g., given to Indian groups in Latin America); and guarantees of participation in the decision-making process by means of communal controls or quota representation in local and national government.

The purpose of all these pledges or privileges is to satisfy the desire of the group for protection against assimilation and integration.

The drafters of such provisions are possibly uncertain whether the goal of constitutional privileges should be to preserve separation or to prepare the ground for integration after communities have coexisted for a long time as equal but separate partners. The drafters of the modern Venezuelan Constitution of 1961, for example, clearly hoped that the special privileges granted the Indian communities would result in "their progressive incorporation into the life of the Nation " (Article 77). The core of the problem is that special privileges may indeed prepare and condition a minority for assimilation, but they may also perpetuate ethnic or linguistic differences. The experience of India, Ceylon and a few other countries that have experimented with proportional communal systems illustrates that problem. The communal or quota system of representation is a constitutional arrangement that assures minority representation in the legislative and executive branches of government on the basis of the minority's percentage of the country's population.

This system was introduced into India by the Morley-Minto reforms in the British-Indian "constitution" of 1909. The reforms were occasioned by the Muslim fear of democracy, which might result in rule by an intolerant Hindu majority. The Muslim spokesman, Aga Khan III, accordingly asked the Viceroy of India, Lord Minto, for separate

Muslim electorates "commensurate not only with their numerical strength but also with their practical importance and the value of the contribution which they make to the defence of the Empire," an allusion to martial qualities of Indian Muslims in contrast to the nonmilitary characteristics of the Hindu majority. The Aga Khan also invoked the past glory of the Muslim Moghul empire when the Muslims dominated India and which the modern Hindu majority was expected to avenge.

In addition to the introduction of separate electorates for Hindus and Muslims in 1909, the British also proposed (in 1931) a separate electorate for untouchables, a possible overrepresentation, and, at least, the reservation of seats for untouchables inside the Hindu bloc of Indian legislatures. Gandhi opposed communal systems because he felt they would perpetuate India's internal divisions. In a letter to the British Prime Minister MacDonald, written in Yeravda prison, Gandhi argued:

> The mere fact of the Depressed Classes having double votes does not protect them or Hindu society from being disrupted. . . . I should not be against even overrepresentation of the Depressed Classes. What I am against is their statutory separation, even in a limited form, from the Hindu fold so long as they choose to belong to it.[38]

Gandhi opposed the principle of communalism in 1932 by taking a six-day fast which resulted in the Yeravda Pact. That complex compromise was negotiated by representatives of caste Hindus and the untouchables, and agreed to by the British. The "Epic Fast," as it came to be called, marked the beginning of the very slow process of improving the conditions of life for untouchables, (They are now called Children of God—*Harijans*—a term coined by Gandhi.)

The British cannot escape the charge that the communal system enfranchised Indians as members of their respective communities rather than as citizens of an indivisible Indian nation. The system was another colonialist device to "divide and rule." It certainly favored pro-British, non-Hindu groups such as the Muslims, Anglo-Indians, and Christians. Nevertheless, it is difficult, if not impossible, to adopt majoritarian solutions when the majority and the minority both refuse to create a consensual community. If each views the other as an unfriendly nation living within a common state framework, if there are no constitutional or other legal protections of the minority's collective rights, integration becomes impossible. Even with guarantees integration may prove impossible, since the privileges granted minorities may perpetuate their separate status and vested interests.[39]

After condemning the British communal system, independent India ironically introduced one of its own to protect underdeveloped and underprivileged (i.e., "Scheduled") tribes and castes. The constitutional protection was also intended to include the Anglo-Indian community.

Seats shall be reserved in the House of the People for the Scheduled Castes; and the Scheduled Tribes (Article 330).

. . . [T]he provisions of this Constitution relating to (a) the reservation of seats of the Scheduled Castes and Scheduled Tribes . . . and the representation of the Anglo-Indian community . . . shall cease on the expiration of a period of twenty years . . . (Article 334).[40]

As a result, 76 of 500 seats in the lower house of the Indian Parliament are reserved for untouchables. The few additional untouchables usually elected on unreserved seats are a modest symbol of change and promise. Roughly 12½ percent of the jobs in the civil service were assigned to qualified untouchables and special educational and economic aid was granted them—free tuition, scholarships, books, and in some cases, midday meals and clothing.[41]

The time limit placed on the duration of the quota system expresses the hope that at the conclusion of the prescribed period (1980) scheduled tribes and untouchables will have been fully integrated into the Indian nation.

However, reality does not always reflect constitutional hope. The granting of special privileges, assistance, and assured quota representation has had an undesirable, nonintegrative effect. It has solidified the differences between groups on new grounds. For example, some Indian Christians and Muslims have reconverted to Hinduism to revive their former lower caste status in order to enjoy the new, compensatory privileges—quota advantages and material support.

To protect the mixed group of Anglo-Indians, the constitution authorizes the president to nominate two members of parliament "if he is of the opinion that the Anglo-Indian community is not adequately represented in the House of the People" (Article 331).

A similar problem of minority representation—and its solution by a quota system—is reflected in the Indonesian Constitution. The president may make additional nominations in case the Malay majority shows a lack of tolerance and political wisdom by failing to place representatives of non-Malay minorities in eligible positions on the party electoral lists.[42]

The case of Cyprus illustrates failure of a communal system.[43] There, the numerical relation between the Greek majority and Turkish minority is roughly seven to three. The short-lived constitution (1959) of independent Cyprus provided for a presidential system with a Greek president and a Turkish vice-president; each had veto power over major laws concerning foreign affairs, defense, and security. A six-to-four ratio of Greeks and Turks was to be reflected in the composition of the Cypriot army, whereas a seven-to-three ratio was to be maintained in the police force, in Parliament, and in the cabinet, in which one of three key ministries (Defense, Finance, or Foreign Affairs) was always to be held by a Turk.

The communal system of Cyprus collapsed. In 1963, intercommunal fighting broke out when President Makarios proposed a change in the constitution that was interpreted by the Turkish community as a threat to its communal rights and the scope of its veto.

Theoretically, the proportional communal formula is logical and sound. In practice, however, it has proven disappointing for two reasons. First, communal separation is a barrier to progressive modernization programs (e.g., the fight against pollution) that often require centralized national and international planning. Highly developed systems cannot be subdivided along communal lines because they are based on an intricate economic web which cannot be disentangled without loss to both the national whole and its communal components. Second, the veto power added to communal representation must be unequivocal to assure each group's all-embracing protection. But, the veto can paralyze government as it did on Cyprus when the Turkish minority claimed the right to veto almost everything in matters vaguely defined as security. Yet, without the veto, even a six-to-five ratio of representation may not protect a minority against the tyranny of a majority when mutual hostility and suspicion continue to separate them. On the other hand, if hostility and suspicion are removed and consensus emerges proportional communal representation may no longer be necessary.

A communal proportional system in the United States intended to assure blacks of proportional participation in government would entitle the black community to roughly eleven percent of the representatives and senators in Congress. In that case political competition within the black community would determine whether black Democrats, black Republicans, black Communists, black Maoists, black Fascists, black Muslims, or black capitalists should represent blacks in national, state, and local governments. Of course, if the black community became unified in ideology and agreed on political goals and the means of achieving them, then a single all-black political party could represent it. That was the apparent hope of the National Black Convention, held on March 11, 1972, in Gary, Indiana. The convention called for an independent all-black political movement to seek a constitutional amendment which would require a minimum of 66 black representatives and 15 senators in the Congress to be elected at large by black Americans. Another aim was to obtain "proportionate black employment and control at every level of the federal government structure." The 55-page Black Political Agenda, an action program published on May 19, 1972, called for control of the black segment of the mass media and all-black schools. The all-black program logically had to condemn the integration of schools by bussing and oppose the merger of white and black colleges in the South. The agenda also demanded the right of blacks in the South to hold plebiscites to determine whether they want to secede and become part of a "republic of New Africa" or "remain under the captive sovereignty of the United States." Black communities would be permitted to become separate political entities, and, under a proposed socialistic transformation of the American economic and political system, blacks would be paid reparations out of the assets of the national economy for "the horrors of slavery and the human indignities visited upon them." The Gary agenda was subsequently repudiated by the Black Congressional Caucus and the National Association for the Advancement of Colored People.

It is debatable whether the American two-party system will be altered by adding a third black political party. In his keynote address to the convention at Gary, Richard G. Hatcher said

> I, for one, am willing to give the two major political parties one more chance in 1972. But if they fail us, a not unlikely prospect, we must then seriously probe the possibility of a third party movement in this country.[44]

That probe will certainly need to consider the fact that neither political parties nor proportional communal systems, however considerate they may be, can transform a minority into a majority. The guarantee of representation in the legislature cannot protect a minority against a tyranny by a majority. Furthermore, once established, the system of quota representation would lead to a possible demand for a quota representing Catholics, Jews, Spanish-speaking Americans, Irish-Americans, and the myriad other minority groups in the United States. The "melting pot" might well burst its communal seams.[45]

RIGHT TO ONE'S OWN LANGUAGE

The Universal Declaration of Human Rights (Article 15) declares "Everyone has the right to nationality. No one shall be arbitrarily deprived of his nationality." The nationalist is bound to see that the loss of nationality begins when the use of his native language is denied in the schools, courts, administration, legislation, mass media, and entertainment. In multilingual and multiethnic states the right to communicate in the language one knows best is an important constitutional right. The freedom of expression and the right to petition have little political value if a linguistic minority is unable to communicate with the authorities. Those groups that dread linguistic oppression, denationalization, and discrimination on the basis of linguistic difference tend to place a high priority on a linguistically separate but equal status (see Document 2.7).

Constitutions which recognize the existence of significant multilingual problems employ a variety of devices to reconcile the need for national unity and rapid communication with the desire of linguistic groups to preserve and perpetuate their identity.[46] Since total linguistic homogeneity does not exist, the identification of a "significant problem" itself may result in controversy. In unitary systems the use of a local vernacular by minorities living in a compact area is authorized by appropriate local, provincial, or national authorities. In China, for example, that commitment is included in the constitution. Another partial solution is a federal constitution that guarantees major ethnic-linguistic groups a territorially defined autonomy (as in the case of the USSR, India, Pakistan, Burma, Yugoslavia, Czechoslovakia, and with qualification in Switzerland and Canada). Polyethnic federalism assures major linguistic groups of their right to conduct ethnic business in their own tongues within autonomous boundaries. However, it does not quite determine which language will be used by the national government in conducting its business or which language the components shall use in communicating with one another. Nor does it define the differences between major groups having the right to linguistic and territorial autonomy and the minor groups lacking autonomy. In the Soviet Union there are about 50 ethnic and linguistic groups (from over 100 million Great Russians to 5,000 Mansi-Vogul people). Yet, according to the constitution, only 15 major ethnic groups have the right to be union republics with the right of secession. The other groups are given a lower form of territorial autonomy or none at all. India has more than 720 languages and dialects, 24 of them spoken by more than 100,000 people, but only 12 are recognized by the constitution as major languages to be used in addition to English and Sanskrit, the classical language of the Hindu holy scriptures. Even a federal guarantee ensuring freedom of expression in one's own language within autonomous territorial boundaries cannot avoid the need to establish a federal or official lingua franca —i.e., the language to be used by the federal government in interstate communication.

All national constitutions whether federal or unitary determine explicitly or implicitly the official national language. In some countries the

Document 2.7

LANGUAGE: THE PRIMARY INSTRUMENT OF SOCIAL COMMUNICATION

Rupert Emerson, *From Empire to Nation* (Cambridge, Mass.: Harvard, 1960), pp. 133–35:

Leaving aside the fascinating if unanswerable query as to the extent of which particular language both mirrors and fashions unique patterns of thought and thus reflects and molds a distinctive national soul, it is evident that language is the primary instrument of social communication. Those who speak the same language have an immense common bond, which also reaches back to a common store of social memories; those who do not, have a gulf of silence between them which can only be bridged by some third intermediary. Where there is linguistic diversity, schools, press, radio, speeches, literature must all employ different languages, making it far more difficult to bring the same influences to bear on all the people and creating the likelihood that the linguistic communities will look to different sets of leaders. . . .

It was one of the aims of the French Revolution to impose a central national language on all the people of France. Since that time, wherever a diversity of languages was involved, the language issue became a major concern to every nation as it came to claim its place in the sun. . . . Nationalist movements have with regularity been accompanied by a flurry of philological activity. . . . Language controversies have everywhere been a central feature of the minority problem. Not without reason national minorities have felt that if they could preserve their language much of the battle for survival was won, while the majority has been persuaded that if its own language could be brought to acceptance the backbone of resistance was close to being broken.

---

national language is self-evident and the constitution can be silent on the subject. In those cases the language of the constitution is the official language, e.g., German in Germany and Austria, Spanish in Spain and Latin American countries, English in Britain, Australia, New Zealand, and the United States. It should be noted that the Hispanic population in New York and the Chicanos in the Southwest may create a new linguistic problem in the United States. In other countries constitutions explicitly name the national language, as in the case of all the Arab countries in the Middle East and North Africa which specify Arabic. The Indonesian Constitution adopted a modernized version of the Malay language (the lingua franca of Singapore and the Indonesian ports) as its national language (*Bahasa Indonesia*). It is written in the Latin alphabet and has been placed above the 114 languages spoken in Indonesia, of which 16 are considered major. The neighboring Philippines have been less successful in phasing out the use of the European languages used during the colonial period (English and Spanish) and replacing them and the local island vernaculars with a modernized version of another Malay language, Tagalog. Israel has successfully revived and modernized ancient Hebrew,[47] which is now used as the national language.

Unlike Israel and the Arab states, many countries cannot rely on the language of their holy scriptures as a choice in certifying the constitutional right to free expression, so difficult and often painful choices are required. In those cases two or more languages may be chosen on equal footing[48] or in hierarchic order.[49] One or more languages may be made official and others described as auxiliary. Auxiliary languages may be earmarked for future official status or eventually phased out (i.e., as in the case of the official languages of colonial rulers).

The Indian Constitution established Hindi as the official federal language to be used in federal administration, the parliament, the judiciary, and official publications (see Document 2.8). English was also to be used for fifteen years (i.e., until 1965) by the federal center; by that time it was hoped that Hindi would replace English. However, the extraconstitutional facts of life prevented the constitutional pledge from being implemented. The main reasons were the opposition and bloody riots which ensued in the south, where languages unrelated to the northern Hindi are spoken. A new law, the Official Language Bill of 1967, provides that English can continue to be used as an "associate" language for official purposes by the federal authorities until its discontinuance is approved by legislatures in those states where Hindi is not the official state language and ratified by each house of Parliament.

The Indian and several other examples demonstrate that a medium of communication understandable to all is the first necessity for building and modernizing a nation. Yet, the individual's right to free expression in his own language is equally important. The conflict between nation building and respect for subnational ethnic and linguistic liberties has resulted in many political-cultural conflicts in Asia and Africa. The controversy over national languages has frequently absorbed the interest and energy of many developing nations more intensely and passionately than any other issue of modernization. In 1958, following some promises hastily made during the preceding election campaign, the government of bilingual Ceylon (Sinhalese and Tamil) enacted the "Sinhalese Only Act." Violent riots resulted, and modernization was slowed. The adoption of one official language proved to be a bloody affair inside Ceylon, although the all-Ceylonese struggle for independence from Britain was peaceful and dominantly legalistic in its procedures. In 1972 Ceylon promulgated its new socialist constitution, changed its name to Sri Lanka (meaning "Great Beautiful Island") in

Sinhalese, the official language, and severed relations with the Commonwealth. The celebration of the new national charter (May 22) was boycotted by the Tamil Federal party that represents the large lingual minority of Tamils. The boycott occurred because the new constitution decreed the official language to be Sinhalese only and not Sinhalese-and-Tamil as the Tamils had demanded.

Similarly, the issue of the national and provincial languages has plagued Pakistan since its inception. Originally, three languages were used as official: Urdu in West Pakistan, Bengali in East Pakistan, and English (to be phased out) in both provinces. In 1972, following the secession of Bangladesh, a new problem arose in West Pakistan: in one of its provinces, Sind, the legislative assembly made Sindhi the only official language of the province against the objection of Urdu-speaking people who make up about 45 percent of the province's total population of 11 million. Widespread rioting followed and at least fifty deaths were caused by this linguistic conflict. Finally, on July 15, 1972 leaders of the Sindhi and Urdu-speaking communities agreed on a formula that kept Sindhi as the official language but granted the Urdu-speaking people a period of twelve years (apparently instead of overnight) in which to learn the official language.

The selection of a national language within a multilingual community becomes, as one might expect, an important political issue. Usually, the language selected is that of the numerically or politically strongest group: the Hindi north in India, the Great Russians in the USSR, the Serbians in Yugoslavia, and the Sinhalese in Ceylon. All other groups inevitably suffer the consequences of that choice, so they resist. Aside from the psychological effects the most obvious practical disadvantage is the need for all members of the other groups to learn a second language in order to compete with the dominant group for access to political, administrative, and economic institutions. In turn, the minority groups may be forced to denationalize their children by sending them to majority-language schools. Another disadvantage that results in those countries that have been administered by a foreign power which used one of the world languages (i.e., English, French, and Spanish are used world-wide in commerce and diplomacy) is that the language of the colonial power is preferred by many minorities over the underdeveloped, unmodern language of the numerically strongest native group. This is one of the reasons the Dravidian south of India prefers English to Hindi.

The problem of language requires practical solutions yet it is emotionally explosive. It is closely connected to the anxieties and pride which characterize emotional nationalism. In that context language and

Document 2.8

HINDI, ENGLISH, OR INDIAN ENGLISH

India, 1949
Article 351. It shall be the duty of the Union to promote the spread of the Hindi language, to develop it so that it may serve as a medium of expression for all the elements of the composite culture of India and to secure its enrichment by assimilating without interfering with its genius, the forms, styles and expression used in Hindustani and in other languages specified in the Eighth Schedule,* and by drawing, wherever necessary or desirable, for its vocabulary, primarily on Sanskrit and secondarily on other languages.

Journal of Constitutional and Parliamentary Studies (New Delhi), 2:1 (January–March 1968), pp. 85–86:
Under the Constitution of India, business in Lok Sabha [House of the People] is required to be transacted in Hindi or in English, though, as a special case, a member who cannot adequately express himself in either of the two languages, may be permitted by the Speaker to address the House in his mother tongue. Never since the enactment of the Constitution did all the members of Lok Sabha know both Hindi and English and therefore whatever happened to be the floor language in the House at any time, there were always some members who, not being bilingual, could not follow the proceedings of the House. . . . On September 7, 1964 started the simultaneous interpretation of the proceedings of the House for the first time in the history of parliamentary institutions in India. The Hindi and English interpreters, seated in two separate booths in a corner of the House, listen to the proceedings through head-phones and render English speeches into Hindi and Hindi speeches into English. . . . Every seat in the House is fitted with a head-phone and a language-selector switch.**

Paul Verghese, "Indian English," *India News,*
September 4, 1970:
The concept of an Indian English is generally pooh-poohed on the grounds that it can only be bad English or *baboo* English. . . . [But] Indian English is only a variety of English whose characteristics stem from the life and culture of India. And the Indianness of it consists in its cultural overtones and undertones and not in a legalization of the ignorant misuse of English.

Perhaps the best definition of Indian English is the one given by Prof. V. K. Gokak. According to him Indian English represents 'the evolution of a distinct standard—a standard the body of which is correct English usage, but whose soul is Indian in color, thought and imagery, and, now and then, even in the evolution of an idiom which is expressive of the unique quality of the Indian mind while conforming to the "correctness" of English usage. It is illustrative of a special type of language phenomenon—a language foreign to the people who use it, but accepted by them because of political and, recently cultural reasons.'

What Prof. Gokak means is that good Indian English is simply good English, English that differs a little in vocabulary and idiom from good English as written

88

in London or New York, so that it brings out the inwardness of Indian life and culture. It rests upon the same basis as that which the standard English of Great Britain rests upon, but it reveals the Indian character and Indian life in all their glory and shame. Furthermore, Indian English establishes an Indian idiom of English as opposed to the English idiom of British English, the American idiom of American English and the Australian idiom of Australian English.***

*In addition to Hindi, English, and Sanskrit, the recognized languages are: Assamese, Bengali, Gujarati, *Kannada,* Kashmiri, *Malayalam,* Marathi, Oriya, *Tamil, Telugu* and Urdu (spoken by Muslims, related to Hindustani, but written in the Persian script). The italicized languages denote the Dravidian group in the south—languages totally unrelated to the northern languages in sound, grammar, style, and script.

**This is an improvement that shows how new technology may be of help. Nevertheless the bilingual system in the Indian Parliament still does not solve the problem of free expression when exercised by political representatives who speak only their regional languages such as Telugu (more than 10 percent of the Indian population), Tamil (more than 8 percent), or Bengali (nearly 8 percent).

***This argument is somewhat similar to the recommendation that black English and Hispanic English be recognized and taught as separate idioms in the United States. A good analysis of this subject is a book written by J. L. Dillard of the University of Puerto Rico, *Black English: Its History and Usages in the United States* (New York: Random House, 1972).

---

the right to nationality may well be valued more than any other constitutional right or liberty. In 1848 the Rumanian patriot, Nicolas Bâlescu, wrote a few lines that illustrate the nature of the problem:

> For my part, the question of nationality is more important than liberty. Liberty can be easily recovered when it is lost, but not nationality.[50]

The alleged ease of regaining lost liberty may be questioned, but the importance of language as an essential ingredient of an ethnic group's collective identity cannot be underestimated.

STATUS OF WOMEN

Most modern constitutions and their bills of rights accord women equal political and economic status. Several bills of rights add special guarantees, advantages, and privileges, such as exemption from combatant duties and the right of rest and compensation during pregnancy. Constitutions obviously cannot eliminate the natural differences between men and women but they can attempt to eradicate sexual discrimination and inequality.

The Soviet Constitution of 1936 (Article 122), for instance, accords women in the USSR equal rights with men "in all spheres of economic, government, cultural, political, and other social activity." Then the article adds special pledges to women:

> The possibility of exercising these rights is ensured by women being accorded an equal right with men to work, rest and leisure, social insurance and education, and by State protection of the interests of mother and child, State aid to mothers of large families and unmarried mothers, maternity leaves with full pay, and the provision of a wide network of maternity homes, nurseries, and kindergartens.

The Polish Constitution of 1952 (Article 66) echoes the Soviet Constitution and adds "the extension of a network of service establishments and restaurants and canteens" and the promise of a network of "maternity homes, creches, and nursery schools."

No doubt, the proportion of women in the Communist countries in professions and jobs that have been considered a primary domain of men in the West for a long time is relatively high. Visitors to Communist countries are usually impressed by the dominant position of women in the medical profession and by the number of women employed as streetcleaners and metal workers.

But that impression is deceptive because the decisively important domain of politics, including membership in the Communist party, is predominantly male. The proportion of women in the party hierarchy becomes progressively smaller at the top. There are, for example, no women in the Politburo, and no woman has ever been a full member of the Politburo in the Soviet Union or China. During Khrushchev's regime one woman, comrade Furtseva, was an alternate member for a short period of time.

The impact of the American women's liberation movement and its questions, arguments, and statistics started to be felt throughout the world in 1972. The impact was reflected in the *Peking Review* when the English edition propagandized China's truly significant record in liberating Chinese women from their traditional bonds. However, in the field of politics, even the Chinese record was less than impressive. The *Peking Review* wrote:

> Chairman Mao said in 1964: "Times have changed and today men and women are equal. Whatever men comrades can accomplish, women comrades can too." . . . There are women members in the Party committees and revolutionary committees at all levels, from commune to provincial level which were established during the Great Proletarian Cultural Revolution. *There are also women members on the Party's Ninth Central Committee* (italics added).[51]

The number of women on the Central Committee was not mentioned; nor was it noted that the Politburo had an exclusively male membership.

The comparative statistics of national political institutions in the Western world are neither better nor worse with regard to top-level participation by women in politics. Male chauvinism in that arena seems to be a universal phenomenon. Except for India (Indira Gandhi) and Israel (Golda Meir), no system in the Western, Communist, and Third world can boast about the role that women are permitted to play in top-level politics.

In the United States, as everywhere else, the struggle for the equal status of women began with a focus on voting rights. From that beginning the struggle has proceeded toward achieving equality for women in active politics, jobs, education, social activities, and sexual relationships.

The Nineteenth Amendment to the United States Constitution, which assured women full voting rights on a national basis, was proposed in 1919 and became effective in 1920. By the time the amendment was adopted, women already enjoyed full suffrage rights in fifteen states and Alaska, and voting rights in presidential elections in an additional fourteen states. Wyoming was the first state to extend voting rights to women in 1890. Nevertheless, it is worth noting Wyoming gave voting rights to women twenty years after the Fifteenth Amendment gave that right to black males.

After 1923 an amendment to the United States Constitution containing the sentence: "Equality of rights under the law shall not be denied or abridged by the United States or by any state on account of sex," was proposed each year. At long last, in 1973, that social-economic provision became the Twenty-seventh Amendment to the United States Constitution. The vote in the Congress (March 1972) was an impressive victory for the cause of American women: 354 to 24 in the House of Representatives, 84 to 8 in the Senate.

The amendment is expected to end sex discrimination previously sanctioned by the law and the practice of federal, state, and local governments. Among the several practices that the amendment was intended to eliminate are discriminatory entrance requirements for women at state universities; differing curricula (home economics and physical education) in public schools; differing rules for service on juries; and the laws that limit the right of married women (but not men) to sell property or engage in business without the consent of their spouses (in existence in a few states).

The list of discriminatory laws and practices which the new constitutional amendment is expected to eliminate is quite long. However, new additions to a bill of rights may change some laws and governmental practices but they cannot be expected to transform the traditional attitudes of society or its behavior overnight. A constitutional amendment can only become the focal point of a web of changed behavior and attitudes yet to be woven—especially since many women find it easier to note past inequities than to predict precisely how different the future place and role of women in society should be.

The women's liberation movement has produced a copious literature ranging from Betty Friedan's *The Feminine Mystique,* Kate Millet's *Sexual Politics,* and the English tradition of Simone de Beauvoir's *The Second Sex* to Susan Lydon's "The Politics of Orgasm" and Rubin's "Woman as a Nigger." These and other writings include extremely valuable studies as well as faddish manifestoes which will be quickly forgotten.

One valuable study, undertaken by two officials in the United States Census Bureau on the basis of 1966 figures, yielded a general picture of consistent discrimination against women in employment.[52] It showed that women in the age group from 30 to 44 who worked continuously since leaving school had much lower incomes than men of the same age, with the same education, and in the same type of jobs:

	MEN	WOMEN
Overall Median Income	$7,529	$5,818
Income by Occupation		
Professional and technical workers	$9,868	$6,705
Clerical workers	$7,006	$5,570
Skilled blue collar workers	$6,452	$3,666
Service workers	$5,778	$3,272
Income by Education		
High school diploma	$7,362	$5,500
1 to 3 years of college	$8,310	$5,608
4 years or more of college	$10,726	$6,862
Less than 4 years of high school	$5,660	$3,132

Other studies have examined male behavior and attitudes toward women; male values built into the English language; male stereotypes in the mass media; and the prevalence of male-centered stories in children's books and elementary school readers. The National Organization for Women (NOW, founded in 1966 and by the 1970s the largest and most influential women's liberation organization with over 260 chapters in 48 states), organized a task force to analyze 134 books published by fourteen major publishing companies in the United States and read in three suburban New Jersey towns. From 2,769 stories read, the following boy-and-girl and male-to-female ratios were derived:

Boy-centered to girl-centered stories	5:2
Adult male to adult female main characters	3:1
Male to female biographies	6:1
Male to female animal stories	2:1
Male to female folk or fantasy stories	4:1[53]

The study found that the stories, even those girl-centered, abounded in stereotypes. Boys were generally described as creative, brave, curious, adventurous, and ingenuous. The typical girl was usually depicted as a frilly thing with a smile on her pretty face and a passive attitude toward life.[54]

The campaign for women's equality regards the use of "Mrs." and "Miss" as discriminatory since those terms distinguish married and unmarried women—while the male "Mr." makes no such distinction. The honorific "Ms." makes no marital distinction and is widely used by women in business correspondence, and by the Republican National Committee (as noted by *Time,* March 20, 1972), and by the federal Equal Employment Opportunity Commission.

The American women's liberation movement is in the vanguard when compared to other countries of the world. It is distinguished by its awareness and systematic study of the problem as well as by the level

Drawing by Hector Breeze; reprinted by permission of *Private Eye.*

"I suppose it will happen just as women get equal pay."

of political activism it has encouraged—and by the inevitable dose of excess which characterizes many reform movements in the United States.

The Muslim countries occupy the opposing pole on a world scale. In those areas under the influence of Islam women are frequently the most underprivileged and inadequately represented group. Constitutional assertions of equality for women in the Muslim countries require a creative, in fact a revolutionary, interpretation of Islamic doctrine and practice. That fact can be especially appreciated by reading the constitution of Morocco, 1962 (Article 8) which states that "men and women enjoy equal political rights." The constitution of Pakistan, 1960 (Article 20) assured Pakistani women of a quota representation in the National Assembly as a protection against under-representation. The quota was not over-generous; six seats out of 156 were guaranteed for women in the event that Muslim males, as expected, failed to elect a female member.

In Spain the Civil Code did not allow women to leave home and live independently (i.e., without parental authorization) until their twenty-third birthday, except to get married or to enter a convent. Men were legally responsible for their acts and decisions, without reservation, at the age of twenty-one. This discriminatory clause in the Civil Code (enacted in 1889) was removed in 1972, thereby granting Spanish women legal adulthood at the age of twenty-one.

Another case deserves special mention here. Switzerland's democratic and egalitarian reputation has rarely been questioned yet voting rights were not granted women in national elections until February 8, 1971. At that time Swiss men reversed a decision made in 1959 and approved the long-debated women's suffrage amendment in a national plebiscite by 621,403 votes to 323,596. However, the status and rights of Swiss women in the economic and social life of their country was often superior to those enjoyed by women in many countries where constitutional bills of rights are quite eloquent on the subject of women's equality.

To sum up: the five freedoms discussed in this chapter—personal liberty, the right to privacy, freedom of thought, freedom of religious creed and practice, and the right to equality, including minority and women's rights—represent only a segment, however essential, of a wider network of guarantees, pledges, and assurances that constitute various bills of rights. It is difficult, if not impossible, to agree on which of these rights are primary and which are secondary. Although comparative analysis requires discussion of them one by one in separate chapters and under separate subheadings, it should be reemphasized that

Document 2.9

THE NEW EGALITARIANISM

Herbert J. Gans in "The New Egalitarianism," *Saturday Review,* May 6, 1972, p. 43. By permission. Copyright 1972 Saturday Review, Inc.:

Although the fundamental idea of the Declaration of Independence is that "all men are created equal," Americans traditionally have been more interested in life, liberty, and the pursuit of happiness than in the pursuit of equality. In the last decade, however, their interests have begun to shift, and equality may be on its way to becoming as significant as liberty in the hierarchy of American goals.

The shift began approximately on the day in 1955 when Mrs. Rosa Parks of Montgomery, Alabama, decided that she was no longer willing to sit in the rear of the bus. Much has been written about the ensuing political and social unrest; however, few observers have emphasized that the revolts of the blacks, the young, and others have a common theme: the demand for greater equality by the less than equal. Blacks have agitated for racial equality through black power; students, in high schools as well as in colleges, have demanded more power on the campus; teen-agers have begun to claim the sexual freedom now available to young adults, and in less public ways they—and even younger children— have sought more equality within the family. And, of course, many women are now demanding equality with men, and homosexuals with heterosexuals.

Similar developments have been occurring in the economy. . . . Wage workers have begun to demand guaranteed annual incomes and other privileges that salaried workers enjoy. Public employees have struck for wage equity with workers in private industry. Assembly line workers have sought better working conditions and more control over the operation of the line. Enlisted men have called for reductions in the power of officers. . . .

Few of these demands have been explicitly phrased in terms of equality; most of those making the demands have spoken of autonomy [such as community controls, consumers' and environmentalists' controls] and democracy. Many have actually asked for more liberty. Still, if all of these demands are put together, they mean more income for some and higher costs for others, more power for some and less for others. If the demands were heeded, the eventual outcome would be greater overall equality.

---

fundamental liberties and rights are simultaneously interconnected and in conflict. They are mutually dependent and reinforce each other even as they threaten and sometimes destroy each other. Albert Camus wisely noted in *The Rebel* that if absolute freedom mocks at justice, so does absolute equality mock at liberty and absolute freedom denies equality (see, in conclusion, Document 2.9).

Drawing from *Tygodnik powszechny* (Cracow), September 12, 1971.

NOTES

1 In 1951 the Economic and Social Council of the United Nations adopted Resolution 350 (XII), inviting the cooperation of the International Labor Organization in the establishment of an *ad hoc* committee whose task it was to "study the nature and extent of the problem raised by the existence in the world of systems of forced or 'corrective' labour, which are employed as a means of political coercion or punishment for holding or expressing political views, and which are on such a scale as to constitute an important element in the economy of a given country." The narrower United Nations definition of forced labor as a result of *political* coercion and the use of forced labor for major national *economic* undertakings was evidently aimed at the practices of Stalin's Russia. The result of the inquiry may be found in the U.N. publication *Report of the Ad Hoc Committee on Forced Labour* (E/2431) (Geneva: International Labour Office, 1953), p. 619.

2 Quoted by the United Nations Secretary General in his memorandum *The Suppression of Slavery,* United Nations, (ST/SOA/4), July 11, 1951, p.3. The Vienna Declaration was reaffirmed by another declaration (Verona, November 28, 1822) signed by Austria, England, France, Prussia, and Russia that described the continuing practice of slave trade as "a scourge which has too long desolated Africa, degraded Europe, and afflicted humanity." Ibid., p.4.

3 The Soviet Constitution (1936), Article 132: "Universal military service is the law. Military service in the armed forces of the USSR is an honorable duty of the citizens of the USSR."

   The Italian Constitution (1947) states in Article 52: "The defence of the country is a sacred duty of the citizen. Military service is compulsory."

4 The Constitution of Brazil (1946), Article 181, states: "No Brazilian, after reaching the minimum military service age, established by law, may hold public office or employment in any state-controlled entity, society, or mixed economy, or undertaking holding a concession for public service, without producing proof of military enlistment, or being a reservist, or of enjoying exemption from such obligation."

5 References to divorce are relatively rare in constitutional texts, since most emphasize the role of family and do not mention its possible dissolution.

The Japanese reference is the more remarkable because of its American source; at the time of the American drafting of the Japanese Constitution the United States, with the exception of Nevada, was not known for an understanding legal attitude toward divorce.

6 The right to privacy, especially on the part of public figures, may conflict with another citizen's right: that to be informed. Chapter 5 will return to this problem under the subheading "The right to be informed."

7 Neither Pasternak nor Solzhenitsyn were allowed by the Soviet government to go to Stockholm and receive their Nobel Prizes. The Soviet press described the granting of the prize a "hostile, anti-Soviet provocation" and an "instrument of cold war." Solzhenitsyn bitterly denounced his country in the lecture he would have delivered if he could have gone to Stockholm to accept the Nobel Prize he won in 1970. The lecture was published in 1972 by the Nobel Foundation in Stockholm. It contained the following warning: "Woe to the nation whose literature is disturbed by the intervention of power. Because that is not just a violation against 'freedom of print,' it is the closing down of the heart of the nation, a slashing to pieces of its memory."

8 Hannah Arendt, *The Human Condition* (Garden City, N.Y.: Doubleday, 1959), pp. 37 and 41.

9 Erich Fromm, *Escape from Freedom* (New York: Rinehart and Co., 1941), pp. 131–34. "The individual is confronted by incontrollable dimensions in comparison with which he is a small particle. . . . People cannot go on bearing the burden of 'freedom from'; they must try to escape from freedom altogether. . . . The principal social avenues of escape in our time are the submission to leaders, as has happened in Fascist countries, and the compulsive conforming in our own democracy."

10 In his *1984* George Orwell described the ultimate horrors of the Thought Police and their ubiquitous instrument of surveillance, the telescreen: "You had to live—did live, from habit that became instinct—in the assumption that every sound you made was overheard and, except in darkness, every movement scrutinized." Already by the 1960s infra-red techniques permitted a room to be watched and photographed from an adjoining room.

11 The extent of privacy invasion in our electronic age, when "the marvels of microminiaturization and circuitry, chemical synthesis and projective psychiatry" unmistakably favor those who conduct physical surveillance is the subject of an excellent study by Alan F. Westin, *Privacy and Freedom* (New York: Atheneum, 1967).

12 In 1965, Representative Cornelius Gallagher of New Jersey, chairman of the House Subcommittee on Invasion of Privacy, introduced a bill (H.R. 9878) to forbid the federal use of lie-detectors (polygraphs). Yet his own proposal was qualified "*except* in cases involving extraordinary necessity in protecting the national interest." (Italics added.)

13 The term "dossier dictatorship" was coined by Professor Arthur S. Miller of the University of Michigan Law School, author of a book, *The Assault on Privacy: Computers, Data Banks, and Dossiers*. Professor Miller used this term

during a hearing held on February 23, 1971, by the U.S. Senate Subcommittee on Constitutional Rights, chaired by Sam J. Ervin, Democrat of North Carolina. According to Miller, as reported by the *New York Times* (February 24, 1971), "Information is being gathered, recorded and disseminated with a let-George-do-it philosophy that is putting us on the pathway toward a dossier dictatorship. It is simply unrealistic to assume that the managers or proprietors of computer systems—government or private—will take it upon themselves to protect the public against misuse of the data in their custody."

14   Carl Kaysen, "Data Banks and Dossiers," *The Public Interest* (Spring 1967), p. 55.

15   Testimony before the Senate Subcommittee on Administrative Practice and Procedure of the Committee of the Judiciary, March 15, 1967. The idea of the federal data center was first officially proposed in October 1966 in a report of the Bureau of the Budget. Representative Gallagher of New Jersey saw the data center as a possible step toward a totalitarian state.

16   In England, tolerance toward the Catholic and Jewish minorities did not become part of the "constitution" until 1829, when Catholics were enfranchised to sit and vote in Parliament and 1846, when Jews were placed in the same position as members of nonconformist Protestant churches.
   The Roman Catholic Emancipation Act of 1829 stated:

> Whereas by various Acts of Parliament certain restraints and disabilities are imposed on the Roman Catholic subjects of his Majesty, to which other subjects of his Majesty are not liable; and whereas it is expedient that such restraints and disabilities shall be from henceforth discontinued; and whereas by various Acts certain oaths and declarations commonly called the declaration against transsubstantiation and the invocation of saints and the sacrifice of the mass, as practised in the Church of Rome, are or may be required to be taken, made and subscribed to by the subjects of his Majesty, as qualifications for sitting and voting in Parliament, and for the enjoyment of certain offices, franchises and civil rights: Be it enacted . . . That . . . all such parts of the said Acts as require the said declarations . . . are . . . hereby repealed.

The Roman Catholic Emancipation Act, 1829, does not affect the position of the sovereign who, by the Bill of Rights, must not be a Roman Catholic nor married to a Roman Catholic.
   Enfranchisement of the British Jews was part of the Religious Disabilities Act of 1846 according to which "Her Majesty's subjects professing to the Jewish religion, in respect to their schools, places for religious worship, education and charitable purposes, and the property held therewith, shall be subject to the same laws as her Majesty's protestant subjects dissenting from the Church of England are subject to. . . ."

17   Sweden, 1809, Article 2: The King shall always profess the pure evangelical faith, as adopted and explained in the unaltered Augsburg Confession and in the Resolution of the Uppsala Meeting of the year 1593.

18   Peru, 1933, Article 232: Respecting the sentiments of the national majority, the State protects the Roman Catholic Apostolic religion. All other religions enjoy freedom in the exercise of their respective beliefs.

19 Burma, 1947, Article 21: The State recognizes the special position of Buddhism as the faith professed by the majority of the citizens of the Union. . . . The State also recognizes Islam, Christianity, Hinduism and Animism as some of the religions existing in the Union at the date of the coming into operation of this Constitution. . . . The abuse of religion for political purposes is forbidden; and any act which is intended or is likely to promote feelings of hatred, enmity or discord between racial or religious communities or sects is contrary to this Constitution and may be punishable by law.

20 Nepal, 1962, Article 3: Nepal is an independent indivisible and sovereign monarchical Hindu State.

21 Afghanistan, 1964, Article 2: Islam is the sacred religion of Afghanistan. Religious rites performed by the State shall be according to the provisions of Hanafi doctrine. Non-Muslim citizens shall be free to perform their rituals within the limits determined by laws for public decency and public peace.

22 The Ugandan Constitution, 1966, Article 25, specifically guarantees "freedom to change religion or belief."

23 Stanley Feingold, "The American Alternative in Church-State Relations," *Midwest Quarterly* 11:2 (January 1970), p. 160. Feingold's insightful study focuses on the American tradition of cooperation, that is the government's helping all faiths and the cause of religion.

　　Compare with Justice Douglas who, dissenting, declared in 1961: "The institutions of our society are founded on the belief that there is an authority higher than the authority of the State, that there is a moral law which the State is powerless to alter, that the individual possesses rights conferred by the Creator which government must respect" (*McGowan* v. *Maryland,* 366 U.S. 420, 562, 1961).

　　According to another scholar, William A. Carroll, the government should be wholly neutral to religion but cannot be so unless religion is defined to include both belief and *nonbelief* in god. Carroll's broad definition of religion for constitutional purposes is "the search for answers to ultimate questions—such as: Who made man and the universe? What is the end of man?" It is based on Justice Frankfurter's opinion in a case involving free exercise of religion (*Minersville School District* v. *Gobitis,* 310 U.S. 586, 593, 1940). Speaking for the Supreme Court, Justice Frankfurter said: "Certainly the affirmative pursuit of one's convictions about the ultimate mystery of the universe and man's relation to it is placed beyond the reach of the laws." William A. Carroll, "The Constitution, the Supreme Court, and Religion," *American Political Science Review* 61:3 (September 1967), p. 664.

24 Stanley Feingold, "The American Alternative in Church-State Relations," p. 161, noted that already "James Madison accepted the congressional and military chaplaincies, while opposing further acts of church-state cooperation."

25 In 1967 India was a scene of serious riots on account of political agitation in favor of a new law or amendment which would prohibit slaughtering of bulls, in addition to cows and calves. The Indian Constitution, written in English, prohibits the slaughtering of cows and calves but does not mention

bulls; the Hindi translation used the word "go" which means both "cow" and "cattle." In 1958, the Indian Supreme Court ruled that a cow is not a cow when it is a bull. In 1967 one of the issues was again whether a bull, although a cow's progeny, could be constitutionally permitted to remain outside the rigidity of the Hindu faith and be slaughtered and consumed by Muslim, Christian and Hindu unbelievers. There are 175 million cattle in India (about one-fifth the world's total); the cattle population competes with the swelling human population for food.

Another special treatment to a religious group is accorded by Article 25 which authorizes the Sikhs, an offshoot of Hinduism, to wear kirpans (daggers) as part of the profession of the Sikh religion which is anti-caste and also violently anti-Muslim.

26 When in 1970 the Italian legislators approved a law permitting divorce, the 1929 concordat was evidently due for revision. The Communist party suggested so on January 14, 1971, in cautious terms, proposing a new dialogue with the church rather than fight.

27 Article 25A: The bleeding of slaughter animals which have not been previously stunned is expressly forbidden; this provision applies to all methods of slaughter and to all kinds of livestock.

28 Article 51: The Order of Jesuits and societies affiliated with it may not be admitted in any part of Switzerland and all activities in church and school are forbidden to their members.

29 *Time,* August 7, 1959.

30 The right to equal economic opportunity will be discussed along with social rights in chapter 3.

31 In 1969 John Lennon returned his M.B.E. award to the Queen in protest "against Britain's involvement in the Nigeria-Biafra thing and against our support of America in Vietnam." He added: "Really, shouldn't have taken it, Felt I had sold out. I must get rid of it, I kept saying. I must get rid of it. So I did" (*New York Times,* November 30, 1969).

32 One understandable departure from the current constitutional principle of equality regardless of race or skin color may be found in the Liberian Constitution (Article 5, Section 13): "The great object of forming these Colonies being to provide a home for the dispersed and oppressed children of Africa, and to regenerate and enlighten this benighted continent, none but Negroes or persons of Negro descent shall be eligible to citizenship in this Republic."

33 The arguments used by the American colonists against England were used in many other cases of interethnic intolerance and enmity. The Serbs, Croats, Slovenes, Czechs, Slovaks, and Poles used the same arguments when they pressed for autonomy and secession from the Austro-Hungarian Empire in 1918, but later the same quotes were used in favor of the right of ethnic-and-territorial self-determination by the Croats against Serbian domination in Yugoslavia, and by the Slovaks against Czech centralism in Czechoslovakia. In 1945 the Indonesians quoted the 1776 document verbatim against the Dutch. The leader of the independence movement, Sukarno, described the revolutionary shots at Lexington as an inspiration for all liberation movements, but in turn the outer islanders in independent In-

donesia, notably in Sumatra and Moluccas, quoted the Declaration of 1776 again, this time against domination by Sukarno's central island, Java. In South Asia the American declaration was invoked by the Indians against the British and again by the Indian Muslims against Nehru. When Muslim Pakistan was formed, the Eastern Pakistanis claimed national self-determination against West Pakistan. In Africa territorial secession was advocated by the English, French, and Belgian colonies. When they gained independence the Katanga province quoted Jefferson to the central Congolese government in Leopoldville (the country is now called Zaire, the capital Kinshasa). Biafra did the same with reference to the central government of Nigeria. During the Hungarian revolution in 1956 the rebels read, at dictation speed, the American Declaration of 1776 in their evening broadcasts in order to mobilize popular and international forces against the Soviet military forces sent to crush the Hungarians and deny their right to secede from the Soviet bloc by abolishing a Stalinist government which they deemed had become "destructive of life, liberty and pursuit of happiness."

34 A more detailed analysis of a polyethnic federal system may be found in Ivo D. Duchacek, *Comparative Federalism: The Territorial Dimension of Politics* (New York: Holt, Rinehart and Winston, 1970), pp. 276–309. See also Ivo D. Duchacek, *Power Maps: Comparative Politics of Constitutions* (Santa Barbara: Clio Press, 1973), the chapter on federalism.

35 J. Gus Libenow, "Liberia," in Gwendolen M. Carter, ed., *African One-Party States* (Ithaca: Cornell University Press, 1962), p. 380.

36 Gary T. Marx in his review of Theodore Draper, *The Rediscovery of Black Nationalism* and John H. Bracey, Jr., et al., "Black Nationalism in America," *Saturday Review,* July 4, 1970, p. 32.

37 This was one of the claims of a convention in March 1968 sponsored by the Detroit Malcolm X Society and held at the Shrine of the Black Madonna (Central United Church of Christ). Another small group of black separatists dedicated a 20-acre farm near Bolton, Mississippi as a capital of the Republic of New Africa, a first step in the eventual takeover of the five southern states. This claim was presented on March 31, 1971. The proposal to set up a "shadow government" with a capital on United States territory in order to qualify for membership in international organizations was voiced at a black conference held in Washington on May 25, 1972, and attended by the representatives of several black American organizations and African states. The main purpose of the conference was to coordinate the American black and African efforts to influence the United States foreign and trade policy toward the white-ruled territories in Africa.

38 Quoted by Louis Fischer, *Gandhi: His Life and Message for the World* (New York: Mentor, 1954), p. 116.

39 After World War I the newly established states in Eastern Europe, in treaties under the League of Nations, pledged their respect for collective minority rights. Thus the right to be equal and separate was made a matter not only of constitutional, but also of international law.

40 In 1959, the Eighth Amendment replaced the original provision for a period of ten years by twenty years. In 1969 the Parliament extended the reservations for the Scheduled Castes and Tribes for an additional ten years.

41 In the late fifties the Backward Classes Commission listed an additional 2,399 backward groups in need of help. It also raised an interesting question: what help can be made available to poor and illiterate members of the Hindu upper castes? So far, no answer has been found.

42 The Indonesian Constitution of 1950 stipulated in Article 56: "The House of Representatives represents the entire Indonesian people and consists of a membership the number of which is determined on the basis of one representative to every 300,000 residents of Indonesian citizenship, without prejudice to the provision in the second paragraph of Article 58."

Article 58: "(1) The Chinese, European [Dutch], and Arab minority groups shall be represented in the House of Representatives by at least 9, 6 and 3 members respectively.

(2) If these numbers are not attained by election in accordance with the law referred to in Article 57, the Government of the Republic of Indonesia shall appoint additional representatives of these minorities. The number of the membership of the House of Representatives referred to in Article 56 shall then, if necessary, be increased by the number of these appointments."

43 This and the following paragraph concerning Cyprus is an abridged version of the author's analysis of the communal system in *Comparative Federalism: The Territorial Dimension of Politics*, pp. 105–6.

44 *New York Times*, March 12, p. 1.

45 An illustration of such an anxiety was manifest in the five-to-three ruling of the Supreme Court on June 7, 1971, that states are not required to carve out separate legislative districts for urban blacks merely because the election of legislators "at large" from a metropolitan area gives inner-city blacks little representation. The case concerned the city of Indianapolis and its failure to eliminate representation at large and subdivide the metropolitan area into single-member districts to assure that the inner-city blacks could elect their own representatives. Otherwise, the court warned, working-class neighborhoods, college communities and religious and ethnic groups, living in compact areas, would next demand their own districts. A week before, however, the same court ruled that Jackson, the capital city of Mississippi, must be divided into single-member districts so that black voters would have a chance to elect their own representatives.

46 In 1966 the Puerto-Ricans who lived in New York State and spoke only Spanish were given the right to vote without the knowledge of English that the New York State literacy test formerly made a prerequisite for voting. Although Spanish-speaking New Yorkers may now pass the electoral literacy test in the language of Cervantes, New Yorkers of German, Italian, or Greek descent cannot use the languages of Goethe, Dante, or Homer for the same test. A further problem (in multilingual situations there is always a further problem) developed when New Yorkers who spoke only Spanish objected to passing a test in English to obtain a driver's license. Cervantes won again. This problem seems somewhat different from that of voting rights: an only-Spanish-speaking driver may read, listen, and vote in Span-

ish but must read road signs which, unlike those in Switzerland, Canada, or India, are mostly in English only.

47 "Only a hundred years ago there was not a single Jew in the world whose mother tongue was Hebrew; today it is the spoken language of hundreds of thousands." Prime Minister David Ben Gurion, *New York Times Magazine,* April 20, 1958, p. 9.

48 In Afghanistan (Article 3) "from among the languages of Afghanistan, Pushtu and Dari, shall be the official languages." In Pakistan (Article 215) the two national languages are Bengali and Urdu. Equality of two languages in principle (although not always in practice) characterizes Belgium (French and Flemish), Canada (English and French), Cyprus (Greek and Turkish), Czechoslovakia (Czech and Slovak), Yugoslavia (Serbo-Croat, Slovene, and Macedonian) and the South African Republic (English and Afrikaan; in the new autonomous area Transkei, the indigenous language of Xhoca is officially used).

49 A hierarchical order between languages may be found in Ireland whose Constitution of 1937 (Article 8) states: "The Irish language as the national language is the first official language. The English language is recognized as a second official language." In the Kenyan Constitution of 1963 (Articles 186-190) English was to be used in Parliament but Swahili was a prerequisite for naturalization. In the Tanganyika part of Tanzania English initially was the official and Swahili the national language. As of 1970 Swahili became the official language in both Kenya and Tanzania. In all former French colonies in Africa, now independent states, French remains either the first, official, or the second, auxiliary, language. Mauritania, for instance, proclaims French the official and Arabic the national language; Madagascar names Malagasy first and French second. The Constitution of Chad, (1962) on the other hand, states in Article 1: *"La langue officielle est le français."* The official text of the constitution is in French only. Similar provisions may be found in the constitutions of Gabon (1961), Dahomey (1964), Ivory Coast (1963), Mali (1961), Niger (1960), Senegal (1963), Togo (1963), and Upper Volta (1960). Switzerland's Article 116 recognizes four national languages (German, French, Italian, and Romansh) but only the first three are official languages on the federal level, i.e., a citizen may communicate in any of them with his government and members of the national legislature may discuss issues and laws in any of them. The equal use of German, French, and Italian is also guaranteed in pleading cases before the Federal Tribunal.

50 Quoted by Hans Kohn, *The Twentieth Century* (New York: Macmillan, 1949), p. 15.

51 "Women Active on Various Fronts," *Peking Review,* March 10, 1972, p. 11. In the same issue Ms. Lu Yu-lan, chairman (or as we now say, "Chairperson") of an agricultural cooperative and since 1969 member of the party's Central Committee, discusses the liberation of women in the process of socialist transformation of society as a whole.

52 The *New York Times,* March 26, 1972, E, p. 6.

53 *Women on Words and Images, Dick and Jane as Victims: Sex Stereotyping in Children's Readers,* Princeton, N.J. The study has this to say about the English language:

> Gender terminology is often used as a means of indicating or underlining characteristics in animals or inanimate things. Soft, delicate fluffy kittens are usually female. So is the lazy magpie. Boisterous, playful dogs are male. Old people who are mean and ugly are female. . . . Wise old people are without exception male, and a human being of any stature is male by definition. Thus, hieroglyphologists are "men" who study Egyptian writings and elsewhere we meet "sayings of Wise Men." We don't want to be unreasonable and hold the [children's] readers responsible for sexism built into the English language, which symbolically has handed over the entire world to men, with pronouns like the bisexual "he" for he-and-she words like "mankind" that stand for all of us. But the [children's] readers don't have to extend this practice by defining archeologists as "men" who dig. Archeologists are also women. . . . The built-in sexism of our common language is loud and clear in a comment made to young Oliver Perry [on the pages of one of the readers]: "You're certainly not up to a man's work, so you'll start as a scrubwoman."

54 "Look Jane Look. See Sex Stereotypes," NJEA Review, March 1972, p. 15.

Right to Economic & Social Progress

It is probably agreed that the general welfare and the pursuit of individual happiness are goals that national constitutions should proclaim and promote. They do so. People often disagree, however, on concrete definitions for these goals, the means of achieving them, and what the mutual relationship between the general welfare and individual happiness should be. There are many reasons for disagreement, poor communications, semantic complexity and the vague meaning of words such as "general welfare" and "happiness." The basic reason, however, is simply that men are endowed with unequal mental dispositions, talents, and skills, and exposed to varying experiences. Men are bound to reach conflicting conclusions as to what is best for them individually and for society collectively—and to be self-righteous about their opinions. In addition men are in conflict not only with other men but also with themselves. They simultaneously desire mutually exclusive goals. Sometimes a balance between partly contradictory goals is possible, often it is not. Men dread both unemployment and employment that is so rigidly planned that it resembles conscripted labor. They want to be free, yet to have a sense of direction; to go it alone and to go it with others. Such inner conflicts in men's hearts, as well as conflicts between individual and general welfare, have been described but not solved in millions of pages written by philosophers, political scientists, psychologists, sociologists, anthropologists, religious leaders—and constitutional lawyers. It is too much to expect that a few articles and paragraphs in a national constitution will do more than add another brave attempt to the general search for an acceptable balance between the conflicting aims and hopes of men.

In eighteenth- and nineteenth-century constitutions individual liberties, protection of private property, and participatory democratic rights were emphasized as preconditions for securing individual and general welfare. References to social and economic matters were general and vague. In the French Declaration of 1789 the need for taxation and its popular control were not related to economic planning but only to the maintenance of public force and the expense of administration (see Document 3.1). Only the seventeenth theme of the French Declaration —which solemnly reaffirmed the sacred and inviolable nature of property—contained a clause which subsequently could perhaps be interpreted as a basis for nationalization of the means of production and economic planning, the right of expropriation of private property "if public necessity evidently demands it."

The "general welfare" provisions in the United States constitutional documents of the same era are also vague although somewhat more specific than the French Declaration. The Declaration of Independence of 1776 labeled the pursuit of happiness an inalienable right—even then that right had a material as well as a spiritual content. The United States Constitution pledges the promotion of general welfare in the preamble and again in Article I which assigns Congress the task of providing "for the general welfare of the United States." Article I also commits Congress to the promotion of "the progress of science and useful arts" in connection with the protection of authors and inventors who are accorded "exclusive rights to their respective writings and discoveries." Article I enumerates the means necessary for the purpose of promoting the general welfare: taxes, borrowing money, building roads, and post offices. In 1791 the Fifth Amendment limited the right of the government to take private property for public use, i.e., eminent domain, by stipulating that private property "cannot be taken without just compensation." Property can, of course, be expropriated with appropriate indemnity.

Eighteenth- and nineteenth-century constitutions implied the fundamental hope that man's rationality and innate goodness, once liberated from oppressive limitations, would establish a community of free, happy, and tolerant citizens. They would, it was hoped, through natural and unfettered competition, with minor assistance from government, achieve the general welfare or a "great society." Collective happiness was perceived to be the result as well as the sum of individual happinesses. In this framework the most important route to progress and happiness seemed to be the protection of private property and free enterprise, along with individual rights and liberties.

Document 3.1

ECONOMIC AND SOCIAL RIGHTS IN THE EIGHTEENTH CENTURY

The French Declaration of the Rights of Man and Citizen, 1789

(12) The guarantee of the rights of man and citizen requires a public force. . . .

(13) For the maintenance of the public force and for the expense of the administration a general tax is indispensable; it ought to be equally apportioned among all the citizens according to their means.

(14) All the citizens have the right to ascertain, by themselves or by their representatives, the necessity of the public tax, to consent to it freely, to follow the employment of it, and to determine the quota, the assessment, the collection, and the duration of it. . . .

(17) Property being a sacred and inviolable right, no one can be deprived of it, unless a legally established public necessity evidently demands it, under the condition of a just and prior indemnity.

This optimistic creed (in essence economic liberalism) was attacked from opposite sides by egalitarian socialism and anti-egalitarian conservatism, both of which advocated resubordination of the individual to the society in the belief that individual happiness issued from the general welfare. Conservatives stressed the need for strong institutions anchored in the proven past, e.g., the family, church, or monarchy, which were to be rededicated to paternalistic reform and welfare. The socialists opposed the laissez-faire optimism of the economic liberals because it seemed to ensure the survival of exploiters through unbridled competition. The socialists thus suggested nationalizing the means of production, enabling the collectivity to prosper, thereby finally profiting the individual.

Between the conservative and socialist extremes which are so critical of liberalism's easy optimism there are many hybrid concepts ranging from "anarcho-syndicalism" to "Christian and humanitarian socialism." Originally these concepts arose from extraconstitutional programs and movements. At the beginning of the twentieth century, and rapidly after World War II, many such concepts found their way into the texts of new constitutions, usually as new bills of economic, social, and educational rights. Carl J. Friedrich called this grafting of new economic rights onto the older concept of liberties "negative revolutions" and identified their four main focal points as:

(1) reaffirmation of human rights; *but* (2) efforts to restrict these rights in such a way as to make them unavailable to the enemies of constitutional

democracy; (3) stress upon social goals and their implementation through socialization; *but* (4) efforts to circumscribe these goals and implementation in such a way as to prevent the re-emergence of totalitarian methods and dictatorships.[1]

The drafters of new constitutional charters have recognized, perhaps belatedly, the truth in Saint-Simon's skeptical analysis of the French Declaration of 1789 voiced in 1816 in his prophetic anticipation of future controversies: "The Declaration of the Rights of Man, which has been regarded as the solution to the problem of social liberty, was in reality a statement of the problem." The new bills of welfare rights are also statements rather than solutions of the problem.

The economic and social articles found in national constitutions have been largely inspired either by Karl Marx's critique of nineteenth-century capitalism or the Roman Catholic papal encyclicals, *Rerum Novarum* (Leo XIII, 1891) and *Quadragesimo Anno* (Pius XI, 1931). Marx and the popes all condemned capitalist liberalism. The postwar Western European constitutions were drafted by coalitions of socialist and Christian democratic parties, so it is small wonder that they contain a mixture of Marxist and Catholic philosophies. Other constitutions have been inspired by social and welfare concepts, the Koran, the Bible, Jeremy Bentham and Harold Laski. Whatever the source, a commitment to economic and social rights and goals is found today in all constitutions. These commitments fall into five broad categories: (1) commitment to economic planning and social welfare, often in conjunction with nationalization of the means of production; (2) protection against exploitation; (3) right to rest; (4) right to education; and (5) the promotion of family and group solidarity.

ECONOMIC & SOCIAL PLANNING

Modern constitutions assign the central political authority a dominant role in promoting economic progress, social justice, cultural development, education, care for the aged, health care, accident and unemployment insurance and the organization of rest and leisure (see Document 3.2). An increase in the regulatory, planning, and mobilizing powers of the national government is assumed to be in the interest of individuals, groups, and their collective, national whole. Unlike the drafters of nineteenth-century constitutions, the writers of modern constitutions expect the role of government not to be limited. On the contrary, the role of modern government is expanded. Political authority is now pledged to adopt policies and enact measures in fields that used to be reserved for private enterprise or benevolent charity. Switzerland amended its constitution so as to assign the government the task

Document 3.2

RIGHT TO REST AND CULTURE

USSR, 1936

Article 119. Citizens of the USSR have the right to rest and leisure. The right to rest and leisure is ensured by the establishment of a seven-hour day for industrial, office, and professional workers, the reduction of the working day to six hours for arduous trades and to four hours in shops where conditions of work are particularly arduous; by the institution of annual vacations with full pay for industrial, office and professional workers, and by the provision of a wide network of sanatoriums, holiday homes and clubs for the accommodation of working people.

Poland, 1952

Article 62. (1) Citizens of the Polish People's Republic have the right to benefit from cultural achievements and to participate in the development of a national culture. This right is ensured on an increasing scale by developing and making accessible to the working people in town and country libraries, books, press, radio, cinemas, theatres, museums and exhibitions, houses of culture, clubs and recreation rooms; by a general fostering and promoting of the cultural creative activity of the people and of the development of creative talents.

Spain, Labor Charter, 1938/1947*

Renewing the Catholic tradition of social justice and human feeling which inspired the laws of the Spanish Empire and the National State inasmuch as it is a totalitarian instrument completely at the service of the whole country, and syndicalist inasmuch as it stands for reaction against both liberal capitalism and Marxist materialism—undertakes the task of carrying out, with militant, constructive, and religious spirit, the revolution of which Spain is in need. . . . To achieve this end . . . the State shall enter the social sphere with the resolve to place wealth at the service of the Spanish people and to subordinate its economy to this purpose. . . .

II. (1) The State . . . shall free married women from the need to work in shops and factories.

(2) The State shall maintain Sunday rest as a condition sacred to work.

(3) The law shall oblige all concerned to keep traditional prescribed religious [Catholic] feasts and declared civil holidays. . . .

(5) Every worker shall be entitled to a yearly holiday with full pay to enable him to take a well-earned rest, and institutions to ensure the fulfillment of this clause shall be established for that purpose.

(6) The necessary institutions shall be set up to give workers access, during their spare time and hours of recreation, to the enjoyment of all the benefits of culture, happiness, military service [!], health and sports.

---

* *Fuero del trabajo,* converted into Basic Law of Spain by a referendum in 1947.

(Article 23A) of "encouraging cultivation of corn in the country and purchasing native corn of good quality fit for grinding at a price which allows the cultivation of the same;" Italy (Article 6) requires the national and local authorities to "safeguard landscape and artistic property of the nation" (one of the first beautification provisions in constitutional history). Nostalgic India expects its government (Article 43) to "promote cottage industries" although its current leaders have quite non-Gandhian dreams about more and more steel mills and atomic plants. Inevitably, the international concern over environmental pollution will be introduced into constitutional texts in the next two decades.

The constitutional commitment to economic and social progress is associated with two more concepts: (1) economic planning, and (2) violability of private property and the rights based on it (such as the freedom of an employer to hire and fire). Implementation of this principle ranges all the way from income taxes to trade unions' rights and nationalization of all or some means of production.[2]

SOCIALIST & MIXED ECONOMIC SYSTEMS

Communist constitutions have elevated planning, along with an almost total socialization of the economy, into the heart of their welfare commitment (see Document 3.3).

Other national systems provide for a mixed economy in which the government either owns and manages or dominantly regulates the means of production, leaving other parts of the economy in private hands.

The differences between the Communist system of total planning and the mixed systems are not as sharp as this description suggests. Even in those economies which seem totally nationalized some aspects of economic life remain unplanned. For example, the artisan and artistic work, and minor items of privately owned property, e.g., household furniture, and private plots on collective farms[3] are generally free of government planning provisions in Communist constitutions. Inheritance is also permitted,[4] although it is severely taxed, and is regarded as a personally unearned income. The practice of inheritance was considered to be a capitalist institution by the revolutionary socialists.

There are powerful arguments for maintaining a mixed economic system in combination with national planning. Nasser, in commenting on the draft of the Egyptian political and welfare program for the future in the so-called Arab Charter of June 30, 1962, said of Arab socialism:

> The private sector has its effective role in the development. . . . The maintenance of the private sector beside that of the public sector renders

Document 3.3

CONSTITUTIONAL SOCIALISM

USSR, 1936

Article 4. The economic foundation of the USSR is the socialist system of economy and the socialist ownership of the instruments and means of production, firmly established as a result of the liquidation of the capitalist system of economy, the abolition of private ownership of the instruments and means of production, and the elimination of exploitation of man by man.

Article 118. Citizens of the USSR have the right to work, that is, the right to guaranteed employment and payment for their work in accordance with its quantity and quality.

The right to work is insured by the socialist organization of the national economy, the steady growth of the productive forces of the Soviet society, the elimination of the possibility of economic crises, and the abolition of unemployment.[*]

Czechoslovakia, 1960

Article 12. The entire national economy shall be directed by the state plan for the development of the national economy.... usually worked out for a period of five years.... A state budget shall be drawn up every year in conformity with the state plan....

Poland, 1952

Article 14. Work is the right, the duty,[**] and matter of honour of every citizen. Exemplary workers enjoy the respect of the whole nation.

---

[*]The Yugoslav Constitution realistically provides for the right to material security during temporary *unemployment* (Article 36) in socialism.

[**]As we have seen (chapter 2), one feature of total national planning, the duty to work ("He who does not work, neither shall he eat"—USSR, Article 12), may result in a new form of forced labor especially in developing countries that cannot afford the wage enticements available to wealthier countries during their planned mobilization of human resources.

---

control over public ownership more effective. By encouraging free competition within the framework of general economic planning, the private sector is also an invigorating element to the public sector.[5]

Similarly, Nehru argued in favor of the private sector when defining a mixed system under Indian socialism in his speech to the Congress party on December 22, 1954:

It is advantageous for the public sector to have a competitive private sector to keep it up to the mark ... there is a risk of the public sector becoming slow, not having the urge and push behind it ... it is a good thing to have a private sector, something where the surplus energies of people who are not employed in the public sector may have some play, provided, of course, we control the private sector in the interest of the National Plan.[6]

The Chinese Constitution (Articles 5, 6, 8, 10, 14 and 101) distinguishes four types of ownership of the means of production and proclaims different attitudes toward each:

(1) *State ownership:* "ownership by the whole people"; "all mineral resources and waters, as well as forest, undeveloped land and other resources which the State owns by law are the property of the whole people"; "public property is sacred and inviolable"; "the State ensures priority for the development of state-owned economy."

(2) *Cooperative ownership:* "collective ownership by the working classes." It is splitting Chinese hairs to distinguish between working masses and the whole people since everyone has the duty of working. Here the phrase basically means peasant collectives. The state "protects peasant ownership of land" but induces the peasants to own it collectively by organizing "producers', supply and marketing, and credit cooperatives."

(3) *Ownership by individual working people,* which means household utensils, furniture, and clothing.

(4) *Capitalist ownership* is recognized and temporarily protected by the Chinese document unlike the practice of other Communist constitutions. Article 14 forbids the use of private property to the detriment of public interest; Article 8 proclaims that the policy of the state is to restrict and gradually eliminate the rich-peasant economy, which has been done. Article 10 reads;

> The State protects the ownership by capitalists of the means of production and other capital according to law. The policy of the State toward capitalist industry and commerce is to use, restrict and transform them. The State makes use of the positive qualities of capitalist industry and commerce . . . restricts their negative qualities . . . encourages and guides their transformation into various forms of state-capitalist economy, gradually replacing capitalist ownership with ownership by the whole people. . . .

This is the constitutional expression of Mao Tse-tung's conception of the difference between the "big bourgeoisie" and the "national bourgeoisie." The big bourgeoisie, according to Mao, has the character of a comprador (i.e., it acts as the agent of the foreign firms engaged in business in China), subservient to the imperialist powers. The national bourgeoisie, on the other hand, is a class having a dual character, it is "oppressed by imperialism and fettered by feudalism," and is, therefore, "one of the revolutionary forces . . . to a certain extent and for a certain period of time." Mao believes that the national bourgeoisie "lacks the courage to oppose imperialism because it is economically and politically flabby."[7]

Planning in Nonsocialist Systems

The most laissez-faire or antisocialist country cannot do without some planning. As soon as a government levies taxes and coins money, it must have at least a one-year plan and a budget to determine what is to be done with them. A national budget and a constitutional commitment to general welfare, even as vague as those mentioned in the United States Constitution, actually prescribe some regulation and initiative from the political center. Even when rugged economic individualism was the rule Americans expected their government to regulate trade, levy taxes, provide for defense—national safety being one of the preconditions of general welfare—and grant homesteads.

Several Western European countries[8] usually not described as socialistic (e.g., France under de Gaulle and Britain under the Conservatives) have planned economies and their governments own and manage several key industries.

In many constitutions it is anticipated that public ownership and management of important sectors of the national economy will grow. This does not necessarily mean state ownership but rather collective ownership by municipalities, cooperatives, and regional governments. English Fabians and Western European Christian Socialists who oppose private ownership dread the totalitarian implications of a centralized, nationalized economy. Their answer is pluralism, or different forms of competitive *public* ownership—local, regional, and cooperative.[9]

Instead of outright expropriation (with or without compensation) and subsequent nationalization, many countries subject private enterprises to the limitations of national planning through credit, tax, and tariff manipulations, price controls, licensing, and by forbidding national or foreign monopolies[10] (in many Latin American constitutions). Extralegal and extraconstitutional private enterprise may be further limited by irresistible *political* persuasion, guidance, and supervision. Some public controls, even where public ownership and management is absent, may be so thorough that ostensibly free and capitalist enterprises become unfree in reality. This has, at least partly, happened to many capitalists under fascist, Nazi,[11] or military regimes and in democracies during wars and economic crises.

BASIC SOCIAL RIGHTS

Modern constitutions protect citizens against economic injustice, unemployment, exploitation and overwork in two ways. First, they grant citizens the right to organize themselves to protect and promote their interests, whatever they may be. The right to trade-unionism, collective bargaining, strikes and demonstrations is granted in all modern constitutions. (This right will be discussed along with freedom of expression in chapter 5 and interest groups in chapter 7.) Some constitutions extend the usual trade union rights to guarantee workers the right to share in profits, and sometimes that is coupled with the right to participate in the administration of enterprises (Algeria).[12] On the contrary some countries specifically deny such rights (Mexico).[13]

The second form of labor protection found in many constitutions is the right to work. The right to work in the context of American labor unionism is a slogan used by employers to restrict union efforts to organize the workers. Elsewhere in the world the term "right to work" simply means the right "never to be unemployed" and in that sense is closely connected with the constitutional commitment to economic planning (see page 108). Constitutional provisions concerning just working conditions, e.g., minimum wages, night shifts, work with dangerous raw materials, pre- and post-pregnancy compensation, annual vacation, sick leave, bonuses, the form and place for payment of wages, and other details of worker-employer relations which in the United States are usually found in collective contracts and state laws are also found under the heading "right to work." Such lists of specific guarantees of working conditions are part of many constitutional texts in addition to, not instead of, trade union rights. For example, the constitution of Mexico (1917) stipulates:

> An employer who dismisses a worker without justifiable cause or because he has entered an association or union, or for having taken part in a lawful strike, shall be required, at the election of the worker, either to fulfill the contract or to indemnify him to the amount of three months' wages. . . . He shall also have the obligation to indemnify a worker to the amount of three months' wages, if the worker leaves his employment due to lack of honesty on the part of the employer or because of ill treatment from him, either to himself or to his wife, parents, children, or brothers and sisters. An employer may not relieve himself of this responsibility when the ill-treatment is attributable to his subordinates or members of his family acting with his consent or tolerance (Article 123 [22], as amended in 1962).
> The following conditions shall be considered null and void and not binding on the contracting parties even if expressed in the contract: (a) Those that stipulate a day's work that is inhuman because it is obviously excessive, considering the kind of work; (b) Those stipulating a period of more than one week before payment of a day's wages; (d) Those indicating as the place of payment of wages a place of recreation, an inn, cafe, tavern, bar, or store,

except for the payment of employees of such establishments; (e) Those that include the direct or indirect obligation of acquiring consumer goods in specified stores or places; (f) Those that permit the retention of wages as a fine. . . . (Article 27).

RIGHT TO EDUCATION

Every modern constitution provides for free compulsory primary and secondary education. The impartation of knowledge and skills is only one of several reasons for including provisions on education in constitutional texts. Another reason is the guarantee of equal economic and career opportunities to all. Education protects against injustice and exploitation by increasing the individual's knowledge and skill to articulate demands. Furthermore, the writers of national constitutions try to determine the broad goals of national education since it is one of the most effective instruments political authorities can employ to introduce their youth into the political culture of the country and promote their support of the existing system.[14] Secular constitutions prescribe the separation of state and school; in some constitutions the freeing of schools from religious influences is enough, but others suggest the scientific, democratic, and patriotic contents of public curricula.[15] Constitutions that establish national churches, on the contrary, insist that education shall have a religious content (Syria). The constitutions of developing countries sometimes contain provisions for a struggle against illiteracy.[16]

Several constitutions describe in detail auxiliary educational facilities such as "scholarships, the development of hostels, boarding schools, and students' homes, together with other forms of material aid for the children of workers, working peasants, and intelligentsia" (Article 61 of the Polish Constitution of 1952). This and similar provisions found in Communist constitutions are aimed at terminating the previously privileged position of children of bourgeois origin in which the relative wealth of parents favored their access to schools over the children of industrial workers. A new class discrimination was current in Communist countries during the 1940s and 1950s under Stalin. Children of recent or distant bourgeois background were directed to manual work irrespective of their academic potentialities, presumably to compensate for past injustices. In the 1970s a similar argument—compensation for past injustice—developed in the United States in connection with the admission of black and other minority students to college. The redress of past wrongs, some observers noted, could result in discrimination against qualified "white Anglo-Saxon Protestants."

The constitution of Liberia (1847, Articles 5/15) anticipated the need for activities that today occupy the Peace Corps, Vista, and Seek. That constitution provides for social guidance in the nation's backward areas:

> The improvement of the native tribes and their advancement in the arts of agriculture and husbandry, being a cherished object of this government, it shall be the duty of the President to appoint in each county some discreet person whose duty it shall be to make regular and periodical tours through the country for the purpose of calling the attention of the natives to these wholesome branches of industry, and of instructing them in the same, and the Legislature shall, as soon as it can conveniently be done, make provision for these purposes by the appropriation of money.

FAMILY & GROUP SOLIDARITY

There are few variations in constitutional pledges to protect the family, marriage, motherhood, and childhood. Even those Communist states that experimented with free love and divorce by correspondence now place an almost Victorian seal of approval on the institution of marriage. The only remnant of the daring period of young communism is the constitutional protection extended to illegitimate children and unmarried mothers (USSR Constitution, Article 122). The rights of children born out of wedlock also are dealt with today in nonsocialist constitutions, such as that of West Germany (Article 6):

> (1) Marriage and the family are under the special protection of the state. (2) The care and upbringing of children are the natural rights of parents and their duty incumbent upon them primarily. The state watches over their performance [of this duty]. . . . (5) For their physical and mental development and for their position in society illegitimate children shall, by legislation, be given the same opportunities as legitimate children.[17]

The constitution of Venezuela (1961) assures the protection of motherhood in Article 74, "regardless of the civil status of the mother," and also calls the family "the fundamental nucleus of society." Consonant with the Catholic concept of family, the Irish Constitution of 1937 (Article 41) makes family rights antecedent and superior to positive law.

> The State recognizes the Family as the natural primary and fundamental unit group of Society, and as a moral institution possessing inalienable and imprescriptible rights, antecedent and superior to all positive law. The State shall, therefore, endeavour to ensure that mothers shall not be obliged by economic necessity to engage in labour to the neglect of their duties at home.

A similar provision is included in the Spanish Labor Charter (see Document 3.2). This contrasts sharply with Communist constitutions, which take it for granted that in a socialist economy, mothers will work along with everyone else, and so pledge to free mothers from home worries and chores by provisions similar to the Polish "creches and nursery schools, service establishments, restaurants and canteens." (See also chapter 2 on the "Status of Women.")

Most modern constitutions recommend and promote producer and consumer cooperatives,[18] trade unionism, and other forms of group cooperation and solidarity.

In the Communist context, cooperatives are not voluntary; they serve as instruments for controlling, indoctrinating, and transforming peasants and artisans into workers in the tightly centralized socialist economy. Agricultural cooperatives are transitional; their future transformation into wheat factories (or rural-urban communes) is anticipated. Article 7 of the Chinese Constitution (1954) stipulates:

> The co-operative sector of the economy is either socialist, when collectively owned by the masses of working people, or semi-socialist, when in part collectively owned by the masses of working people. Partial collective ownership by the masses of working people is a *transitional* form by means of which individual peasants, individual handicraftsmen and other individual working people organize themselves *in their advance towards collective ownership* by the masses of working people.
>
> The state protects the property of the co-operatives. . . . It regards the development of co-operation in production as the chief means of the *transformation* of individual farming and individual handicrafts.

The hope for re-education through cooperative endeavors is also expressed in other Communist constitutions. The preamble of the Yugoslav Constitution (1963) describes the inviolable foundation of man's position and role as "self-management by the working people in the working organization . . . in the commune and in other social-political communities." In Article 59 the constitution proclaims a Communist version of "Love Thy Neighbor": "It shall be the duty of every person to come to the assistance and help of any person in danger, and to participate in the elimination of general danger."

FORMS OF SOCIAL GUARANTEES

Enjoyment of social and economic rights obviously depends on the availability or future mobilization of resources. The right to be employed presupposes national planning just as the right to education presupposes schools and teachers. The right to health means little if hospitals and doctors are unavailable.[19] Sufficient funds must precede the enjoyment of the right to social security, better housing, rest, and leisure. Unlike political rights, welfare rights are not enforceable in a court of law. They are merely desirable goals that everyone should keep in mind when voting, rule making, rule applying, debating, articulating demands, or opposing authority. A bill of welfare rights therefore often means nothing more than the right to invoke the constitution and so strengthen or legitimize an argument for or against a welfare proposal.

Nineteenth-century rights enabled a citizen or group to petition a judge to *prevent* government or private persons from encroaching upon their constitutional rights. Judges cannot, however, force a government to enact and finance welfare provisions. Several constitutions (Ireland, Pakistan, India, and Burma) explicitly state that the welfare principles "shall not be enforceable by any court." The constitution of Pakistan (1960) eliminated any parallel between the judicial enforceability of political rights and nonenforceability of welfare rights frankly and bluntly. Furthermore, it added a cautious warning that the political authority shall carry out its duties to attain the social and economic goals only insofar as economic development and its financial resources permit.

> The Principles set out in this Chapter shall be known as the Principles of Policy and it is the responsibility of each organ and authority of the State, and of each person performing functions on behalf of an organ or authority of the State, to act in accordance with those Principles in so far as they relate to the functions of the organ or authority (Article 7/1).
>
> Insofar as the observance of any particular Principle of Policy may be dependent upon resources being available for the purpose, the Principle shall be regarded as being subject to the availability of resources (Article 7/2).
>
> The validity of an action or of a law shall not be called in question on the ground that it is not in accordance with the Principles of Policy, and no action shall lie against the State, any organ or authority of the State or any person on such a ground (Article 8/2).

Social goals and rights may be listed in national constitutions in three ways: as an integral part of the bill of rights, as a separate list, or as a reference to extraconstitutional sources.

When new social and economic guarantees are added to the list of nineteenth-century liberties and incorporated into a constitutional bill of rights it grows in size and acquires a mosaic-like quality. Traditional rights and freedoms alternate with specific provisions on better housing, paid vacations, health services, and unemployment insurance. The Japanese constitution, Chapter III, "Rights and Duties of the People," is an example. It has forty articles, which include the usual guarantees of criminal justice, universal suffrage, equality, separation of state and church, freedom of thought and expression, as well as (Article 28) "the right of workers to organize and to bargain and act collectively," and (Article 25) "the right to maintain the minimum standards of wholesome and cultured living." It includes, inspired by its American constitutional muses, a modified version of the American Declaration of Independence (see Document 2.4).

Constitutional guarantees of welfare rights are sometimes grouped separately into a title and a chapter clearly separate from the traditional bill of political rights and civil liberties.[20] Many constitutions have adopted this form, although conceptually it is not always easy to distinguish among participatory, individual, and welfare rights. Where does the right to trade unionism and collective bargaining belong? In the chapter dealing with participatory rights? Or in that guaranteeing the freedom to articulate demands? Or in social or economic rights? Since this right properly belongs under any of those three headings, it is an editorial problem for many authors of constitutional texts—or of books like this.

The Irish Constitution based its Directive Principles of State Policy on the social doctrine expounded in two papal encyclicals, *Rerum Novarum* (1891) and *Quadragesimo Anno* (1931). These encyclicals have restated the social teaching of the Roman Catholic Church for modern industrial societies. In both, the church criticizes the excessive individualism connected with liberal capitalism for neglecting the moral factor in human relations. The encyclicals recognize the merits of free competition and they warn against the results of unbridled competition, i.e., the failure to recognize man's needs for security; the neglect of his human personality; waste, duplication, and an artificial stimulus of wants; and, above all, economic power consolidated in the hands of a few. *Quadragesimo Anno* states:

> This concentration of power and might . . . is the fruit that the unlimited freedom of struggle among competitors has of its own nature produced, and which lets only the strongest survive; and this is often the same as saying, those who fight the most violently are those who give least heed to their conscience.

The criticism of unregulated capitalism is accompanied by a strong condemnation of Marxian materialism and the Communist concept of class struggle leading to inevitable violence and totalitarian controls. The church finds, however, that socialism which has modified and tempered the concept of materialism and class struggle is related to Catholic social doctrine. *Quadragesimo Anno* reads as follows:

> Socialism . . . in a certain measure approaches the truth which Christian tradition has always held sacred; for it cannot be denied that its demands

at times come very near those that Christian reformers of society justly insist upon . . . It can even come to the point that imperceptibly these ideas of a more moderate Socialism will no longer differ from the desires and demands of those who are striving to remold human society on the basis of Christian principles.

Socialism as mentioned by the 1931 papal encyclical is, indeed, a broad and quite controversial term. Socialism has been variously defined by scholars, political leaders, and ideologists and the meaning varies from country to country (Russia, Cuba, Scandinavia, China, or Czechoslovakia) and from time to time. Marxists believe that scientific socialism is the only true socialism, as expounded by Karl Marx and Friedrich Engels. Yet, they differ greatly as to its intermediate goals and methods. Communists believe socialism is a phase preceding communism. Their emphasis is on elitist parties, revolution, and a dictatorship of the proletariat. Western social democratic parties define socialism as a final goal with emphasis on mass parties, elections, evolution, and democracy. The central point of each belief and definition is social control of the means of production. According to some men, therefore, socialism begins with any governmental activity in the economic sphere. In the late thirties some Americans labeled Roosevelt's New Deal and the Tennessee Valley Authority as examples of "creeping socialism." A similar reaction was recorded in 1971 when President Nixon introduced price controls and a wage freeze to curb inflation, and again in the 1972 presidential campaign when President Nixon's opponent, Senator McGovern, proposed a new tax program directed against the propertied classes and suggested a minimum income for the underprivileged.

On the other hand, many liberals, radicals, and the New Left, including Herbert Marcuse, tend to use the term "socialism" as an opposite to the overly materialistic preoccupations of capitalism, communism, Western European labor parties, and other establishments. In such a context socialism shades off into humanism, individualistic utopianism and anarchism. Often it seems that socialism is what its advocates say it is. The anti-capitalist (anti-semitism is often a sort of vulgar anti-capitalism) program of the National *Socialist* German Workers' Party (NSDAP—the Nazi Party) contained elements of socialism which Adolph Hitler and his left-oriented Nazi associates, such as Gregor Strasser, emphasized when addressing German labor.

Some communist intellectuals argue that Christianity may conduct a useful dialogue with present-day communism. Before his expulsion in 1970 Roger Garaudy, a member of the Central Committee of the Communist party of France, suggested that "a Christian can become a better Christian and a Marxist a better Marxist if we can learn from each other how best to develop our own beliefs."[21] The connection between fundamental Christian ideals and socialist utopias undoubtedly facilitated the migration of the Irish Bill of Welfare Rights, based on papal encyclicals, into the constitutions of socialist and Hindu India (see Documents 3.4 and 3.5), socialist and Buddhist Burma, and welfare-oriented Muslim Pakistan. There are differences only in a few specifics but not in substance. Some of the differences were already noted in the introduction.

The Catholic doctrine that inspired the democratic constitution of Ireland and found its way, with minor modifications, into those of India, Burma, and Pakistan, was also made part of the Latin American constitutions, the Portuguese, and the Fundamental Laws of Franco's Spain. In the two latter examples paternalistic and authoritarian overtones are particularly evident. The Spanish Labor Charter promises small holdings to every peasant family, special care for those who earn their living on the sea, social security, and organization of the nation's economic life into branches of production or service, the so-called "vertical syndicates." In other words, it suggests central planning through corporations in which the state (in a dominant position), employers, and workers participate. This form of organization would be unacceptable to free trade unionism. The Spanish vertical syndicates resemble the communist trade unions as extended hands of the party and the state employer.

A third method of incorporating social, economic, and cultural rights into a constitution is to proclaim adherence to a document, revealed truth, doctrine, religion, or ideology that has already dealt with general welfare and man's material and spiritual rights or aims. Such adherence is usually proclaimed along with a detailed bill of welfare rights, but sometimes, as in several African states, instead of it. Many African states save themselves the ordeal of writing their own bills of political and welfare rights, as noted in the introduction, by simply declaring their adherence to the Universal Declaration of Human Rights (see Document 3.6) which, as a mixture of political and economic guarantees, contains all that is necessary in its 30 articles.

RELIGION AS A BILL OF SOCIAL RIGHTS

An established religion may also be viewed as an extraconstitutional source of standards for the political authority to observe when making or applying rules in matters of material and spiritual needs. An American scholar has related both Labor Zionism and the welfare orientation of the state of Israel to the ancient roots of the Jewish religion:

> Social idealism is deeply rooted in Jewish tradition. Jews glimpsed the vision of a moral order of society at an early date, and the Bible is a living

Document 3.4

IRISH DIRECTIVE PRINCIPLES OF SOCIAL POLICY

Ireland, 1937

Article 45. The principles of social policy set forth in this Article are intended for the general guidance of the Oireachtas [the President and the two Houses of the National Parliament]. The application of those principles in the making of the laws shall be the care of the Oireachtas exclusively, and shall not be cognisable by any Court under any of the provisions of this Constitution.

(1) The State shall strive to promote the welfare of the whole people by securing and protecting as effectively as it may a social order in which justice and charity shall inform all the institutions of the national life.

(2) The state shall, in particular, direct its policy toward securing

(I) That the citizens (all of whom, men and women equally, have right to an adequate means of livelihood) may through their occupations find the means of making reasonable provisions for their domestic needs.

(II) That the ownership and control of material resources of the community may be distributed amongst private individuals and the various classes as best to subserve the common good.

(III) That especially, the operation of free competition shall not be allowed so to develop as to result in the concentration of the ownership or control of essential commodities in a few individuals to the common detriment.

(3) The State shall favour and, where necessary, supplement private initiative in industry and commerce.

(4) The State pledges itself to safeguard with especial care the economic interests of the weaker sections of the community, and, where necessary, to contribute to the support of the infirm, the widows, the orphans, and the aged.

The State shall endeavour to ensure that the strength and health of workers, men and women, and the tender age of children shall not be abused and that citizens shall not be forced by economic necessity to enter avocations unsuited to their sex, age or strength.

---

testimony both to the intensity of their striving for this ideal and their power to express the yearning in lofty prose and poetic imagery. . . . Poverty and the humiliation attendant upon economic inequality and inferior social status preyed upon their minds and goaded them to proclaim injunctions against oppression and exploitation.[22]

Some Muslim constitutions provide for a judicial and religious review of the laws, as passed by the national legislature, to determine their conformity with Islam. According to the Iranian Constitution, Iran's doctors of theology together with the National Assembly are to select a court, composed of "at least five devout doctors of Islamic Law and

Document 3.5

INDIAN DIRECTIVES OF STATE POLICY

India, 1949

Article 37. The provisions contained in this Part shall not be enforceable by any court, but the principles therein laid down are nevertheless fundamental in the governance of the country and it shall be the duty of the State to apply these principles in making laws.

Article 38. The State shall strive to promote the welfare of the people by securing and protecting as effectively as it may a social order in which justice, social, economic and political, shall inform all the institutions of the national life.

Article 39. The State shall, in particular, direct its policy towards securing

(a) that the citizens, men and women equally, have the right to an adequate means of livelihood;

(b) that the ownership and control of the material resources of the community are so distributed as best to subserve the common good;

(c) that the operation of the economic system does not result in the concentration of wealth and means of production to the common detriment;

(d) that there is equal pay for equal work for both men and women;

(e) that the health and strength of workers, men and women, and the tender age of children are not abused and that citizens are not forced by economic necessity to enter avocations unsuited to their age or strength.

Article 43. The State shall endeavour to secure, by suitable legislation or economic organization or in any other way, to all workers, agricultural and otherwise, work, a living wage, conditions of work ensuring a decent standard of life and full enjoyment of leisure and social and cultural opportunities, and, in particular, the State shall endeavour to promote cottage industries on an individual or cooperative basis.

Article 46. The State shall promote with special care the educational and economic interests of the weaker sections of the people, and, in particular, of the Scheduled Castes and the Scheduled Tribes, and shall protect them from social injustice and all forms of exploitation.

Article 48. The State shall endeavour to organise agriculture and animal husbandry on modern and scientific lines and shall, in particular, take steps for preserving and improving the breeds, and prohibiting the slaughter, of cows and calves and other milch and draught cattle.

---

jurisprudence who shall at the same time be conversant with the exigencies of their age." Their task is to veto any bill that may "contravene the holy principles of Islam."

The Constitutional Law of 1906 specifically proclaims in Article 2:

At no time may the enactments of the sacred National Consultative Assembly, which has been constituted with the aid and favor of His Holiness

Document 3.6

UNIVERSAL DECLARATION OF HUMAN RIGHTS, 1948

Article 22. Everyone, as a member of society, has the right to social security and is entitled to realization, through national effort and international cooperation and in accordance with the organization and resources of each State, of the economic, social and cultural rights indispensable for his dignity and the free development of his personality.

Article 25. (1) Everyone has the right to a standard of living adequate for the health and well-being of himself and of his family, including food, clothing, housing, and medical care and necessary social services, and the right to security in the event of unemployment, sickness, disability, widowhood, old age or other lack of livelihood in circumstances beyond his control.

Article 26. (1) Everyone has the right to education. Education shall be free, at least in the elementary and fundamental stages. Elementary education shall be compulsory. . . .

(2) Education shall be directed to the full development of the human personality and to the strengthening of respect for human rights and fundamental freedoms. It shall promote understanding, tolerance and friendship among all nations, racial or religious groups, and shall further the activities of the United Nations for the maintenance of peace.

Article 28. Everyone is entitled to a social and international* order in which the rights and freedoms set forth in this Declaration can be fully realized.

---

*Even a person with a particularly poetic or revolutionary imagination would find it hard to suggest how such a welfare right might be enforced.

---

the Imam of the Age—may God immortalize his reign!—and under the supervision of the learned doctors of theology—may God increase their number!—and by the whole Iranian people, be at variance with the sacred precepts of Islam and the laws laid down by the Prophet (His Holiness the Best of Mankind)—may the blessings of God rest upon him and his descendants! . . . This clause may not be modified until the Advent of the Imam of the Age, may God hasten his reappearance!

The Advent of the Imam of the Age refers to the day when "the Twelfth Imam shall return to establish the reign of perfect justice."[23]

The constitution of Pakistan of 1960 enumerates sixteen Principles of Policy that must not be violated in law making. They include both the traditional liberties and civil rights and the new welfare guarantees. First on the list is: "No law should be repugnant to Islam." The constitution provides for an appropriate mechanism to determine whether a law is or is not in accordance with Islam.

There shall be an Advisory Council of Islamic Ideology. (Article 199)
Members of the Council shall be appointed by the President. . . . The President shall, in selecting a person for appointment to the Council, have

regard to the person's understanding and appreciation of Islam and of the economic, political, legal, and administrative problems of Pakistan.[24]

The Islamic Council may either recommend to the government "means of enabling the Muslims of Pakistan to order their lives in all respects in accordance with the principles and concepts of Islam" or advise the National Assembly, the President, and provincial organs on this question: "whether the proposed law disregards or violates . . . the Principles of Law-making."

EXTRACONSTITUTIONAL STANDARDS FOR CONSTITUTIONAL PROVISIONS

Constitutional references to extraconstitutional sources such as the Universal Declaration of Human Rights, the holy scriptures, or political ideology are found frequently in connection with the bills of political and economic rights.[25] These references raise a broader question. Many constitutional legal provisions are ambiguous and vague but how much more controversial and unclear are the holy scriptures and ideological manifestoes when it comes to their exact meaning and implementation in terms of concrete goals and means? The Swedish Constitution of 1807 (see chapter 2, footnote 17) proclaims that the Swedish King "shall always profess the pure evangelical faith, as adopted and explained in the unaltered Augsburg Confession in 1453. . . ." It seems to expect that the meaning of the Lutheran faith will always be clear and unaltered—ecumenism and the atomic age notwithstanding. Similarly, when the drafters of Communist constitutions refer to "socialism" and its final phase "communism" they assume that their meaning is immutable and that it has the same meaning in Moscow, Peking, Havana, Prague, Belgrade, and in Paris, Milan or Berkeley. The Iranian Constitution anticipates that the coming of the Imam of the Age will be followed by the establishment of "perfect justice" and that then a constitution may not be needed. Similarly, Communist constitutions anticipate the coming of communism—when a perfect society will produce limitless wealth, and men, "freed from the surviving influence of a society based on exploitation" (preamble, the Czechoslovak Constitution of 1960) will be transformed into socialist angels who will work to the best of their abilities and take freely only according to their needs. Having forgotten their past capitalist selfishness,[26] men will obviously need neither state nor constitution. The state may then wither away.

The hopes expressed in both extraconstitutional and constitutional programs for human happiness and welfare are great indeed; the reality, as we all know, is simply different.

NOTES

1 Carl J. Friedrich, "Political Theory of New Democratic Constitutions," in Arnold J. Zurcher, *Constitutions and Constitutional Trends Since World War II* (New York: New York University Press, 1951), p. 18.

Compare also Herbert J. Gans, "The New Egalitarianism," *Saturday Review*, May 6, 1972, p. 46. In his article, Professor Gans writes: "Models and methods for achieving equality have generally been *collectivist*; they call for replacing private institutions with public agencies that will take over the allocation of resources, typically through a nationalization of industry. This approach assumes that all resources belong equally to all people and that public ownership will bring about equality. When all the people own everything, however, they really do not own anything, enabling the officials who govern in the name of the people to make themselves more than equal politically and to restrict others' political liberties. . . . An American equality model must be *individualist;* it must achieve enough equality to allow the pursuit of liberty to continue but not restrict equal access to liberty to others."

2 Philippines, 1935 (Independent, 1946), Article 13: The State may, in the interest of national welfare and defense, establish and operate industries and means of transportation and communication, and upon payment of just compensation, transfer to public ownership utilities and other private enterprises to be operated by the Government.

West Germany, 1949, Article 15: Land, natural resources and means of production may, for the purpose of socialization, be transferred to public ownership or other forms of publicly controlled economy by means of a law regulating the nature and extent of the compensation.

3 Article 7 of the Soviet Constitution (1936) provides: "Every household in a collective farm, in addition to its basic income from the common, collective farm enterprise, has for its personal use a small plot of household land and, as its personal property, a subsidiary husbandry on the plot, a dwelling house, livestock, poultry, and minor agricultural implements."

Article 9: "Alongside the socialist system of economy, which is the predominant form of economy in the USSR, the law permits the small private economy of individual peasants and handicraftsmen based on their own labor and precluding the exploitation of the labor of others."

4 The 1963 Constitution of Yugoslavia states in Article 55: "The right of inheritance is guaranteed. No one shall have real estate and means of work on grounds of inheritance in excess of the limit determined by the Constitution or law."

5 Quoted by Paul E. Sigmund, Jr., *The Ideologies of the Developing Nations* (New York: Praeger, 1963), pp. 133–34.

6 Sigmund, *The Ideologies of the Developing Nations,* p. 103.

7 Mao Tse-tung, "Chinese Revolution" in *Selected Works,* vol. III (New York: International Publishers, 1954), pp. 88–89. This idea is repeated in Mao's "On New Democracy," in which he contrasts the partly and temporarily revolutionary role of national capitalists with the Russian bourgeoisie,

which "had no revolutionary quality to speak of . . . since tsarist Russia was itself already a country of militarist and feudalist imperialism." *Selected Works*, pp. 116–117.

8 In Britain, when a conservative party is in power, it continues to manage the previously socialized sectors of the British economy: broadcasting, telephone, telegraph, coal mines, electricity, civil aviation, the Bank of England, cable communication, gas, and a portion of surface transportation. Only the steel industry has reverted from its nationalized status to one privately owned but government supervised, (and then back again to nationalization).

In France the government owns and manages civil aviation, water power development, shipping, broadcasting, railroads, major banks and insurance companies, coal, gas, electricity, a part of the aviation industry, some automobile factories (Renault and Gnome-et-Rhône), tobacco, matches, importing and sale of industrial alcohol, and the French lottery.

9 Article 44 of the constitution of Burma (1947) stipulates: "The State shall direct its policy towards operation of all public utility undertakings . . . all natural resources in the Union of Burma by itself, by *local* bodies or by people's *cooperative* organizations" (italics added).

In 1971 the Christian Democrats of Chile, fearing an authoritarian rule inherent in the excessive concentration of both economic and political powers in the hands of a Marxist coalition under Allende, promoted different types of collective ownership of the means of production (a cooperative, in particular) as an alternative to state ownership. A political declaration, adopted by the Chilean Christian Democrats on May 10, 1971, rejected Allende's concept of "statist socialism" and proclaimed its adherence to "communitarian socialism" and a noncapitalist road for Chilean development. In particular this meant the promotion of cooperative ownership of the agricultural and industrial means of production, as opposed to state ownership, especially of farms.

10 Communist constitutions manifest uneasiness over the possibility of monopolies *within* the socialist economic system. The Yugoslav Constitution of 1963 (Article 30) contains the following antitrust clause: "Merger or association between working organizations, or any other activity of an organization or state organ aimed at preventing or restricting free commerce in goods and services for the purposes of material and other advantages not based on work, or violating socialist economic relations, or promoting other relations of inequality in business, or causing damage to the general interest determined by federal law shall be prohibited."

11 The original program of the German National Socialist Party contained some socialistic provisions. Its Twenty-Five Points of 1920 stated: "We demand . . . (Article 13) the nationalization of all business combines . . . (Article 14) that the principle of profit sharing be introduced in all big firms. . . . (Article 17) the adoption of a programme of land reform . . . and the enactment of a law for expropriation without compensation of land for public use." The last sentence was reinterpreted in 1928 as being primarily directed against Jewish-owned real estate companies. Later, any kind of

enterprise was either praised as an "Aryan creative enterprise" if it was owned and developed by racially "pure" Germans or condemned as "sinister Jewish usury" when owned and operated by non-Aryans.

12 Algeria (1963) states in Article 20: "Trade union rights, the right to strike, and participation by the workers in the administration of enterprises are recognized and shall be exercised within the framework of the law."

13 Mexico, whose constitution was amended in 1962, states in its new Article 123 (9): "The right of workers to participate in profits does not imply the power to intervene in the direction or administration of an enterprise." President de Gaulle enacted a similar formula in 1967 by a decree based on legislative delegation.

14 In Communist Czechoslovakia school teachers at all levels were required from 1972 on to take a "solemn oath of faithfulness" to Marxism-Leninism so that the children could be brought up "in the spirit of proletarian internationalism and love for the Soviet Union" from kindergarten through their universities. According to the same source, the problem often seemed to be that many teachers were "good Marxist-Leninists" but had no training in education (*Učitelské Noviny,* Prague, January 1, 1972).

15 Mexico, 1917, Article 3 (as amended in 1946): The education imparted by the Federal State shall be designed to develop harmoniously all the faculties of the human being and shall foster in him at the same time a love of country and a consciousness of international solidarity, in independence and justice . . . education shall be maintained entirely apart from any religious doctrine, and, based on the results of scientific progress, shall strive against ignorance and its effects, servitude, fanaticism, and prejudices.

16 Syria, 1950, Article 28: Education shall be directed at creating a generation strong physically and mentally, believing in God, morality and virtue, proud of Arab legacy, equipped with knowledge, conscious of its duties and rights, working for the public interest, and full of the spirit of solidarity and brotherhood that should prevail among all citizens.

Article 160: Illiteracy must be eradicated within ten years, at the most, of the coming into force of the provisions of this Constitution.

India, 1949, Article 35: The State shall endeavor to provide within a period of ten years from the commencement of this constitution for free and compulsory education for all children until they complete the age of fourteen years. (Statistics show that 16.6 percent of India's population was literate in 1951. Ten years later, 23.7 percent. Now, 30 percent.)

17 Compare with the Universal Declaration of Human Rights, Article 25 (2): "Motherhood and childhood are entitled to special care and assistance. All children, whether born in or out of wedlock, shall enjoy the same social protection."

18 Article 51 of the constitution of Turkey (1961) states: "The State shall take measures conducive to the promotion of cooperative attitudes." See also Note 9 on Burma.

19 Senator Edmund Muskie, addressing physician graduates at Albert Einstein College of Medicine, proposed a medical bill of rights (*New York Times,* May

28, 1971). In his speech Senator Muskie proposed the following gradation of American medical rights: (1) care within one's means; (2) care within one's reach; and (3) care within one's needs. In connection with the second and third rights, Senator Muskie observed that "even if we guaranteed the payment of health costs to all Americans, millions of our citizens could not find sufficient medical service" unless the number and facilities of medical schools expanded through the infusion of federal financial incentives and unless needy students received federal scholarships.

20 Constitutional bills of welfare rights bear many names: Directive Principles of Social Policy (Ireland, Burma, India, and Pakistan, which, however, after revising its constitution in 1960 significantly dropped the adjective "Directive" from the title); Economic and Social Rights (Morocco and Turkey, which adds "Duties" to the "Rights"); Rights and Duties of the People (Japan); National and Social Guarantees (Peru); Ethical and Social Relations (Italy); Labor and Social Security (Mexico); Labor Charter (Spain); Economic and Social Order (Brazil); etc. Whatever the name, all have grown in length and specifics. The chapter on economic and social order in the constitution of Brazil (1967) occupies sixty-nine paragraphs grouped into nine major articles; in addition, a separate chapter, with five articles and numerous subdivisions, deals with family, education, and culture.

21 *New York Times,* December 1, 1966.

22 Oscar I. Janowsky, "Israel: A Welfare State in the Making," *Middle Eastern Affairs* X (1959), p. 271. See also *Foundations of Israel: Emergence of a Welfare State* by the same author. The tension and conflict between modern welfare planning, secular mass culture, nationalism, and the magnetism of city life as opposed to the early religious messianism of a kibbutz, as well as the continuing orthodox insistence on the public observance of the sabbath and the dietary laws in the army and official establishments are analyzed by Leonard J. Fein, *Politics in Israel* (Boston: Little, Brown, and Co., 1967). His chapter on "Political Culture" is a thought-provoking analysis of the clash between religion and secular nationalism and welfare.

23 A. P. Saleh's translator's note *The Iranian Constitution with Amendments,* a mimeographed copy distributed by the Iranian Embassy in Washington, 1960, p. 14.

24 As in the constitution of Iran, theological experts are required to be in tune with the changing times (Article 201).

25 It may be cogently argued that constitutional references to extraconstitutional documents make them an integral part of constitutional law and practice.

26 Lenin described how it will be when communism arrives: "The narrow horizon of bourgeois law which compels one to calculate with the pitilessness of a Shylock, whether one has not worked half-an-hour more than another, whether one is not getting less pay than another—this narrow horizon will then be left behind."

CHAPTER **4**

Impartial Justice

۞ Guarantees of impartial justice are an essential part of most national constitutions for two reasons. First, they are an expression of the concept of limited, constitutional government, limited by a rule of law to which citizens as well as government are equally subject. The courts apply the same standards to both citizens and political authorities. Second, impartial justice rendered through independent and easily accessible courts is a fundamental precondition for the exercise and protection of all other political rights and liberties which have meaning only if they are either universally respected (which is highly improbable) or enforceable by a court when violated by citizens or government. Modern constitutions provide social and economic rights such as the rights to health, literacy, and housing which differ from political rights and liberties precisely because they are judicially nonenforceable (see chapter 3).

The role of the court in interpreting and enforcing constitutional provisions in response to changing political and economic circumstances varies in accordance with the legal tradition and source of law. Those countries (e.g., France) influenced by the Roman law tend to resolve political conflicts (i.e., conflicts over what the law "ought to be") through the legislature and not by the courts. In those countries the translation of new political and economic values into law is not regarded as a proper function of the judge—it is a matter reserved to the legislator. The judge is generally considered, quite properly, as a captive of the law as it is written. His role is to interpret the law, not to change it. In fact, those judges who endow old laws with new meanings are condemned for usurping the legislative function—or they are regarded as quasi-revolutionaries.

The countries strongly influenced by common law traditions (e.g., England, the United States, and several Commonwealth nations) tend to have a contrasting view of the proper role of the court. In England, the royal judges were initially the most important law makers. Their role was to detect and translate the community's customs and concepts of justice into generally enforceable rules based on precedent. The American acceptance of a quasi-legislative role for the Supreme Court is, to some extent, explained by the tradition of judge-made law brought to the colonies by English settlers. That role would be highly debatable in countries influenced by the Roman law tradition.

The function of the courts in all systems is to settle conflicts between individuals and between society and individuals which can be resolved by judicial action within the established framework of law. However, the individual often prefers non-judicial settlement—negotiation, compromise, arbitration, or, at the opposite extreme, violence. Frequently, the resolution of human conflict behavior is left to group, peers, or family for settlement. In rural Japan many conflicts are settled informally which, in the United States, would appear in the courts. That fact partially explains the relatively low number of lawyers in Japan. Informal "comrades' courts" in the Communist countries take care of many conflicts arising from labor and housing situations. Some issues, of course, must necessarily be left to the individual's artistic sense and conscience—conflicts involving esthetic and ethical values are rarely amenable to judicial arbitration. The Argentine Constitution of 1853 (Article 19) refers non-justiciable conflicts to God:

> The private actions of men that in no way offend public order and morality, nor injure a third party, are reserved to God and are exempt from the authority of the magistrate.

Articles and chapters dealing with the right to impartial justice, like any other portion of a constitution, are important since they communicate symbols and pledges from the political system to the society, and so increase public support. Even when political authorities are not interested in maintaining an impartial and effective judiciary for the sake of transcendent justice, they make every effort to enhance the prestige of the judiciary since the courts are an effective instrument for maintaining peace and order and keeping conflicts between citizens within bounds. The constitutional guarantee of an impartial and accessible judiciary is likely to encourage citizens to settle their grievances and conflicts of interest by orderly legal procedures. Thus civil conflicts and disputes are transferred from the streets to the courts and the use of force is discouraged. "No one may take the law into his own hands," warns the Mexican Constitution of 1917 (Article 17), "or resort to violence in the enforcement of his rights." Certain constitutional provisions are expected to deter criminal activity by instituting public trials, which are supposed to restore confidence in public order by dramatically reenacting crime and punishment. The effect of a criminal trial, other than the exploitation of gruesome thrills by the mass media, "is affirmation of the public order through the instrumentalities of the trial."[1]

Beyond serving the political authority's need to preserve domestic tranquility, constitutional guarantees of justice are presumably effective in preventing the political authority itself from abusing its coercive power. The judicial system and its legitimate authority to coerce and punish have too frequently been employed by political authorities in their own interests, mostly to silence dissent. Stalin, Hitler, and Castro are not the only political leaders who have channeled predetermined guilt and penalty through seemingly judicial procedure—ostensibly "fair" trials have frequently been used to eliminate or punish political opponents.

CIVIL LAW

Constitutions are invariably written by individuals who first assume that conflicts of interest and opinion are inevitable in society and then try to prevent their sometimes violent and disruptive effects. Both the assumption and the means of prevention are found in the legislative and judicial chapters of national constitutions. Legislative chapters provide for the peaceful adjustment of society to new concepts and environmental changes by adoption of new laws. Judicial chapters establish independent courts to administer criminal justice and to judicially arbitrate civil conflicts among citizens. Bills of rights, with their guarantees of impartial procedure and substantive justice, are therefore directly linked to both the legislative and judicial provisions.

Some constitutions laconically refer to an obvious need for justice and a system of courts, and leave the details of structure and scope to be subsequently provided in ordinary laws. The constitution of the State of Singapore (1963) contains no judicial article. The constitution of Guinea (1958) describes the Guinean system and concept of justice in only 135 words. The United States Constitution, on the other hand, is elaborate and specific. The judicial Article III has more than 400 words, and references to substantive and procedural justice appear in other articles and amendments, especially the Fifth, Sixth, Seventh, and Eighth as well as Fourteenth (which has extended most of the federal justice guarantees to the fifty state judicial systems). The constitution of Mexico (1917) has one of the world's longest articles on the judiciary. Half of it, about 2,000 words, is used to describe the writ of *amparo*,[2] the unique feature of Mexican law which, like an injunction, is intended to prevent damage through preliminary judicial decision rather than to establish the right of a claim. In Mexico a writ of *amparo* may be granted in civil and criminal cases, and labor matters.

Constitutions outline procedures for obtaining justice in civil law disputes over mutual grievances between citizens or groups in general terms. Modern constitutions simply reassert the "freedom to seek one's rights" and "litigate and defend one's case as plaintiff or defendant before judicial authorities by availing oneself of all legitimate procedures" (Article 31, Turkish Constitution, 1961). The Italian Constitution of 1947 (Article 24), states: "All are entitled to institute legal proceedings for the protection of their own rights and legitimate interests." Some constitutions try to guarantee the right of easy access to the courts and low-cost legal assistance. However, the courts in many countries, including the United States, are accessible in principle, but not always in practice because of the costs and delays involved. The Mexican constitution of 1917 (Article 17) provides that the service of the Mexican courts be "gratuitous" and adds that "all judicial costs are, accordingly, prohibited."

CRIMINAL LAW

Those acts of the individual which are in conflict with other individuals and with the public order and social values are defined as crimes in either a penal code or in specific criminal laws. They are the proper domain of public criminal law.

Two general principles of criminal law are recognized by practically all modern legal systems:

(1) Criminal offenses must be defined with clarity and *precision* by a properly enacted and published law *prior* to the commission of criminal acts. However, constitutional references to high treason, sedition, sabotage, or rebellion rarely meet this standard of precision. They are often so vague that they can be extended or contracted—like an accordion—to play any political tune.[3] Most constitutions expressly prohibit *ex post facto* laws, recognizing the principle that there is no crime without a preceding law (United States Constitution, Article 1, Section 9). *Ex post facto* laws declare an act criminal after the fact of commission, or retroactively increase the penalty. In a legal sense, even the most repulsive cruelties (e.g., the Nazi death camps) are not crimes unless they are defined as criminal by an existing law which provides for punishment. Retroactive laws that favor an accused person, however, are often permitted. The Brazilian Constitution of 1946 (Article 141/29) states: "Penal law shall determine the individualization of the punishment and shall only be retroactive when it shall so benefit the accused."

(2) An accused person is presumed innocent until proven guilty (see the French Declaration of the Rights of Man and Citizen, Document A.4). Guilt is personal and must be established beyond any reasonable doubt by an appropriate court, following prescribed procedures. Any

other form of determination of guilt and punishment is inadmissible. For instance, some constitutions specifically ban bills of attainder (i.e., punishment by legislative action), or the imposition of sentences by extraordinary tribunals (Switzerland)[4] and special commissions (Argentina).[5]

Constitutions provide the general principles of impartial justice[6] but leave the definition and determination of punishment of such crimes as murder, robbery, arson, kidnapping, rape and theft to either statutory laws or a criminal code. There are two exceptions to this general rule. National constitutions often define the crime of high treason, and occasionally add related crimes such as subversion and sabotage. Communist constitutions define damage to socialist property as a serious crime.[7]

The second exception to the usual constitutional silence on specific crimes concerns the treatment of criminal practices which used to be an abhorrent and widespread practice in the past. The Brazilian Constitution of 1946 (Article 146) proclaims "usury, in any form," punishable by law. On the other hand some constitutional drafters have transferred some acts from the domain of criminal law to that of civil law. Several modern constitutions thus prohibit imprisonment for indebtedness,[8] a former penalty which continued well into the nineteenth century.

In criminal cases the defender of the public order (prosecutor) brings a violator of the law to court, thus personifying and reenacting a conflict between the accused and his community. Usually, the judge is either assisted by other judges in serious cases (e.g., in France) or by representatives of public attitudes: by lay assessors in Communist countries, or by juries in countries inspired by the Anglo-American legal tradition.

The judges and prosecutors are instruments of public order and interest and both receive their salaries from the same source. Consequently, an accused is often at a great disadvantage, psychologically and procedurally. Constitutions try to compensate this danger by guaranteeing that judges will be independent and impartial, by assigning the burden of proof to the prosecution, and by assuring an accused all reasonable means of defense. The Anglo-American judicial system is most thorough in providing these guarantees, reflecting the English and American history of struggle against royal abuses of judicial powers. Justifiably, there is always the fear in that system of possible mistakes that would result in the death of an innocent accused denied an adequate defense.

The fundamental principle that accused are innocent until proven guilty is observed in countries inspired by the Anglo-Saxon common law by placing them on the same level as the prosecutor. The judge then presides over their confrontation as an arbiter, elevated above them both. The judge's symbolic role is stressed by solemn rituals, and his appearance in wig or robe.

When a great government treats the lowliest of criminals as an equal antagonist, strips itself of the executive power which it possesses, and submits the case to twelve ordinary men, allowing the judge only the authority of an umpire, we have a gesture of recognition to the dignity of the individual which has extraordinary dramatic appeal. Its claim is on our emotions, rather than our common sense.[9]

All constitutions today provide for the rights of a person accused of violating fundamental social norms in some detail. However, controversy is always possible over the question of whether the social values expressed in the existing legal norms are really fundamental and worth perpetuating.

Most constitutions differentiate between guarantees of *procedural* fairness and guarantees of *substantive* due process of law. The *manner* in which laws are enforced and disputes settled constitutes procedural due process—the subject *matter* of law is substantive due process. Some constitutions withdraw some matters (e.g., religious heresy or retroactive criminal laws) from legislative regulation. Nevertheless, if an unconstitutional law is the basis of a trial which follows all the procedural requirements it would remain *substantively* unfair. Some lawyers maintain that the Nuremberg war crime trials were procedurally fair trials based on substantively unfair law (retroactive criminal law proclaimed by the victorious allies). A study of past experience reveals examples of trials that were procedurally and substantively fair in their own time but which now seem unfair because the definition of crime has been changed due to changing conditions and ethos. The trial of Jeanne d'Arc in 1431 was, for example, relatively fair procedurally, yet it seems substantively unfair today.[10]

PRETRIAL GUARANTEES

Most constitutions contain the following guarantees:

(1) No one may be arrested or detained, except by virtue of a written order (warrant). No warrant is necessary when a person is caught in *flagrante delicto* (in the act of committing a crime). One of the earliest pretrial rights in England and in other common law countries was the writ of *habeas corpus* which prevents a person's illegal detention without the bringing of charges or the granting of a trial. The English Habeas Corpus Act of 1679 (see Document 4.1) reaffirmed the procedure devised by English judges centuries before to protect the individual against the frequent practice of royal officials who arrested and illegally imprisoned persons without a proper judiciary writ. The Act of 1679 is considered to be one of Great Britain's great constitutional documents.

In different forms, it has traveled far from its verbose original source (see Document 4.2).

(2) To ensure inviolability of residence, letters and private communications, constitutions specifically prohibit *unauthorized* searches and seizure; this problem and its electronic dimension was discussed in another context in chapter 2.

(3) Protection against self-incrimination—the right of silence—and the right to legal counsel during *pretrial* interrogation and investigation[11] are only occasionally stipulated in constitutional texts. Both principles, of course, are considered rights of an accused person during the trial. In many countries, including the United States, trial guarantees are now being extended into the vital pretrial period.

(4) "Excessive bail shall not be required," states the Eighth Amendment to the United States Constitution. This idea is repeated in many constitutions in a slightly different form. "Excessive" usually means an amount higher than necessary to ensure the presence of a defendant (presumed innocent until proven guilty) at a trial—bail is allowed to give the defendant time and freedom of movement to prepare his defense. In the case of crimes for which the penalty is death or in the case of dangerous criminals,[12] bail may be denied.

(5) In countries inspired by the English common law, an indictment by grand jury has been long considered to be a fundamental protection against over-eager or politically biased prosecutors. Grand juries must find the evidence presented by a prosecuting officer sufficient to indicate that a crime has been committed and that the accused person may have committed it, before a trial is sanctioned. The United States Constitution (5th Amendment, clause 1) expresses this principle as follows:

> No person shall be held to answer for a capital, or otherwise infamous crime, unless on a presentment or indictment of a Grand Jury. . . .

This traditional shield against trial on trumped-up charges in the absence of sufficient evidence is being seriously questioned in the United States, where the following objections have been noted: (a) Grand jury proceedings resemble trials in secret and by inquiry. (b) The accused is not allowed counsel in the grand jury room. (c) No judge or other impartial arbiter is present during grand jury proceedings, only a government counsel and volunteer grand jurors (usually picked by court officials, and quite frequently their friends). (d) Minority groups and blue-collar workers are under-represented on grand jury panels. (e) The rights of bail and appeal are limited and the privilege against self-incrimination is curtailed. (f) Grand jury decisions often have an eroding effect upon the basic assumption that an accused is "innocent until found guilty," although they are only empaneled to sanction future trials.

A research paper on the subject of grand juries in the 1970s, presented by two legal experts, Michael Tigar and Madeleine Levy, at the Center for Democratic Institutions at Santa Barbara, severely criticized grand jury indictment procedures (*New York Times,* January 8, 1972):

> The evils which were disowned in the creation of the right to a fair trial are, in fact, quite at home in the grand jury room: there is no right to notice of the scope and nature of the crimes being investigated; there is no confrontation of the witnesses who have laid the trail of investigation to the witnesses' doorstep and, collaterally, there is no possibility, much less a right, to cross-examine those witnesses. In essence, there is trial in secret, and by inquiry.

In Roman law countries, a special investigating judge (*juge d'instruction* in France) conducts the preliminary interrogation of an accused and the chief witnesses and sifts the evidence. This procedure seems to favor investigating judges, the trial judges, and the prosecutor over the accused. On the other hand, grand juries are not entirely immune to public passions or an occasional collusion with the prosecution.

(6) *Statutes of limitations* are not part of constitutional, judicial guarantees. Most countries have laws that limit prosecution of offenses to a specified period of time, three to twenty years, after commission of an act which would call for prosecution and punishment. The United States Supreme Court explained the doctrine as follows:

> Statutes of limitation find their justification in necessity and convenience rather than in logic. They represent expedients, rather than principles. They are practical and pragmatic devices to spare the courts from litigation of stale claims, and the citizen from being put to his defense after memories have faded, witnesses have died or disappeared, and evidence has been lost (*Chase Securities Corp.* v. *Donaldson,* 325 U.S. 304, 1945).

The statute of limitations was extended by West Germany in 1969 to close off a potential escape route for undetected Nazi criminals. The bill which extended the statute of limitations from twenty to thirty years had obvious political and moral overtones since those individuals suspected of genocide and other war crimes during the Nazi regime may now be prosecuted until December 31, 1979.

INDEPENDENT JUDGES

The right of an individual to be tried before an impartial and independent judge is not usually found in constitutional bills of rights

Document 4.1

THE RIGHTS OF THE ACCUSED:
THE SEVENTEENTH AND EIGHTEENTH CENTURIES

Britain (The Habeas Corpus Act), 1679

Be it enacted ... that whensoever any person or persons shall bring any *habeas corpus* directed unto any sherrif or sherrifs, gaoler, minister or other person whatsoever for any person in his or their custody, and the said writ shall be served upon the said officer or left at the gaol or prison with any of the under-officers, under-keepers or deputy of the said officers or keepers, that the said officer or his officers, his or their under-officers, under-keepers or deputies shall within three days after the service thereof ... bring or cause to be brought the body of the party so committed or restrained unto or before ... the judges or the barons of the said court from whence the said writ shall issue, ... and shall then likewise certify the true causes of his detainer or imprisonment ...*

France (The Declaration of 1789)

(4) Liberty consists in the power to do anything that does not injure others; accordingly, the exercise of the natural rights of each man has no limits except those that secure to the other members of society the enjoyment of these same rights. These limits can be determined only by law.**

(5) The law has the right to forbid only such actions as are injurious to society. Nothing can be forbidden that is not interdicted by the law, and no one can be constrained to do that which it does not order ...

(7) No man can be accused, arrested, or detained, except in the cases determined by the law and according to the forms that it has prescribed. Those who procure, expedite, execute, or cause to be executed arbitrary orders ought to be punished; but every citizen summoned or seized in virtue of the law ought to render instant obedience; he makes himself guilty by resistance.

(8) The law ought to establish only penalties that are strictly and obviously necessary, and no one can be punished except in virtue of a law established and promulgated prior to the offense and legally applied.

(9) Every man being presumed innocent until he has been pronounced guilty, if it is thought indispensable to arrest him, all severity that may not be necessary to secure his person ought to be strictly suppressed by law.***

---

*The act has twenty-one long articles that list the exceptions in cases of treason, felony, and certain types of debts, and prevent jailers from pleading ignorance or moving the prisoner to another jail.

**Compare with the constitution of Brazil of 1967 (Article 150) which states: "No one may be obliged to do or refrain from doing anything except by virtue of the law."

***Other themes from the French document, consisting of seventeen major points, were reproduced in Document A.4.

Document 4.2

THE RIGHTS OF THE ACCUSED:
THE TWENTIETH CENTURY

Rumania, 1965

Article 31. .... No person can be detained or arrested if there are no well-grounded proofs or indications that he committed a deed listed and punished by the law. The organs of inquiry can order the detention of a person for a maximum of 24 hours. No one can be arrested except on the basis of an order of arrest issued by a court or the Procurator.

Turkey, 1961

Article 30. Taking into custody is resorted to only *in flagrante delicto* or in cases where delay is likely to thwart justice. .... The person taken or held in custody shall be arraigned within 24 hours excluding the time taken to send him to the court nearest to the place of arrest, and after the lapse of this time, such person cannot be deprived of his freedom without a court judgment. When a person is taken or held in custody, or is so arraigned, his next of kin shall be immediately notified thereof.

Pakistan, 1964

Article 9. No law should authorize the punishment of a person for an act or omission that was not punishable by law at the time of the act or omission.

Italy, 1947

Article 27. Punishment must not consist of measures contrary to humane precepts and shall aim at reforming the condemned person.

West Germany, 1949

Article 104. The freedom of the individual may be restricted only on the basis of a formal law and only with due regard to the forms prescribed therein. Detained persons may be subjected neither to mental nor to physical ill-treatment.*

USSR, 1936

Article 127. Citizens of the USSR are guaranteed inviolability of the person. No person may be placed under arrest except by decision of a court or with the sanction of a procurator.

Uganda, 1966

Article 24. Every person who is charged with a criminal offense shall be presumed to be innocent until he is proved or has pleaded guilty; shall be informed as soon as is reasonably practicable, in a language that he understands and in detail, of the nature of the offence charged.

*This article aims at preventing by a constitutional prohibition any return to the Gestapo-like methods of interrogation and detention.

along with the listing of inalienable, individual rights. That right can usually be found expressed as a general principle in the articles which deal with the judicial system. Independence and impartiality require that the judge be impervious to executive pressure or other influences in criminal cases, and neutral in his attitude toward both defendant and plaintiff in civil cases.[13]

The independent judge is, nonetheless, *dependent* on the law. He is also *partial* to the law as it exists because that is the basis of his interpretations and applications. Although he may have doubts about the law and the constitution, express dissent as a voter, and hope for changes in the supreme or statutory law—he must still apply the law as it is until it is changed by amendment or legislative processes. When a new constitution and new laws are imposed by revolution, a coup d'état, or other illegitimate means they may contain concepts and goals abhorrent to the judge. He must then decide whether to apply the law regardless of content and origin or refer to the previous supreme law or a supraconstitutional standard of justice and decency according to his own conscience. German judges were criticized for their docile application of Nazi laws and because they failed to challenge those laws in the name of international law and morality. The criticism suggests that under exceptional circumstances a judge may refuse to apply the existing law and constitution and sabotage them. How, for example, should a jurist having Communist convictions apply the laws of a Western democracy, or a liberal judge apply those of a Communist country? The constitution of Communist Poland (1952), for instance, equates the will and program of the Communist party of Poland with the supreme law of the land. The Polish courts are, according to Article 48, "custodians of the political and social system of the Polish People's Republic" (as imposed by the Communist party) as well as "independent and subject only to the law" (as enacted by Communist legislators). Neither the party nor the legislators are necessarily representative of the will of the majority.

The issue is beyond the scope of this study. However, it should be remembered that judicial impartiality and independence does not mean that judges are independent of legal systems established and maintained by political processes.

Judges are usually appointed for life, pending good behavior, or they are popularly elected to assure that they are independent of the executive. Judicial salaries and positions are sometimes specifically ensured in the constitution. The constitution of Belgium (1831) states:

> Judges are appointed for life. No judge may be deprived of his office or suspended except by a specific judgment. The transfer of a judge can only be made on the basis of a new appointment and with his consent (Article

100). . . . The salaries of members of the Judiciary are fixed by law (Article 102).

Many countries appoint judges with or without the concurrence of legislative bodies, from among practicing lawyers. In the Anglo-American system, judges are usually former court-lawyers (barristers in England). In countries which adhere to the Roman codified law (e.g. France), judgeship is a profession for which law students prepare by taking a series of special examinations. That method is eminently suited to legal systems where law is codified into civil and criminal codes (i.e., simplified digests of general, abstract principles of law that may be applied to concrete situations). The application of codified law requires legal training but less experience in specific cases than required by those systems which are dependent on case law and judicial precedent.

Judges are still elected in some countries (e.g., in some states of the United States, Switzerland, and the Communist countries). The outcome of those elections is determined by the influence of political parties, particularly the dominant party. Recent statistics indicate that American voters are indifferent to prospective judges proposed by the political parties.[14]

Obviously, judges cannot be immunized against political influence through either the elective process or by lifetime appointment. Consequently, some systems combine these requirements of judicial independence with some form of subsequent popular control. The device most frequently used is the recall. The Japanese Constitution drafted by General MacArthur's staff makes it possible for Japanese voters to recall members of the Supreme Court.[15] According to the Japanese Constitution Supreme Court judges are appointed by the cabinet, and the chief justice by the emperor on the basis of a cabinet decision. All of them are subject to recall every ten years at the time of general elections. To date not a single Supreme Court justice has been recalled, partly because of party dominance in the elections, and partly because the voters are indifferent or unable to evaluate the complex records of their justices.

JURIES & LAY ASSESSORS

The practice of trial by an impartial jury or by a combination of a judge and lay assessors may be traced to a concession obtained from the English King John by his barons at Runnymede in 1215. The Magna Carta (Chapter 39) states:

> No freeman shall be arrested and imprisoned, or dispossessed, or outlawed, or banished, or in any way molested; nor will we set forth against him, nor send against him, unless by the lawful judgement of his peers. . . .

Direct participation in a trial by nonjudicial persons has undergone two changes since 1215.

First, modern juries no longer emphasize the selection of knowledgeable peers. On the contrary, they are chosen from a cross-section[16] of the population. Jurors are selected at random, not for their knowledge of the case but for their ignorance of it and therefore, presumably, their lack of bias. In some American trials, jurors have been eliminated because they read about the crime in newspapers and formed opinions about it. In the 1970s, for instance, it was extremely difficult to secure jurors for trials involving members of the Black Panther party. Some citizens were simply unwilling to serve, others were intimidated by black militants, and few could be considered unbiased and impartial by both the defense and the prosecution. The national chairman of the Black Panther party, Bobby G. Seale, was on trial for six months, charged with kidnapping and murder in the torture-slaying of Alex Rackley. The trial took four months and a venire of 1,500 persons before a jury of twelve could be formed. Eventually the jury was dismissed without reaching a verdict. The judge dismissed all charges against the defendant because "massive publicity" about the trial made it "impossible to believe that an unbiased jury could be selected without superhuman efforts."

Many lawyers and journalists felt it would be impossible to find an unbiased and untainted jury for the second trial. Others disagreed. Lesley Oelsner wrote (*New York Times*, May 30, 1971):

> Was it really impossible to get a fair jury, in all of Connecticut, to retry the Panther leader and his young co-defendant, Mrs. Ericka Huggins? What if the defendant here were Lee Harvey Oswald, the assassin of President John F. Kennedy? And in an era studded with politically tainted trials, all publicized, would there come a time when some defendants are simply let go because jurors could not be found?

Lesley Oelsner also quoted a constitutional expert, Yale Kamisar, who admitted that in the Panther case it was easy to say the "good guys" won, but "what about cases where the 'bad guys' win? What if some civil rights workers are murdered in Mississippi, and the judge says 'I find it impossible to get a jury'?"

In a related trial, also in New Haven, 242 persons were questioned before twelve jurors and three alternates were selected. In New York, 212 prospective jurors were examined over a five-week period before a jury was seated to try a group of Panthers on trial in the state Supreme Court. In 1970, during his trial in Los Angeles, Charles M. Manson waved a newspaper at the jury in an effort to disqualify its members.

Drawing by Ed Fisher; © 1972 The New Yorker Magazine, Inc.

"Where's all that prejudicial pre-trial publicity you promised me?"

That newspaper headlined President Nixon's opinion that Manson was the murderer. The president's prejudgment violated the principle that an accused is "innocent until proven guilty" and it threatened to destroy the jurors' impartiality. In this case, however, the jury reached a verdict and condemned Charles M. Manson to death.[17]

Secondly, there has been a sharp decline in the use of the jury system in all countries, including the country of its origin, Britain. The jury is used in some European countries only in the gravest cases (France) or in cases in which the public interest is particularly involved. The Belgian

Constitution of 1831 (Article 98) prescribes that "a jury is empanelled for all criminal affairs and for political and press misdemeanors." The United States is the only country in which there is general belief in the jury system. It is still used in federal and state courts and in criminal as well as in civil cases.[18]

On May 20, 1968, the United States Supreme Court ruled that trial by jury in *serious* criminal cases is fundamental to the American judicial system and that the provisions of the Sixth Amendment are therefore binding on the states. The question of how to define petty as opposed to serious crime remains. In many states misdemeanors (e.g., possession of narcotics, possession of stolen property, gambling, assault in the third degree, etc.) are disposed of without a jury. Each of these acts may result in sentences of up to one year in prison, which exceeds the federal guideline which defines "petty" (i.e., crimes carrying a maximum sentence of six months in prison and a $500 fine). The hearing of misdemeanor cases by jury, which are now heard by a judge or panel of judges, would cost New York City millions of dollars for several new courthouses, assistant district attorneys, court clerks and stenographers (according to the *New York Times,* June 1, 1968). In 1968 New York's criminal courts tried 480,000 new cases; by the end of the year 520,000 were still unsettled.

Many countries, including the Communist states, have replaced the jury with two or three lay assessors. Unlike the juries, which only evaluate facts and leave the application of the law to the judge, lay assessors sift the evidence and apply law jointly with the judge. Lay assessors, however, tend to be awed by the professional judge's knowledge and expertise and become passive assistants rather than partners. In the Soviet Union, a professional judge and two lay assessors (all three selected by the party) preside over most trials. The lay judges rarely dare to overrule the professional.

There are several sources of opposition to participation by laymen in the judicial process, because the public is now well informed by the mass media. The most frequent argument arises from the cumbersome and lengthy procedures of trial by jury and its resulting cost, especially in civil cases. Other arguments are contradictory. A study made at the University of Chicago shows that judge and jury agreed in 81 percent of the criminal cases; disagreement occurred mostly in statutory rape cases and first-offense, drunken driving cases. The study indicates that the twelve wise and just men, if they are of German and British background, may be quite vindictive, while those of Negro and Slavic descent seem to favor acquittal more often.

Except for the United States and Communist countries, there is a tendency which seems to favor professionally trained judges who will, in full public view, decide cases alone. Serious cases would be tried before a panel of two or three professional judges. The underlying reason for this trend appears to be that professional training can be trusted to make judges at least as immune to passion and bias as jurors. Foreign observers may venture the tongue-in-cheek comment that Americans cannot trust a judge to evaluate an insurance claim in an automobile accident case without the help of twelve jurors, but they can trust a majority of one in Supreme Court decisions, which treat really explosive and delicate issues of justice under the constitution.

Joint decisions made by three or more judges in European courts rarely reveal that they have not been unanimous. Dissent among judges over the meaning and application of law could be construed as a challenge to its supreme majesty and precision and raise prejudicial questions concerning the decisions made under it. This is in sharp contrast with the common law practice of indicating dissent and publicizing the opinion of the minority. Probably both practices have merit, but the American practice of publicizing judicial dissent may signify a humble admission that there is rarely only one correct and just solution to a conflict of private and public interests in matters of human justice. The constitutional provisions described above demonstrate once more the difference between justice in the abstract and the realities of justice administered by human beings. The latter is relative, changing, and quite often inaccurate.

SELF-INCRIMINATION & DEFENSE

Protection against self-incrimination is viewed as the cornerstone of a fair trial in practically all constitutions of the Western Hemisphere[19] and a few others that have adopted the principle of the American Fifth Amendment: "Nor shall any person . . . be compelled in any criminal case to be a witness against himself."

In many European countries, and in those portions of Asia and Africa which have long been under Europe's legal influence, protection against self-incrimination is not felt to be as essential to a fair trial. In many European systems the accused is not put under oath and therefore cannot commit perjury; it is assumed that he may lie in self-defense. His truthfulness is treated as an alleviating circumstance.[20] In Communist countries, dramatic self-accusation often becomes an essential portion of a purge trial. The last Stalinist trial in Czechoslovakia is a case in point. That trial eliminated all Jews from leading positions in the party and the state, and the public self-incrimination of Rudolf Slánský, former secretary-general of the party, and other former leaders was *the* cornerstone of the judicial proceedings (see Document 4.3).

Document 4.3

SELF-INCRIMINATION IN A COMMUNIST TRIAL

According to the official organ of the Czechoslovak Communist party, *Rudé Právo,* November 21, 1952, p.3, the following exchange took place between the accused former Secretary-General of the Communist party, Rudolf Slánský, and the Public Prosecutor:

Slánský: " . . . and so it happened that through Trotskyism and opportunism I have finally become an enemy of the Communist party and an agent of the bourgeoisie . . . "

Public Prosecutor: "You wanted to proceed as Tito did, by Titoist methods?"

Slánský: "Yes."

Public Prosecutor: "This means: to place the agents of imperialism in the government, honest Communists into jail, and the whole country into chains. Is that so?"

Slánský: "Yes."

Public Prosecutor: "You have engaged in treasonous activities in the service of Western imperialists and, above all, American would-be conquerors of the world."

Slánský: "I admit it."

Public Prosecutor: "The aim was to become a Czechoslovak Tito?"

Slánský: "Yes."*

*Slánský was executed by hanging.

"Defense is an inalienable right at every stage of legal proceedings," states the Italian Constitution of 1947 (Article 24). Practically all national constitutions, in one way or another, proclaim this basic right which usually includes (a) the right to be informed of the nature and cause of the accusation, (b) the right of an accused to be confronted with witnesses against him, (c) the right to compulsory procedure for obtaining witnesses in one's behalf, and (d) the right to have the assistance of counsel for one's defense (Sixth Amendment to the United States Constitution). In multinational states such as Russia or China[21] the right to have an interpreter may be as important as the right to legal counsel.

Does the right of defense include the right to use every possible trick on behalf of an accused? Should a self-confessed murderer be freed because a minor technicality in the criminal procedure was neglected? What is a minor point in a procedure that may lead to life imprisonment? Many controversies have evolved around these and similar issues. Generally, however, the criminal system in most countries tends to provide less rigorous protection for those facing criminal charges than does the United States Constitution as interpreted by the Supreme Court.

Even in England, where the writ of habeas corpus and the jury system originated, some second thoughts on the subject of defense and self-incrimination have appeared in recent times. In 1972, for instance, a committee composed of judges, prominent lawyers and professors of law and chaired by Sir Edmund Davies, a Lord Justice of Appeal, recommended drastic changes in English criminal procedures. Most of them favored removing some of the defendant's built-in advantages. The recommendations were based on nearly eight years of deliberation and wide consultation. The final report frankly stated that one of its objectives was to prevent acquittals for the "increasing class of sophisticated professional criminals" who refused to answer police questions and who manufactured elaborate false evidence. The report then added:

> We need hardly say that we have no wish to lessen the fairness of criminal trials. But it must be clear what fairness means in this connection. It means, or it ought to mean, that the law should be such as will secure as far as possible that the result of the trial is the right one. . . . We disagree entirely with the idea that the defense have a sacred right to the benefit of anything in the law which may give them a chance of acquittal, even on a technicality, however strong the case is against them.

The report further recommended limiting the defendant's right of silence, especially if he fails to mention facts he later brings up at his trial, thus preventing the police and the prosecution from checking these facts in time. The committee also favored abolishing the right of the defendant to make unsworn statements which, in England, can be read to the court but cannot be subject to cross-examination by the prosecution. If the defendant then refuses to be cross-examined under oath, his refusal could be counted as corroboration of evidence against him.

SPEEDY & PUBLIC TRIAL

"In all criminal prosecutions, the accused shall enjoy the right to a speedy and public trial," states the Sixth Amendment to the United States Constitution and, similarly, so do almost all national constitutions. Two qualifications must be added. First, in many countries cases involving national security or those offending public morals may be held in secret. The dictatorial systems usually interpret national security rather broadly, so that any type of offense may have security overtones and therefore many cases are tried in secret. Second, in those democracies where the mass media may sometimes operate with irresponsible freedom, the right to a public trial may not always favor an accused. The practice of televising trials, for instance, may be so distracting that it can deny a defendant due process.[22] The right to a public trial is intended to protect defendants and does not belong to television and newsreel cameramen, photographers, and newspaper reporters. It has been alleged that "more constitutional questions have been raised by too much rather than too little public involvement in trials,"[23] but a recent Twentieth Century Fund study[24] does not confirm that statement. Except for a few widely publicized cases where prejudicial publicity was clearly possible (e.g., the trials of Lee Harvey Oswald and Dr. Samuel Sheppard) there is simply no press coverage whatsoever. The authors of the study suggest that the disadvantages of excessive publicity should be weighed carefully against the usefulness of the press as "public watchdog" in protecting the rights of defendants.[25] The impact of modern publicity on the jury system was already discussed above.

EXCESSIVE PUNISHMENT

The protection against excessive fines and cruel and unusual punishment provided in the Eighth Amendment to the United States Constitution is repeated in less laconic form in many national constitutions. The Mexican Constitution of 1917 (Article 22) is quite specific:

> Punishment by mutilation and infamy, branding, flogging, beating with sticks, torture of any kind, excessive fines, confiscation of property and any unusual or extreme penalties are prohibited. Capital punishment for political offenses is likewise prohibited; as regards other offenses, it can be only imposed for high treason committed during a foreign war, parricide, murder that is treacherous, premeditated, or committed for profit, arson, abduction, highway robbery, piracy and grave military offenses.

The Mexican Constitution also forbids imposing fines on day laborers or workmen if the fine exceeds their wages for one week. Many constitutions forbid confiscation of property as a criminal penalty. The Venezuelan Constitution (Article 60/7) bans any sentence to "perpetual or infamous punishment" and sets a maximum of thirty years for imprisonment. Evidently, the humane words of national constitutions must be ever so often compared with the actual treatment of prisoners and convicts by the police or prison wards. A gruesome example of such a contrast between constitution and practice was reported from the Central African Republic, a former French colony whose constitution had been modeled after the French. On July 31, 1972, President Jean-Bédel Bokassa visited a prison in Bangui where he ordered his soldiers to beat men imprisoned for theft with clubs. Of the forty-six men beaten, three died on the spot. The following day their corpses were put on public display with the battered survivors, many of whom appeared near death. President Bokassa justified beating to death by proclaiming: "Thieves must all die. There will be no more theft in the Central African Republic."

The death sentence is the most controversial issue. All constitutions ban torture, which may or may not result in death. Most national constitutions, however, seem to permit execution by guillotine, firing squad, electrocution, hanging, or lethal gas as penalty for certain crimes and under some circumstances, i.e., during war or national emergency. Many nations, however, have modified and softened their constitutional attitudes toward the death penalty. These changes are the result, at least partly, of new theories which suggest that mental health and the social environment are the major and truly relevant factors in fixing direct responsibility for crime. Furthermore, constitutions reflect uncertainty regarding criminal penalties—are they meant to avenge a death, deter crime, or reform the individual?

Since World War II, some countries have abolished the death sentence (Austria, Australia, Nepal, and New Zealand, for instance). Many have abolished the death penalty for murder only but have retained it as a punishment and deterrent for military cases (several Latin American countries and Italy).[26] The death penalty may be used to punish wartime treason, collaboration with the enemy, piracy, and arson in royal dockyards and arsenals (Britain), and desertion and serious crimes in wartime (Switzerland and the Scandinavian countries). In some countries the death penalty was abandoned *de facto;* it is never used in some countries and rarely imposed in others. In Belgium, for instance, other than one soldier executed in 1918, no execution has taken place since 1863. In Liechtenstein the last execution took place in 1798, and in the past one hundred years in Luxembourg one man was executed in 1948 (for war crimes). In Israel a major Nazi war criminal, Adolf Eichmann, was executed in 1962. Ten years later, however, Israel did not impose the death penalty on Kozo Okamoto, one of three gunmen who killed twenty-four passengers in the arrival hall at the Tel Aviv airport on May 30, 1972. The state prosecutor, Lt. Col. David Israeli, explained:

> Okamoto certainly deserves death but Israel should not execute him. This country has a moral force. That force should impose a restraint on the country, even in a case such as this. Israel should not put a man to death, even if the law permits it, not even if the prisoner deeply desires it.

It should be noted, of course, that in general, it is the Israeli government's policy not to send Arab terrorists to the gallows; it is believed that such a policy may save Israeli lives because it induces Arab guerillas to give up when cornered rather than fight on in desperation.

The death penalty was abolished in the Soviet Union in 1947 but was restored in 1950 for spies, traitors, and "wrecker diversionists"—a broad category which subsequently included all types of political offenders. In 1950 the death penalty could be imposed on persons favoring Tito (see Document 4.3). In the United States, eleven states[27] have outlawed capital punishment and three retain it for special cases only, such as murder of policemen or prison guards.

Following the assassinations of President John F. Kennedy, Reverend Martin Luther King, and Senator Robert F. Kennedy, Attorney General Ramsey Clark advocated abolition of the death penalty for all federal crimes, including assassination. In his testimony at a Senate hearing (July 2, 1968) he said, "In the midst of anxiety and fear, complexity and doubt, perhaps our greatest need is reverence for life, mere life, our life, our lives, the lives of others, all life."[28] He added, "A humane and generous concern for every individual, for his safety, his health, and his fulfillment will do more to soothe the savage heart than the fear of state-inflicted death which chiefly serves to remind us how close we remain to the jungle."

His main argument seemed to be that there was no evidence that the death penalty deterred crime; communities where it is imposed have no better records on violent crime than those where it is banned.

Between 1968 and 1972 nobody was executed in the United States. On February 23, 1972, the Supreme Court of California ruled by a six-to-one majority that capital punishment violated the constitution of the state of California which prohibits "cruel and unusual punishment." The court's argument was that death "is, literally, an unusual punishment among civilized nations," and that "society can be protected from convicted criminals by far less onerous means than execution." As a result, 107 men and women awaiting death in California prisons, including Sirhan Sirhan, Charles Manson, and four of his accomplices, were spared.

Finally, on June 29, 1972, the Supreme Court of the United States ruled that capital punishment, *as now administered* in the United States, was unconstitutional. The historic decision came on a vote of five to four. The four negative votes were cast by the four judges named by President Nixon. The five justices who voted in the majority issued separate opinions and disagreed on the reasons for their conclusion. Three justices (William O. Douglas, William J. Brennan, Jr., and Thurgood Marshall) concluded that executions in contemporary America

Drawing by Ross; © 1972 The New Yorker Magazine, Inc.

"The way I see it, when you start tempering justice with mercy, you've had it!"

violated the constitutional prohibition against "cruel and unusual punishment." The other two (Potter Stewart and Byron R. White) argued that the present system gives judges and juries excessive discretion to decree life or death and that they impose it so erratically that the result is "cruel and unusual punishment" (see Document 4.4).

Document 4.4

THE U.S. SUPREME COURT ON DEATH PENALTY
(June 29, 1972)

Concurring Opinions

Justice Brennan: In sum, the punishment is inconsistent with . . . four principles. Death is an unusually severe and degrading punishment; there is a strong
probability that it is inflicted arbitrarily; its rejection by contemporary society
is virtually total; and there is no reason to believe that it serves any penal
purpose more effectively than the less severe punishment of imprisonment. . . .

Justice White: When imposition of the penalty reaches a certain degree of
infrequency, it would be very doubtful that any existing general need for
retribution would be measurably satisfied. Nor could it be said with confidence
that society's need for specific deterrence justifies death for so few when for so
many in like circumstances life imprisonment or shorter prison terms are judged
sufficient, or that community values are measurably reenforced by authorizing
a penalty so rarely invoked. Most important, a major goal of the criminal law
—to deter others by punishing the convicted criminal—would not be substantially served where the penalty is so seldom invoked that it ceases to be the
credible threat essential to influence the conduct of others.

Justice Stewart: I simply conclude that the Eighth and Fourteenth Amendments cannot tolerate the infliction of a sentence of death under legal systems
that permit this unique penalty to be so wantonly and so freakishly imposed.

Justice Douglas: We know that the discretion of judges and juries in imposing the death penalty enables the penalty to be selectively applied, feeding
prejudices against the accused if he is poor and despised, poor and lacking
political clout, or if he is a member of a suspect or unpopular minority, and
saving those who by social position may be in a more protected position. In
ancient Hindu law a Brahmin was exempt from capital punishment . . .gener-
ally . . . punishment increased in severity as social status diminished. We have,
I fear, taken in practice the same position. . . .

Justice Marshall: At a time in our history when the streets of the nation's
cities inspire fear and despair, rather than pride and hope, it is difficult to
maintain objectivity and concern for our fellow citizens. But the measure of a
country's greatness is its ability to retain compassion in time of crisis. . . . In
striking down capital punishment. . . . in recognizing the humanity of our fellow
beings, we pay ourselves the highest tribute. . . .

Dissenting Opinions

Chief Justice Burger (with whom Mr. Justice Blackmun, Mr. Justice Powell
and Mr. Justice Rehnquist join): Today the Court has not ruled that capital
punishment is *per se* violative of the Eighth Amendment; nor has it ruled that
the punishment is barred for any particular class or classes of crimes. . . . Since
the two pivotal concurring opinions turn on the assumption that the punishment of death is now meted out in a random and unpredictable manner, legisla-

tive bodies may seek to bring their laws into compliance with the Court's ruling by providing standards for juries and judges to follow in determining the sentence in capital cases or by more narrowly defining the crimes for which the penalty is to be imposed. If such standards can be devised or the crimes more meticulously defined, the result cannot be detrimental. . . . Since there is no majority of the Court on the ultimate issue presented in these cases, the future of capital punishment in this country has been left in an uncertain limbo.

POSTTRIAL GUARANTEES

Constitutions typically provide two basic post-trial guarantees: (1) the right of appeal, which provides the person convicted of a crime a second chance in case the trial procedure was faulty or a mistake or some other irregularity is invoked; and (2) the right of a person acquitted not to be tried again for the same crime within the same jurisdiction. In the absence of this provision a person could be tried again and again by a vindictive prosecutor until the desired verdict is reached. The protection against unlimited number of trials on the same charge is usually referred to as the "double jeopardy clause," following the words of the Fifth Amendment to the United States Constitution, "nor shall any person be subject for the same offense to be twice put in jeopardy of life and limb."

SEMI-JUDICIAL AGENCIES & OMBUDSMEN

The regular court systems which deal with civil law suits and criminal proceedings are supplemented by quasi-executive and quasi-judicial agencies which ensure impartial justice in the domain of administrative rules. These agencies are usually independent of both the executive and legislative branches of government but are responsible to both.

The names[29] and the scope of their functions and powers vary greatly, but the reason for their recent growth in numbers and importance is obvious. The need for the additional protection of individuals and groups against administrative arbitrariness and injustice in the modern welfare state as well as the growing bureaucratic apparatus and its power to make enforceable rules is well recognized. E. Emmett Tyrrell succinctly expressed that need in an article commemorating the administrations of President Calvin Coolidge (1923–1929) by saying "The government claimed to do less good in those days and hence did less harm." His tongue-in-cheek article appeared in the *New York Times*

(July 8, 1972) under the title "Calvin Coolidge, the Last Great President." Coolidge was described as a leader who "probably spent more time napping than any President in the nation's history."

Many European countries (e.g., France, West Germany, Sweden, and Finland) maintain administrative court systems which effectively deal with complaints against administrative injustice and neglect, as well as with conflicts between segments of public authority. These administrative courts are criticized by Anglo-Saxon observers who argue that the personal responsibility of bureaucrats is decreased if a different law and a separate court system are applied to them. Administrative courts are thus viewed with suspicion because they extend an already growing bureaucratic power, for it seems that bureaucrats may have delegated to themselves legislative as well as judicial prerogatives. The French experience does not confirm this pessimism because French administrative courts, although manned by bureaucrats with legal training, have not been prejudiced in favor of the administration.

The supreme French administrative court is the Council of State *(Conseil d'Etat)*. The litigation selection of the council deals with appeals from lower administrative courts. At the same time, according to the constitution, the Council of State is an influential, although only advisory agency of the executive. Its personnel, rigidly trained in jurisprudence, advise the government on bills to be submitted to Parliament for approval or modification. In the words of the French Constitution (Articles 38 and 39), the Council of State must be consulted on ordinary bills as well as ordinances that are based on the frequent parliamentary delegation of legislative powers to the Council of Ministers.

In the United States, the independent regulatory agencies perform important executive and judicial functions. There are about sixty in all, including the "big seven": the Civil Aeronautics Board, Federal Communications Commission, Federal Power Commission, Federal Trade Commission, Interstate Commerce Commission, National Labor Relations Board, and Securities and Exchange Commission. These agencies are supposedly independent of the legislative and the executive branches (although some are associated with the executive branch, e.g., the Food and Drug Administration is part of the Department of Health, Education and Welfare). The former chairman of one of them, William L. Cary, writes that "their total independence is a myth, but the myth is worth preserving."[30] Even a myth, it seems, may generate the reality of independent impartiality. These semijudicial agencies, like the Western European administrative courts, permit speedy and rational rule making and adjudication in response to demands articulated by an interested public and various interest groups.

In the Scandinavian welfare states, Britain, New Zealand, (and in West Germany in military matters only), Guyana,[31] and Mauritius[32] the ombudsman, a new agency to protect citizens against bureaucratic injustice, seems to have proved its worth. The ombudsman is a parliamentary delegate or agent of justice, i.e., a commissioner who *investigates* but does not adjudicate, individual complaints against bureaucratic abuse. Sweden was the first country to introduce the *Justitieombudsman* into constitutional theory and practice (and in abbreviated form, into our language).

The ombudsman in Britain and New Zealand, called the Parliamentary Commissioner for Administration, usually does not substitute his judgment for that of bureaucrats. He inquires about the way in which a law or rule was implemented. His main weapons are persuasion and publicity rather than enforcement in the narrower sense of the word. His primary effectiveness, it is argued, lies in his sheer existence; it is often the *possibility* of investigation that keeps bureaucrats on their toes. The effectiveness of the ombudsman is a powerful argument for the establishment of civilian review boards or ombudsmen in American city and state governments, where the opportunity for administrative abuse is as great as on the federal level.[33] An ombudsman's investigation is usually started by a simple letter of complaint sent by a citizen. In Britain, citizen complaints are sifted and channeled by members of Parliament to the Parliamentary Commissioner who is appointed by the Parliament and responsible to it. The British white paper issued on October 12, 1965, listed fifty-one ministries and departments that are now subject to the commissioner's investigations. Ministerial files, excepting cabinet documents, are accessible to him. The commissioner's duty is described as "protection of individuals from mal-administration of the central government." The extension of protection to local government is expected to follow the experience at the central level.

In 1968, the Indian cabinet introduced a bill for the creation of an agency to inquire into complaints based on actions of all federal public servants, including ministers. The Indian ombudsman (called *Lok Pal*), assisted by a network of assistants throughout India, is to be appointed by the president of India after consultation with the leader of the opposition and the chief justice.[34]

In several constitutions, the agency for administrative justice is combined with the office of a Prosecutor General. This practice is followed in several Latin American countries. The Venezuelan Constitution (1961) for instance, established a hybrid agency called the Public Ministry for that purpose under the direction of the Prosecutor General (*Fiscal General*) who is elected by the chambers of the Venezuelan Congress to which he must report annually. According to Article 220, the powers of the Public Ministry are:

(1) to see that constitutional rights and guarantees are respected; (2) to see that there is speed and proper conduct in the administration of justice . . . (5) to initiate actions on which there are grounds for enforcing civil, criminal, administrative, or disciplinary liability incurred by public officials in carrying out their functions . . .

ADMINISTRATIVE CONTROLS
IN DICTATORSHIPS

Dictatorships, like democracies, need to keep their administrators in line and on their toes. In contrast to the democracies, which primarily need to prevent administrative rule makers from arbitrarily abusing individual and group rights, administrative controls in the dictatorships are dominantly concerned with ensuring that the administrative structures adhere to government plans and directives. That was the role of the censorate under the Manchu Empire in China, and it is the main function of the complex control systems maintained in Communist countries. Those countries are characterized by competing and overlapping bureaucratic hierarchies penetrated and watched by both the party informers and the secret police, which simultaneously pervade and control administration and the armed forces. The resulting interplay of authority holds both controllers and the controlled responsible for the fulfillment of state plans and directives.[35]

The Soviet centralized control system has undergone several changes which are reflected at several levels and in various functions. The main problem has been an overlap between party control over the administration and police and the administrative-police control over the party itself. The question is: who should control the performance of the millions of Soviet citizens who are civil servants and employees and who should control the elite (i.e., the 12 million members of the party)? In addition, there is the familiar question, who should control the controllers?

The Soviet Constitution is silent with regard to the important and all-pervading party controls. It does, however, provide an important and powerful Procurator General of the USSR, who is concerned with criminal justice and with the control of administrative performance. The Procurator General is elected by the Supreme Soviet (parliament) for a seven-year term. According to the constitution he has the following functions:

Supreme supervisory power to ensure the strict observance of the law by all Ministries and institutions subordinated to them, as well as by officials and citizens of the USSR generally, is vested in the Procurator General of the USSR (Article 113).

Procurators of the Republics, Territories, Regions, Autonomous Regions, and Autonomous Republics are appointed by the Procurator General of the USSR for a term of five years (Article 115).

The system of soviet procurators is the Russian[36] version of a network of ombudsmen. The procurators may participate in the sessions of the soviets in their area of jurisdiction and challenge the legality of ordinances passed by local governmental units (executive committes of soviets). They are also entitled to receive copies of all orders and decrees issued by all segments of the administrative apparatus. The existence of the procurators along with the controlling functions of state planning organizations, and general party surveillance, would seemingly preclude administrative corruption, inefficiency, and injustice. However, human ingenuity in finding shortcuts, bypassing controls, and engaging in irregular practices, corruption, favoritism, and negligence is limitless. It is unlikely that any constitutional institution will ever be invented to outsmart individuals determined to commit crimes or injustices.

A CONCLUDING NOTE[37]

The actual work of any judicial system, including its semijudicial agencies, cannot be stated entirely in the wording of a constitution. The nature of political systems, international circumstances and pressures, and the customs and ethos of the community each have an effect. The judicial procedure reflects not only the laws as they appear in statutes but other influences as well—a recent study concludes that there are many *inputs* into the judiciary; the law is only one of them.[38]

Judges, in addition to their knowledge of and dependence on the law, bring the influence of political and social environments with them to court. So do juries, lay assessors, and the mass media. Mill's statement concerning the mechanics of politics in general may be applied to any national judicial system: "The power which is to keep the engine going must be sought for outside the machinery; and if it is not forthcoming . . . the contrivance will fail."[39]

NOTES

1 Otto Kirchheimer, *Political Justice* (Princeton: Princeton University Press, 1961), p. 49.

2   Article 107 (as amended in 1950): "A trial in *amparo* shall always be held
at the instance of the injured party. The judgment shall always be such that
it affects only private individuals, being limited to affording them redress
and protection in the special case to which the complaint refers, without
making any general declaration as to the law or act on which the complaint
is based."

3   Time and again, the Supreme Court of the United States has held that vague
laws violate the constitution. For example, the wide use by state and local
authorities of the so-called *vagrancy* laws to justify arrest of "undesirable"
persons such as youth groups and minorities at the whim of local sheriffs
was held to be unconstitutional. American vagrancy laws date back to
fourteenth century England when it was illegal for able-bodied men to be
footloose and without work in the wake of the plague epidemic which
depleted England's labor supply.

New York's legislature erased the "vagabond" provisions from the state's
vagrancy law in 1967, leaving only a prohibition against loitering in circumstances that suggest criminal intent. On February 24, 1972, the United States
Supreme Court declared unanimously that it is unconstitutional to punish
persons under vague laws that prohibit "loafing," "nightwalking," and
"avoiding work." The decision was based on a case in which the Jacksonville
police stopped a car carrying two young black men and two white girls and
charged them with "prowling by auto" in violation of Florida's vagrancy
law.

4   The Swiss Constitution of 1848 (Article 18) states: "No person may be
withdrawn from his natural judge. Accordingly, no extraordinary tribunals
may be established."

5   The Argentine Constitution of 1853 (Article 18) states: "No inhabitant of
the Nation may be . . . tried by special commissions, nor removed from the
judges designated by law before the date of the trial."

6   A good example of such a general provision is Article 14 in the Mexican
Constitution of 1917: "No person shall be deprived of life, liberty, property,
possessions, or rights without a trial by a duly created court in which the
essential formalities of procedure are observed and in accordance with laws
issued prior to the act. In criminal cases no penalty shall be imposed by mere
analogy. . . . The penalty must be decreed in law in every respect applicable
to the crime in question."

7   The Soviet Constitution of 1936 (Article 131): "Persons committing
offenses against public socialist property are enemies of the people." The
Polish Constitution of 1952 (Article 77): "Persons who commit sabotage,
subversion, inflict damage or otherwise injure social property, are punishable with all the severity of law."

8   The Swiss Constitution of 1948 (Article 59): "Imprisonment for debt is
abolished." The Brazilian Constitution of 1967 (Article 17): "There shall be
no civil imprisonment for debt, fines, or costs, except in the case of an
unfaithful custodian and the failure to fulfill one's obligation to alimony."
"Unfaithful custodian" refers, for example, to a custodian who has misap-
propriated funds left for the upkeep or education of children.

9 Thurman W. Arnold, *Symbols of Government* (New York: Harcourt, Brace & Co., 1935), p. 145.

10 Compare Arnold, *Symbols of Government,* pp. 135–40.

11 The constitution of Colombia (1886) states (Article 25): "No one may be compelled in criminal, correctional, or *police proceedings* to testify against himself or against his relatives within the fourth civil degree of consanguinity or the second degree of affinity" (italics added).

The United States Supreme Court ruled in 1966 (*Miranda* v. *Arizona* 384 U.S. 436, 1966) that any evidence, including material obtained by the police in pretrial "custodial interrogation," would be admissible only if the police properly informed the defendant that he could remain silent and terminate the police interrogation at any time, that anything he said could be used against him, and that he had a right to have his attorney present during the interrogation. If he could not afford an attorney, the authorities would have to provide one for him. The Miranda decision was subsequently attacked by law-enforcement officials as a serious obstacle to effective criminal investigation and prosecution since nearly 90 percent of all criminal convictions in the United States result from guilty pleas. Congress diluted the Miranda ruling by passing the Omnibus Crime Control Act in 1968 which, basically, admitted voluntary confession as evidence whether a Miranda warning had been given or not. Trial judges were merely instructed to determine to what extent a confession was voluntary, without being bound by any specifics stipulated in the Miranda decision. In 1972 the new Supreme Court (i.e., with four new justices appointed by President Nixon) confirmed that the dilution of the Miranda warning reflected in the 1968 Crime Control Act was constitutional. The case in review involved a voluntary confession by Paul D. Ware to four murders committed in Pennsylvania.

The Supreme Court upheld (five to two) the constitutionality of a provision of the Organized Crime Act of 1970 that permits grand jury witnesses to be compelled to testify as long as their testimony is not subsequently used against them. It also ruled that witnesses can be subsequently prosecuted for crimes mentioned in their testimony, if the prosecution does not use their testimony or leads developed from it (*Zicarelli* v. *New Jersey* and *Kastinger* v. *United States,* both on May 22, 1972).

A good comparative study on the subject of the rights of defendants is David Fellman, *The Defendant's Rights* (New York: Holt, Rinehart and Winston, 1958).

12 In the Mississippi trial of 1967 in which seven men were found guilty of conspiring to deny three murdered civil rights workers their constitutional rights, federal Judge Cox denied bonds to two of the convicted men and stated: "I'm not going to let any wild man loose on a civilized society."

In the case of Angela Davis, a former philosophy professor at the University of California and a member of the Communist party, bail was first denied according to the California law that prohibits bail in "capital cases." The Supreme Court of California ruled on February 18, 1972 that capital punishment violated the constitution of California which prohibits "cruel and unusual punishment," and Miss Davis, who had been in jail since her arrest in 1970, was released on a $102,500 bail five days after the court's decision. The judge in her case ruled that the decision invalidated the California law prohibiting bail in capital cases. Angela Davis was charged with criminal conspiracy, kidnapping, and murder, and specifically with purchasing the guns that were smuggled into a courtroom and used to take the judge, an assistant district attorney, and jurors as hostages. The ensuing gun battle left four persons dead, including one of the Soledad brothers and a judge of the Superior Court. On June 4, 1972, an all-white jury in San Jose, California, found Angela Davis not guilty on all charges of murder, kidnapping, and conspiracy.

13 Perhaps reflecting previous dubious practices, the Brazilian Constitution of 1946 (Article 96/III) forbade the judge "to receive percentages, under any pretext, in the cases subject to their handling and judgment."

14 A survey taken in New York City indicates that only 25 percent of the people voting for a judge paid any attention to the identity of his opposing candidate. After the election, only 4 percent could remember the name of the person for whom they had voted. According to the chairman of an American Bar Association study committee, a former chief justice of the Supreme Court of California, Roger J. Traynor, suggested to a judicial conference in Lake Placid, N.Y.: "The greatest single improvement that could be made in the administration of justice in this country would be to get rid of the popular election of judges" (*New York Times,* October 5, 1970).

15 The constitution of Japan (1949) states in Article 79: "The appointment of the judges of the Supreme Court shall be reviewed by the people at the first general election of members of the House of Representatives following their appointment, and shall be reviewed again at the first general election of the House of Representatives after a lapse of ten years, and in the same manner thereafter."

16 Recent American studies in Baltimore, Milwaukee, and Los Angeles indicate that the working class is grossly underrepresented on juries and that professionals, managers and proprietors are overrepresented. In Baltimore, the latter group contributed 40 percent of the jurors although they represented only 18.7 percent of the population.

17 Compare the 1961 ruling of the Supreme Court (*Irvin* v. *Dowd*): "The mere insistence of any preconceived notion as to the guilt or innocence of accused, without more" is not enough to keep someone off a jury. The test is whether a prospective juror can "lay aside" his impressions and decide the case on the basis of facts put into evidence during the trial.

Compare also the ruling by Federal District Judge William Matt Byrne in the trial of Dr. Daniel Ellsberg and Anthony J. Russo. Judge Byrne rejected defense demands to disqualify as jurors all persons who had government security clearances. The defense noted that Dr. Ellsberg and Mr. Russo were accused of releasing the top secret Pentagon study of the United States involvement in the Vietnam war to unauthorized persons. It argued, therefore, that jurors who had been indoctrinated to follow strict security rules might be biased against the defendants. On the other hand, Judge Byrne did dismiss two aircraft industry officials who, in his opinion, had *special* expertise in security matters, and therefore, as potential jurors, could be deemed potentially biased.

18 The right to a trial by impartial jury is guaranteed three times in the United States Constitution: in Article III(2), and Amendments VI and VII. The latter prescribes the right of trial by jury in common law suits when the value of controversy exceeds twenty dollars.

A new controversy on the subject of the jury system in the United States concerns the wisdom of requiring jury verdicts to be made by unanimous vote. In several countries only a substantial majority is required. Majority votes can convict defendants in Louisiana (nine to three) and in Oregon (ten to two). Comparative study reveals that the Louisiana and Oregon systems result in more convictions and fewer deadlocked juries. On May 22, 1972, the Supreme Court held (five to four) that unanimous jury verdicts are not required to convict in state criminal courts. Unanimous verdicts in federal juries apparently are still required.

19 The Mexican Constitution of 1917 (Article 20/11): "The accused . . . may not be forced to be a witness against himself; wherefore denial of access or other means tending to this end is strictly prohibited." The Venezuelan Constitution of 1961 (Article 60/4): "No one may be required to take an oath nor compelled to make a statement or to acknowledge guilt in a criminal case against himself, nor against his spouse or the person with whom he lived as married, nor against his relatives within the fourth degree of consanguinity or second of affinity."

20 The United States Compulsory Testimony Act of 1954, the constitutionality of which has been challenged, represents a step toward the European concept. The act provides that an individual may be compelled to testify by a district attorney on the application of the attorney general or a congressional committee. However, the individual cannot be prosecuted for any matter covered by his testimony.

21 The Chinese Constitution of 1954 states in Article 77: "Citizens of all nationalities have the right to use their own spoken and written languages in judicial proceedings. The people's courts are required to provide interpretation for any party unacquainted with the spoken or written language commonly used in the locality. In an area where people of a minority nationality live together, hearings in people's courts should be conducted in the language commonly used in the locality."

22 *Estes* v. *Texas,* 381 U.S. 532 (1965).

23 Edward S. Corwin and J.W. Peltason, *Understanding the Constitution,* 4th ed. (New York: Holt, Rinehart and Winston, 1967), p. 126.

24 Alfred Friendly and Ronald L. Goldfarb, *Crime and Publicity* (New York: The Twentieth Century Fund, 1967).

25 Herbert Jacob concludes that juries, interest group activity in judicial matters, and the media "do not damage the judicial process as many lawyers and

judges claim. Instead, they have broadened the popular base of the judicial process and brought popular support to the judiciary." *Justice in America* (Boston: Little, Brown, and Co., 1968), p. 128.

26 The constitution of Italy (1947) states in Article 27, "The death penalty is not admitted, *save in cases provided for by military laws in time of war"* (italics added).

27 The eleven states are: Alaska, Hawaii, Iowa, Maine, Michigan, North Dakota, Minnesota, Oregon, Rhode Island, West Virginia, and Wisconsin. The three special cases are New Mexico, New York, and Vermont. The New York State Legislature abolished capital punishment in 1965, except for the murder of policemen and murders committed by convicts serving life sentences. The assembly added the death penalty for the murder of firemen by a 107–32 vote in 1968. Some legislators protested that this action opened the way to a general restoration of the death penalty. In fact, such an attempt was made in 1972 when Robert F. Kelly, Republican-Conservative of Brooklyn, sponsored a bill, subsequently endorsed by the Codes Committee of the New York State Assembly (April 18, 1972), which was to restore the death penalty in most homicide cases. Under the bill, a convicted murderer was to face the electric chair unless the jury recommended life imprisonment. Mr. Kelly's argument was that people had become "fed up with wanton killings."

28 This seems to be a paraphrase of André Malraux's famous: "Life is worth nothing, but nothing is worth a life."

29 Administrative courts (West Europe), Council of State (France), independent regulatory agencies (United States), Parliamentary Commissioner for Administration (Britain and New Zealand), *ombudsman* (Sweden, Norway, Denmark), *Lok Pal* (India), *oikeusiamies* (Finland), procurator general (USSR), *Fiscal General* (Venezuela), Supreme Control Chamber (Poland), ministry of state control (Communist countries), Council of Censors (Pennsylvania, 1776), Censors (Imperial China before 1911), control *yüan* (Taiwan), etc. In the United States a bill proposed by Representative Reuss calls the American counterpart of the Scandinavian ombudsman "Administrative Counsel." Senator Long of Missouri, who had Professor Gellhorn's study of the Swedish *ombudsman* included in the *Congressional Record* (January 29, 1966, pp. 1407–22), started his remarks by affirming that the Swedish word "ombudsman" has become part of our vocabulary.

30 *New York Times,* October 28, 1967.

31 The ombudsman's jurisdiction in Guyana extends to Ministers, according to Article 35 of the Constitution.

32 The powers of the ombudsman are described in the constitution of Mauritius (1968), Article 97.

33 The first locally appointed ombudsman in the United States appears to be Sam Greason in Nassau County, New York. In 1968, the City College of New York was one of the first universities to have both a faculty and a student ombudsman.

34 "Bill on Ombudsman Introduced in Lok Sabha" (House of the People, the Indian Lower House), *India News*, New Delhi, May 24, 1968, p. 4.

35 Merle Fainsod, *How Russia is Ruled* (Cambridge, Mass.: Harvard University Press, 1953), p. 478.

36 The Polish Constitution of 1952 was amended in 1957 to include the Supreme Control Chamber, which (Article 28b) "comes under the jurisdiction of the *Seym*." The function of the Supreme Control Chamber as a collective body is "to exercise supervision over the economic, financial, and organizational-administrative activity of the higher and local organs of State administration, as well as agencies subordinate to them, from the point of view of legality, good management, utility and honesty" (Article 28a). Its controlling functions may be extended also to the nonsocialized units of the economy.

37 This chapter makes an admittedly controversial attempt to give an American reader a few insights into the Roman law systems of criminal justice through the prism of common law assumptions. Some of the challenges to the jury system or even the Fifth Amendment may surprise an American reader. No final value judgment on the relative merits of the European system (imported into Asia and Africa) as opposed to the merits of the Anglo-American system is intended.

Peter H. Merkl made the following point: "Judicial systems must stand judicial tests, such as the speedy and inexpensive availability of judicial remedies, the easy and equal access to counsel . . . , and the freedom of criminal trials from emotional community pressures. The common law system does not always compare favorably on these counts with French judicial practice. There is no statistical evidence that would indicate which of the two systems of criminal trial leads more often to wrongful convictions, but there can be little doubt that common law courts and juries more often let a guilty person go unpunished than is likely to happen, say, in France." *Political Continuity and Change* (New York: Harper and Row, 1967), p. 325.

38 Herbert Jacob, *Law and the Federal Courts* (Boston: Little, Brown, and Co., 1967), p. xii.

39 John Stuart Mill, *Considerations of Representative Government* (New York: Holt, Rinehart and Winston, 1882), p. 21.

CHAPTER 5

Freedom of Expression

All modern constitutions recognize the importance of free expression. Their bills of rights guarantee freedom of speech, of the press, and of the right for citizens peaceably to assemble. Undoubtedly, some of those provisions were drafted by men who would violate their own guarantees if the freedom of political expression was claimed by somebody other than themselves.

The etiquette of constitution writing, even in a frankly authoritarian framework, calls for a bill of rights which guarantees the freedom of expression. The attitude of authoritarians toward the freedom of expression is sometimes symptomatic of schizophrenia. Constitutions are frequently drafted by revolutionaries who have come to power partly because they were given the right to freely express their opposition to the system they replaced; yet after assuming power they often dread the consequences of perpetuating a constitutional ritual that might be taken seriously by a new generation of revolutionaries. A new opposition group could breathe life into what the rulers hope is a dead letter. The rulers, former revolutionaries, know that granting freedom of speech, the press, and assembly and making political authority openly responsive and responsible could mean the end of their system.

During the initial movement toward liberalization of the Communist system in Eastern Europe during the sixties there was a resurgence of references to long-forgotten constitutional bills of rights. Students and intellectuals demanded assurance that the old Communist constitutions would be implemented in practice, in particular that their bills of rights and the guarantees of freedom of expression would be observed.[1] The demands were made with tongue in cheek, partly to legitimize the charge that the drafters and guardians of the constitution had proved to be its most callous and consistent violators. The effort of the protestors to transform the constitutions from mere organizational charts and Marxist-Leninist manifestoes into standards of desired reform and benchmarks of official behavior largely failed.[2]

Nonauthoritarians understandably regard the freedom of expression as the most precious constitutional guarantee. They know that men are unhappy unless they can freely communicate and share their fears and hopes. Free expression is part of the pursuit of happiness; its absence stifles artistic creativity, scientific research, and the philosophical search for truth. Most importantly, citizens cannot really participate in politics, they cannot instruct, criticize, control, and recall political authority unless they are free to express differing points of view. In this sense, the freedom of expression is a precondition for all participatory rights, especially the right to vote and form political parties and interest groups. Without free expression elections become authoritarian rituals, similar to the *ja-oder-nein* plebiscites à la Hitler or Stalin.

The right to speak up implicitly presupposes that it is the corresponding duty of the political authority to be responsive—to listen.

It is possible, of course, to achieve a politically *sterile* freedom—the freedom to talk or dissent without perceptible result. In contrast *productive* freedom elicits response and action by public authority. Obviously, a sterile freedom is better than none at all, just as it is preferable for a prisoner to have company and books rather than to be idle in solitary confinement. After Stalin's death, many Communist intellectuals and students and a majority of the Soviet people enjoyed newly gained freedoms, but they were still captives of their system. Life in the Soviet Union became more livable and was thus preferred to the Stalinist past. However, the new-found freedoms were politically sterile; they produced personal satisfaction but no real change in the system, and therefore they proved frustrating in the long run.

Even an unproductive freedom may perpetuate hope that a political system may be transformed in a distant future under the cumulative effect of criticism. Such hopes are frequently entertained by radical minorities in democratic countries even when there is no chance they will become the decisive majority. Ordinarily, they can only try to influence the views and goals of the majority. Thus, for the time being, the freedom of expression may seem to be a politically sterile promise to student radicals in France and the United States.

The freedom to voice an opinion requires a concomitant freedom of assembly and petition if it is to become truly effective. A politically productive freedom of expression also needs access to instruments of power, i.e., political organization. This thought was stated succinctly by a Czech playwright in the spring of 1968:

> We hear quite often that, because of our present and future freedom of speech (which is said to be the essence of democracy), the natural function of opposition will be exercised simply by public opinion with access to mass

communications media. Such a concept assumes the *faith* that the government will draw from public criticism all the necessary inferences. But democracy is a matter not of faith but of *guarantees*. Even though we admit that the public competition of views is the first condition, the most important factor in, and the natural result of, democracy, its very essence—and the true source of our guarantees—is something else, namely a public and legitimate *competition for power*. Public opinion can effectively control and influence the performance of the ruling power only if it has recourse to effective means of control—in other words, if it can share in public decision making (e.g., in elections). When all has been said, it is a fact that power respects power, and an authority can be made to improve itself when its *existence* is at stake, not just its good name![3]

Modern bills of rights go well beyond the general statement contained in the First Amendment to the United States Constitution which enjoins the Congress to "make no law . . . abridging the freedom of speech, or of the press; or the right of the people peaceably to assemble, and to petition the Government for a redress of grievances." After World War II, aware of technological developments, the drafters added new communication techniques to the traditionally guaranteed freedoms of speech and the press: photography (Egypt), graphics (Syria), radio and motion pictures (West Germany), television (Czechoslovakia), pickets, mass meetings, protest marches, and street demonstrations (Turkey)[4] and other forms of what is sometimes called "symbolic speech." Communist constitutions usually guarantee free access to printing presses and other mass media facilities—the freedom of the press otherwise seems to be an empty constitutional gesture. Many constitutions prohibit confiscation of printing presses (Mexico). In addition, some constitutions provide higher constitutional protection of the freedom of expression for specific groups. Peru has a special article on the "freedom of the professorate"; others speak of academic freedom of expression and the special rights of journalists and writers. Mexico extended the constitutional protection of freedom of expression to newspaper vendors and newsboys. Poland (Article 65) grants "special protection to the creative intelligentsia—to those working in science, education, literature and art, as well as pioneers of technical progress, to rationalizers, and inventors." West Germany (Article 5) proclaims: "Art and science, research and teaching are free." It adds, however: "Freedom of teaching does not absolve from loyalty to the Constitution." Article 100 of the constitution of Venezuela (1961) protects "the rights in scientific, literary, and artistic works, inventions, names, trademarks, and slogans." The Brazilian Constitution of 1946 (Article 203) also guarantees freedom from taxation to "authors' royalties and remuneration of teachers and journalists." Brazil's constitution evidently combines a guarantee of the freedom of expression with the constitutional protection of property rights, i.e., the financial reward for published expressions. Several countries (e.g., France) exempt writers' royalties from income taxation.

These samples illustrate the elaborate detail used in modern constitutions to guarantee the freedom of expression. The quantity and variety of constitutional guarantees alone might lead to the conclusion that the freedom of expression is more protected today than ever before. Nothing could be further from the truth. Actually, constitutional texts, as well as extraconstitutional practice, treat the freedom of expression as a relative, and not an absolute, right.

IS THE FREEDOM OF EXPRESSION
RELATIVE OR ABSOLUTE?

The attitudes toward constitutional guarantees of free expression can be identified in three categories: (1) "absolutist" or "libertarian perfectionist"; (2) "maximalist"; and (3) "relativist."

(1) The *absolutists,* an infinitesimal minority, consider freedom of all expression, political as well as nonpolitical, to be a fundamental and "nonnegotiable" right. They argue that political and nonpolitical expression cannot be inhibited by governments. Since any infringement of free expression in a nonpolitical sphere may be easily transferred to the political, they believe that the censorship of movies leads to censorship of editorials—because the line between nonpolitical and political speech is almost impossible to draw in practice. Furthermore, they hold that limits on freedom are contagious. A free society must be free in all aspects of expression in order to guarantee the free trade of political ideas.

The absolutists would, to be consistent, equally protect any form of expression: obscenity, libel, slander, incitement to murder, advocacy of genocide, and false claims in commercial advertising. The libertarian perfectionist makes no distinction in the circumstances under which free expression is used; he approves the right to shout "fire" in a packed theater or "burn, baby, burn" in a crowded ghetto; to conspire to rob a bank or commit murder (conspiracy in this context means planning under the protection of free speech and assembly); and to engage in street demonstrations that would cause traffic accidents. A criminal *act* resulting from free speech remains, of course, punishable.

(2) The *maximalist* differentiates between the freedom to express political ideas which he believes is absolute, and the freedom of expression in nonpolitical fields, which he believes is relative to other social

values such as honesty, morality, decency, and public order. Professor Alexander Meiklejohn insisted vehemently that the First Amendment (freedom of speech, the press, and assembly) protects only *political* communications, and that the protection is absolute.[5] The distinction between political and nonpolitical expression, however, is unclear. Furthermore, political expression is, by definition, inextricably enmeshed with action—that is its very purpose.

The relationship between the freedom of expression and action is, of course, one of the most difficult and controversial issues in constitutional government. The maximalist who believes in an absolute freedom of expression does not advocate the protection of criminal acts. He does not support assassination, arson, and looting if they result from the free exercise of speech on politics. Lord Bertrand Russell's statement, made in his early period, has been constantly quoted ever since: "If an act is illegal, it is logical to make it illegal to advocate it."

"Symbolic speech," that is, conduct closely related to verbal expression, creates an additional problem since it communicates ideas and concepts through symbolic acts which are shorthand messages of sorts. As speech or printed words symbolic communications should not, by themselves, be criminal. The Supreme Court of the United States protected the flying of a red banner by left-wing workers as "symbolic speech" (the California law prohibiting such actions was nullified in 1931 as a violation of the First Amendment). The Court similarly recognized a refusal to salute the flag (the Jehovah's Witnesses school childrens' case), and the carrying of placards by union pickets as symbolic speech protected by the First Amendment. In 1968 the Court, however, refused to accept the view, in Earl Warren's words, "that an apparently limitless variety of conduct can be labeled 'speech' whenever the person engaging in the conduct intends thereby to express an idea." This statement by the Court reversed a lower court decision that held draft card burning to be a constitutionally protected form of symbolic speech. The spring 1968 decision on draft cards (seven to one) was handed down two days before a few participants in the "Poor People's Campaign" threw stones through the windows of the Supreme Court. Was this manifestation of protest against poverty and injustice "symbolic speech" too? During the era of protests and riots demonstrators have used ever more daring stunts to publicize their causes. They have dumped garbage on throughways, staged "stall-ins" on busy bridges, and invaded housing projects, universities, museums, and television stations—public and private buildings. The protestors have claimed that these acts are constitutionally protected "expressions." Federal courts have approved black sit-ins in a public library but have disapproved pouring blood on draft board files as "symbolic speeches."

What these cases show is that many types of conduct can be used to express ideas, and that there is no easy way to separate those which should not be protected by the First Amendment from those that should by labeling the latter "symbolic speech."[6]

In March 1968 while lecturing at the Columbia University Law School, Associate Justice Hugo L. Black, a vigorous defender of free speech, tried to draw the line between conduct and speech:

> It has long been accepted constitutional doctrine that the First Amendment presents no bar to the passage of laws regulating, controlling or entirely suppressing such a course of marching conduct even though speaking and writing accompany it. But recently many loose words have been spoken and written about the alleged First Amendment right to picket, demonstrate, or march, usually accompanied by singing, shouting, or loud praying, along the public streets, in or around government-owned buildings, or in and around other people's property including their homes, without their owners' consent.

It is conceivable that defense lawyers will eventually try to invoke the First Amendment (or its counterpart in other countries) to place hijacking, terroristic bombing, arson, and the taking of political hostages under the protection of free speech and symbolic acts. Political assassinations are frequently described by their perpetrators as protests and symbolic acts rather than murder; they transmit their political messages by means of bullets, rather than ballots.[7]

These absurd extensions of the boundaries of "symbolic speech" may be rejected as an exercise in legalistic sophistry. Nevertheless, they emphasize the real difficulty of disentangling constitutionally protected speech from prohibited, criminal action. Justice Black's distinction between free speech and street demonstrations may not prove as clear in actual practice as his statement seems to suggest.

(3) The *relativists* clearly represent an overwhelming majority amongst founding fathers on all continents, judging by the texts of bills of rights. In the following articles political and unpolitical expression often loses in competition with other societal values. Most guarantees of freedom of speech and the press are surrounded by ingenious, qualifying words such as:

unless ("The expression of ideas shall not be subject to any judicial or administrative investigation, *unless* it offends good morals, infringes the rights of others, incites to crime, or disturbs the public order"— Mexico, 1917, Article 6).

subject to ("public order, morality, and health"—Burma, 1947, Article 192).

save for ("the punishment of offenses perpetrated in exercising these liberties"—Belgium, 1831, Article 14).

Drawing by Ed Fisher; copyright 1967 Saturday Review, Inc.

"Don't you see, by protesting and making it look like this is still a free country, we play the power structure's game. . . ."

as long as ("it does not endanger public safety"—Tunisia, 1959, Article 5).

except as ("prohibited by religious law"—Iran, 1906, Article 18).

in so far as ("this does not contravene the law"—Czechoslovakia, 1960, Article 32).

within the limits of law ("Every individual has the right to express his opinion and publicise it verbally or in writing or by photography or by other means within the limits of law" —United Arab Republic, 1964, Article 35).

"Everyone has the right freely to express and to disseminate his opinion by speech, writing, and pictures. . . . There shall be no censorship. These rights are limited by the provisions of the general laws, the provisions of law for the protection of youth, and by the right of inviolability of personal property"— West Germany, 1949, Article 5).

These references to ordinary laws that qualify the grant of rights or the guarantee of freedom are constitutional devices which make seemingly absolute principles quite relative. They date back to the French Declaration of the Rights of Man and Citizen in 1789. Its eleventh theme stated:

The free communication of ideas and opinions is one of the most precious of the rights of man; every citizen then can freely speak, write, and print, subject to responsibility for the abuse of this freedom in the cases determined by law.

In the American context constitutional relativism is found in the so-called *balancing doctrine* which aims at discovering an appropriate equilibrium between competing societal values:

> . . . the nation's interests in freedom of speech and press is in competition with its interests in some other valued things that sometimes are endangered by unrestrained expression . . . the competing interests ought to be evaluated and balanced out, and therefore a test of *reasonableness* ought to be applied in litigation where abridgement of speech or press is charged[8] (italics added).

The key word is "reasonableness"; its operational meaning varies according to the political culture, from time to time, from person to person within the same political culture and the same period, and according to the age and personal experience of the individual. The many reversals by a one-vote majority in the United States Supreme Court illustrate how varied the meaning can be.[9]

In addition, many constitutions simultaneously proclaim a solemn dedication to principles and goals that conflict with the freedom of speech. Their texts let future conflicts determine whether the principles or the freedom shall be first under all circumstances. Many bills of rights place other values above or in competition with freedom of speech and the press, e.g., *peace* (which interdicts the freedom to advocate war),[10] *polyethnic harmony* (which prohibits tribal and ethnic agitation and regionalism in polytribal Africa,[11] and racial agitation in Asia),[12] and *socialism* (which prohibits advocacy of other than the socialist ideology and system).

EXTRACONSTITUTIONAL LIMITS

In addition to the explicit qualifications of freedom of expression found in constitutional texts, other factors add limitations that were not originally intended. These extraconstitutional, sometimes unconstitutional, factors include judicial interpretations of ambiguous constitutional provisions; new media technology which has affected the freedom of communication in ways that could not have been foreseen by the drafters of the bill of rights; and administrative and judiciary practices, e.g., police and investigative agencies, the licensing of the mass media, and, in socialist countries, the party's role in determining which groups will be provided printing presses, distribution facilities, telephones, electric power, newsprint, and access to radio and television microphones and cameras.

In the United States, for instance, all these factors, judicial interpretation in particular, have qualified freedoms which the absolutists and many maximalists hold to be unqualified—i.e., the freedom of speech and the press as expressed in the First Amendment. In this context the prior restraint and censorship of news and views *before* they are uttered should be distinguished from limitations on words or symbolic acts *after* they have been communicated. The freedom of expression from prior restraint seems generally broader and less controversial than free expression of views that may damage others. (See also the "right to be informed" on page 182.) Some of the qualifications and limitations of free expression *after* words have been uttered have been accepted with less opposition than others. Qualifications such as "slander,"[13] "libel,"[14] and advertisements that present false claims have aroused less controversy than "obscenity," "fighting words," "advocacy of forcible overthrow of government," "clear and present danger," and "seditious[15] speech." There is a passionate controversy centered around the freedom to engage in political agitation in order to replace free political competition with a dictatorship which would censor all expressions except those approved by the political authority. Those opposed to imposing any limit on political speech seemingly assume that people accustomed to a free market of political ideas would not knowingly vote themselves into unfreedom. Skeptics note that it is possible to deceive the credulous masses[16] and they question the wisdom of extending the constitutional protection of free political speech when that freedom includes teaching antidemocratic doctrines, the techniques of sabotage, guerrilla warfare, and other violent means of achieving ideological goals. Justice Douglas reaffirmed that the freedom of speech was not absolute in his opinion on the Dennis case (1951). The leadership of the Communist party of the United States (then solidly Stalinist)[17] was convicted for violating the Smith Act (1950)[18] which made advocating a violent overthrow of government unlawful. Justice Douglas added that "the teaching of methods of terror and other seditious conduct should be beyond the pale along with obscenity and immorality."[19] Nevertheless, he refused to uphold the conviction of the American Communist leaders since he found that they had engaged in nothing more than teaching themselves a revolutionary doctrine. There was no proof that they committed acts of sabotage or engaged in other unlawful conduct, according to Justice Douglas.

The majority of the Supreme Court differed. They ruled, along four different lines of reasoning, that the conviction should stand. Chief Justice Vinson presented the following major arguments:

> The leaders of the Communist Party in this country were unwilling to work within our framework of democracy, but intended to initiate a violent revolution whenever the propitious occasion appeared. . . . Overthrow of the Government by force and violence is certainly a substantial enough interest for the Government to limit speech. Indeed, this is the ultimate value of any society, for if a society cannot protect its very structure from armed internal attack, it must follow that no subordinate value can be protected. . . . If Government is aware that a group aiming at its overthrow is attempting to indoctrinate its members and to commit them to a course whereby they will strike when the leaders feel the circumstance permit, action by the Government is required. . . . it [needs not] wait until the *putsch* is about to be executed, the plans have been laid and the signal is awaited. . . . An attempt to overthrow the Government by force, even though doomed from the outset because of inadequate numbers or power of the revolutionists, is a sufficient evil for Congress to prevent. The damage which such attempts create both physically and politically to a nation makes it impossible to measure the validity in terms of the probability of success, or the immediacy of a successful attempt. . . . The obvious purpose of the statute [Smith Act] is to protect existing Government, not from change by peaceable, lawful and constitutional means, but from change by violence, revolution and terrorism. That it is within the *power* of the Congress to protect the Government of the United States from armed rebellion is a proposition which requires little discussion. Whatever theoretical merit there may be to the argument that there is a "right" to rebellion against dictatorial governments is without force where the existence of the structure of the government provides for peaceful and orderly change. We reject any principle of governmental helplessness in the face of preparation for revolution, which principle, carried to its logical conclusion, must lead to anarchy.[20]

Recalling another case in the Supreme Court's history, Chief Justice Vinson reaffirmed the relativist interpretation of the First Amendment and said:

> The basis of the First Amendment is the hypothesis that speech can rebut speech, propaganda will answer propaganda, free debate of ideas will result in wisest governmental policies. It is for this reason that this Court has recognized the inherent value of free discourse. An analysis of the leading cases in this Court which have involved direct limitations on speech, however, will demonstrate that both the majority of the Court and the dissenters in particular cases have recognized that this is not an unlimited, unqualified

right, but that the societal value of speech must, on occasion, be subordinated to other values and considerations.[21]

The American Civil Liberties Union intensified its recruitment campaign in 1968 by running the following statement as an advertisement in major newspapers:

> Dear Friend of Freedom . . . This is A.D. 1968 . . . 179 years after the Bill of Rights became an integral part of our American heritage. We dare not take our liberties for granted! . . . Pickets displaying placards protesting war are arrested for disorderly conduct. University students are classified 1-A for taking part in a peace demonstration. A false "confession" of murder is pressured out of a retarded teenager. Distinguished professors are required to sign a "loyalty oath" as a condition for employment. Negroes are convicted by juries drawn from panels from which Negroes have been excluded. . . . Join *now*. . . . You are helping to buy someone's freedom. It may be your own.

Such repressive measures certainly cannot be dismissed or self-indulgently ignored. Actually, one of the merits of the American Civil Liberties Union and other such institutions is that their collective libertarian vigilance has never permitted constitutional practice in the United States to approach the lack of freedom that characterizes most of our world. In particular, compare the practice of the socialist-authoritarian, fascist, military and one-party systems of Asia, Africa, Latin America, and Eastern Europe. It is impossible to imagine, for example, that a "Civil Liberties Union" in Rumania, Spain, Poland, Cuba, Portugal, East Germany, Afghanistan, Ethiopia, Liberia, the Soviet Union, Egypt, Nationalist China or Communist China could run a similar advertisement in their leading newspapers. The freedom of expression, however incomplete it may be in the United States, Britain, Canada, Australia, New Zealand, and most West European countries, is still separated by an abyss in comparison to the complete suppression of free speech in most of the modern world.

FREEDOM OF SPEECH & COMMUNIST CONSTITUTIONS

The constitution of Communist Yugoslavia (1963) proclaims in Article 40 that "freedom of the press and other media of information, freedom of association, freedom of speech and public expression, freedom of meeting and other public assemblage shall be guaranteed," but then immediately enumerates values constitutionally superior to free expression and public assemblage:

These freedoms and rights shall not be used by anyone to overthrow the foundations of the socialist democratic order determined by the Constitution, to endanger the peace, international cooperation on terms of equality, or the independence of a country, to disseminate national, racial, or religious hatred or intolerance, or to incite to crime, or in any manner that offends public decency.

Similarly, Article 29 of the Rumanian Constitution (1965) grants freedom of speech, freedom of the press, and the freedom of reunion, meeting and demonstration but forbids the use of freedom for "aims hostile to the socialist system." It also prohibits any association of "a fascist or antidemocratic character," leaving the Communist party to decide what is, or is not, democratic according to Marxism-Leninism.[22] Articles 19 and 87 of the constitution of China (1954) grant all the modern freedoms of expression and further pledge the state to provide the "necessary material facilities" to implement them. Yet, Article 19 promises to suppress and punish all counter-revolutionary activities, leaving it to the secret police and the Communist party to determine when a critique becomes counter-revolutionary activity or treason. The East German Constitution (1949), Article 6, exempted "incitement to boycott democratic institutions and organizations" and "incitement to attempts on the life of democratic politicians" from the constitutional guarantees of freedom of expression. Undemocratic politicians, it seems, are not constitutionally protected.

The Soviet Constitution (1936), Article 125, deals with freedom of expression quite generously and liberally:

In conformity with the interests of the working people, and *in order to strengthen the socialist system,* the citizens of the U.S.S.R. are guaranteed by law: (a) freedom of speech; (b) freedom of the press; (c) freedom of assembly, including the holding of mass meetings; (d) freedom of street processions and demonstrations. These civil rights are ensured by placing at the disposal of the working people and their organizations printing presses, stocks of paper, public buildings, the streets, communications, facilities, and other material requisites for the exercise of these rights (italics added).

Clearly, none of these civil rights could be enjoyed if, in the opinion of the Soviet Communist party, the exercise of any of these rights could *weaken* the socialist system. To avoid misunderstanding on this point, the official interpretation when the constitution was promulgated emphasized: "We shall not give a scrap of paper nor an inch of space to those who think differently from the Party."[23] How Article 125 works in practice was dramatically illustrated in 1968, after the Soviet invasion of Czechoslovakia. Pavel Litvinov (son of former Soviet Minister of

Foreign Affairs Maxim Litvinov and a leading Communist) went to Moscow's Red Square to publicly voice his opposition against the Soviet armed intervention in an allied Communist country. He was arrested, tried, and condemned. His final trial statement, invoking Article 125, was circulated in the Soviet Union and abroad (see Document 5.1). Litvinov's main point was that his critique of the Soviet foreign and military policies was in the interests of socialism, and not, as the prosecutor maintained, against those interests.

PROCLAMATIONS OF EMERGENCY

Among all the constitutional qualifications applied to freedom of expression, the most general and sweeping are proclamations of national emergency and martial law. Such constitutional authorizations place national security and public order above the essential ingredients of a constitutional government when necessary.

The guarantees of personal liberty and impartial justice are the first casualties of an emergency proclamation. Civil courts are replaced by military tribunals and the writ of habeas corpus is usually suspended. The United States Constitution (Article 1/9) permits this action "when in cases of rebellion or invasion the public safety may require it." In several countries the writ of habeas corpus may not only be suspended but replaced by constitutionally sanctioned preventive detention. The police may not even be required to disclose to the detained person the reasons for his detention, "facts which such authority considers to be against the public interests to disclose" (Article 22/6, Indian Constitution of 1949).[24]

An American scholar commented on the frequent use of preventive detention in developing countries, and the consequences for the constitutional guarantees of personal liberty and freedom of speech, by saying:

> Preventive detention . . . which sanctions the confinement of individuals in order to prevent them from engaging in activity considered injurious to the community and likelihood of which is indicated by their past actions . . . and insufficient defense of procedural safeguards in criminal law are the most important modes which infringement of personal liberty assumes."[25]

An emergency proclamation and martial law usually affects freedom to move through the country and to travel abroad as well as the freedom of speech, the press, and assembly. Under martial law the mere gathering of more than three persons in the street may be forbidden and treated as though it is the beginning of an uprising.

One of the most detailed provisions for an emergency proclamation is found in the Indian Constitution. Article 352 authorizes the president,

SOVIET ARTICLE 125 AND FREEDOM OF EXPRESSION

Pavel Litvinov, Moscow, October 11, 1968:

I will not take your time by going into legal details; the attorneys have done so. Our innocence of the charges is self-evident; and I do not consider myself guilty. At the same time, that the verdict against me will be "guilty" is just as evident to me.

I knew this beforehand, when I made up my mind to go to Red Square. Nothing has shaken these convictions, because I was positive that the employes of the KGB* would stage a provocation against me. I know that what happened to me is the result of provocation.

I knew that from the person who followed me. I read my verdict in his eyes when he followed me into the metro. The man who beat me up on Red Square was one whom I had seen many times before. Nevertheless, I went out into Red Square.

I shall not speak of my motives. There was never any question for me whether I should go to Red Square or not. As a Soviet citizen, I deemed it necessary to voice my disagreement with the action of my government, which made me very indignant. . . .

"You fool," said the policeman, "if you had kept your mouth shut, you could have lived peacefully." He had no doubt that I was doomed to lose my liberty. Well, perhaps he is right and I am a fool.

The indictment is too abstract. It does not say what, in actual fact, was subversive to our social and state systems in the slogans we displayed. . . .

The prosecutor also says that we were against the policy of the party and government but not against the social and state system. Perhaps there are people who consider all our policies and even our political errors as the logical outcome of our state and social system. I do not think so.

I do not think that the prosecutor himself would say this, for then he would have to say that all the crimes of the Stalin era resulted from our social and state system.

The prosecutor reversed the sense of Article 125 of the Constitution. He said that liberties are to be used if they work in the interests of the state. But it is in the interests of socialism and of the toilers that people are given these rights.

[The prosecutor interrupted to complain that this argument was not relevant.]

This *is* relevant. Who is to judge what is in the interest of socialism and what is not? Perhaps the prosecutor who spoke with admiration, almost with tenderness, of those who beat us up and insulted us . . .

This is what I find menacing. Evidently it is such people who are supposed to know what is socialism and what is counter-revolution.

This is what I find terrible, and that is why I went to Red Square. That is what I have fought against and what I shall continue to fight against for the rest of my life, by all lawful methods known to me.

*The Soviet Secret Police

acting on the basis of a cabinet decision, to issue a proclamation of emergency in case of internal disturbance, external aggression, or a threat of war. The imminence of danger is sufficient since a belated adoption of emergency provisions could defeat their preventive purpose. Article 358 specifically authorizes the government to suspend the "Right to Freedom" (Article 19) which guarantees Indian citizens "freedom of speech and expression, to assemble peaceably and without arms, ... to move freely throughout the territory of India." Article 359 permits the courts to suspend the enforcement of those rights.

It is frequently argued that proclamations of emergency are not warranted, not that constitutional rights and freedoms should never be curbed or suspended, rather that a given situation does not justify such action. The government's motives are attacked—false and panicky estimates of danger and deliberate distortions of facts are used to silence the opposition. The constitution of Venezuela (1961) states in Article 24 that the president may declare a state of emergency in the event of "internal or external conflict or whenever well-founded reasons exist that either of these may occur." Obviously, the president's judgment, well-founded or not, becomes the pertinent issue.

The *duration* of the state of emergency or siege itself becomes a problem. Constitutions usually limit periods of emergency to a few months and require legislative approval to prolong it. In systems where both the executive and the legislative branches are dominated by one party approval may be arranged with relative ease. India is a good example. Under the Congress Party the emergency provisions lasted for more than a decade during the 1960s. Some leaders in developing countries (e.g., President Nyerere of Tanzania in defending his single-party rule) feel that the period of rapid modernization and nation building is the time of greatest emergency. In a sense, modernization in a postcolonial context is indeed a long-term national emergency.

GOVERNMENT'S RIGHT TO BE HEARD

Granting freedom of expression in conjunction with the right to vote and organize for the purpose of formulating political demands implies that it is government's duty to be receptive and listen. Then is it correspondingly the duty of the mass media to read, hear, and disseminate what the authorities have to say? Or does the freedom of expression, including the right to broadcast, televise, or print the news include a right to silence the government[26] and voice views of the opposition? (see Documents 5.2 and 5.3).

The advanced communications technology and the ever-increasing cost of building and operating mass media has raised a number of additional problems which current constitutions either ignore or mention only casually. One such problem is the possibility that monopolistic groups could so control mass media, as Spiro Agnew suggested, (Document 5.2) that government could be excluded from contact with the public; another problem inherent in the modern mass media is the possibility that a selected few with access to microphones and television cameras could exclude the public from political participation and transform them into passive spectators of a game played between government and mass communicators (see Alexander Klein in Document 5.3). On the other hand, if the mass media are owned and operated by government, as is the case in most countries, there is a danger that the constitutional guarantee of free expression may become meaningless.

The freedom of expression can become an empty promise if it is financially prohibitive and technically impossible for citizens to disseminate their views. Consequently, some constitutions couple grants of free expression with the pledge to provide printing presses, newsprint, and meeting halls and other facilities. Many Communist constitutions contain such a pledge (see Article 125 of the Soviet Constitution, quoted on page 175). Facilities of this kind are meant for mass organizations (e.g., trade unions, womens' associations, writers' and youth organizations, and the armed forces) to run newspapers which reflect their corporate interests within the Communist framework. Communist mass organizations are, as Lenin wrote, "transmission belts" between the party and the society, so the Soviet Constitution, as well as the other Communist constitutions, in reality has guaranteed party control over all mass media, not the freedom of expression for citizens or non-Communist groups.

In nonauthoritarian systems in which newspapers are owned and operated by several political parties or interest groups another problem may arise. In countries where radio and television stations are owned and operated by the government, the press may remain free but its voice may be reduced to a whisper. The French socialist and liberal press in the 1960s complained that there was an excessive projection of de Gaulle's towering (literally) personality through government-controlled radio and television. News programs exclusively covered the French government's (that is, de Gaulle's) point of view on domestic and foreign issues. The free exchange of ideas was distorted since the mass French television and radio audience could not compare with the limited audience a party daily newspaper can conceivably reach in France. A government-controlled mass media, which understandably reports the government's actions and views, is actually a propaganda medium for a political party which won the last elections and tries not to lose the next. An elected government is not above political competition and

Document 5.2

VICE PRESIDENT SPIRO AGNEW v. MASS MEDIA

Address, November 14, 1969, at Des Moines, Iowa:

Every American has a right to disagree with the President of the United States and to express publicly that disagreement. But the President of the United States has a right to communicate directly with the people who elected him, and the people of this country have the right to make up their own minds and form their own opinions about a President's address without having a President's words and thoughts characterized through the prejudices of hostile critics before they can even be digested. . . . Monday night a week ago President Nixon delivered the most important address of his Administration, one of the most important of our decade. His subject was Vietnam. His hope was to rally the American people to see the conflict through to a lasting and just peace in the Pacific. . . . When the President completed his address—an address, incidentally, that he spent weeks in the preparation of—his words and policies were subjected to instant analysis and querulous criticism. The audience of 70 million Americans gathered to hear the President of the United States was inherited by a small band of network commentators and self-appointed analysts, the majority of whom expressed in one way or another their hostility to what he had to say. It was obvious that their minds were made up in advance. . . . The purpose of my remarks tonight is to focus your attention on this little group of men who not only enjoy a right of instant rebuttal to every Presidential address, but, more importantly, wield a free hand in selecting, presenting and interpreting the great issues in our nation. Gresham's Law seems to be operating in the network news. Bad news drives out good news. The irrational is more controversial than the rational. Concurrence can no longer compete with dissent. One minute of Eldridge Cleaver is worth 10 minutes of Roy Wilkins. . . . Normality has become the nemesis of the network news. Now the upshot of all this controversy is that a narrow and distorted picture of America often emerges from the televised news. . . . the loudest and most extreme dissenters on every issue [in the Congress] are known to every man in the street. . . . How many marches and demonstrations would we have if the marchers did not know that the ever-faithful TV cameras would be there to record their antics for the next news show? . . . A single, dramatic piece of the mosaic becomes in the minds of millions the entire picture. And the American who relies upon television for his news might conclude that the majority of American students are embittered radicals. That the majority of black Americans feel no regard for their country. . . . We know that none of these conclusions is true. Perhaps the place to start looking for the credibility gap is not in the offices of the Government in Washington but in the studios of the networks in New York. . . .

Every elected leader in the United States depends on these men of the media. Whether what I've said to you tonight will be heard and seen at all by the nation is not my decision, it's not your decision, it's their decision. . . . Now, my friends, we'd never trust such power as I've described over public opinion in the hands of an elected Government. It's time we questioned it in the hands of a small and unelected elite. The great networks have dominated America's airwaves for decades. The people are entitled to a full accounting of their stewardship.

Document 5.3

MEDIA v. AGNEW

A. B. C. (Leonard H. Goldenson):
In our judgment, the performance of A.B.C. news has always been and will continue to be fair and objective. In the final analysis, it is always the public who decides on the reliability of any individual or organization. . . .

C. B. S.:
No American institution, including network news organizations, should be immune to public criticism or to public discussion of its performance. In a democracy this is entirely proper. We do not believe, however, that this unprecedented attempt by the Vice President of the United States to intimidate a news medium which depends for its existence upon Government licenses represents legitimate criticism. . . . Since human beings are not infallible, there are bound to be occasions when [our newsmen's] judgment is questioned. Whatever their deficiencies, they are minor compared to those of a press which would be subservient to the executive power of Government.

N. B. C. (Julian Goodman):
Vice President Agnew's attack on television news is an appeal to prejudice. More importantly, Mr. Agnew uses the influence of his high office to criticize the way a Government-licensed news medium covers the activities of Government itself. Any fair-minded viewer knows that the television networks are not devoted to putting across a single point of view but present all significant views on issues of importance. It is regrettable that the Vice President of the United States would deny to television freedom of the press.

Alexander Klein, introduction to *Natural Enemies???*
(Philadelphia: J. B. Lippincott, 1970):
The media more and more become not guides and spurs to action, but *substitutes* for action. Receiving "information," sharing a newscaster's, columnist's or Senator's indignation and venting it to friends is for most of us vicarious action, our only sustained "action" on public matters. Thus, most of us are *consumers* of politics; and commentators and editorial writers are primarily processors and purveyors of political drama, creators of shared pseudo-action, turning off real action. Indeed, election-day excepted, commentators rarely, if ever, channel us to take specific actions. The Republic is bleeding to death and we stand by watching as though it were a spectator sport.

"To the American People," a report of President Nixon's Commission on Campus Unrest, chaired by William W. Scranton (September, 1970):
We recommend that the President seek to convince public officials and protesters alike that divisive and insulting rhetoric is dangerous. . . . throughout the years ahead, the President should insist that no one play irresponsible politics with the issue of "campus unrest" . . . We recommend that he articulate and emphasize those values all Americans hold in common. At the same time we urge him to point out the importance of diversity and co-existence to the nation's health.

debates, it is part of them and therefore partisan. Thus, the advanced and costly technology of the mass media, combined with a mass public, may almost absent-mindedly produce what an authoritarian party produces deliberately—a mass dissemination of government-approved news and views.

THE RIGHT TO BE INFORMED

The danger of streamlining information to the point of censorship has caused several constitutional drafters to add the right of a citizen "to inform himself from generally accessible sources" to their new bills of rights (e.g., the West German Constitution of 1949, Article 5). The Universal Declaration of Human Rights (Article 19) specifies that the right to freedom of opinion and expression includes the freedom "to seek, receive, and impart information and ideas through any media and regardless of frontiers." The United States Freedom of Information Act (effective July 4, 1967) is designed to prevent the withholding of information from the public except in such specific areas as records involving the national security or those which might involve invasions of privacy. The act provides that individuals denied access to documents have the right to seek injunctive relief from the courts.

The increasing number of unlisted telephones in the United States during the 1970s raised a curious side issue in the debate concerning the citizen's right to be informed. Individuals who sought protection from telephone salesmen, enemies, fans, and cranks included the president, cabinet members, film stars and celebrities, and elected government officials. The notion that it is a "constitutional" right to telephone an elected representative fanned a mild controversy. Chicago's Mayor Richard J. Daley, for example, kept an unlisted telephone number and changed it when it became known to too many people. During the same period, Governor Edgar D. Whitcomb of Indiana published his private number and in a statement to the *New York Times* (December 21, 1971) maintained that it was part of his responsibility in public office to be accessible by telephone:

> The main trouble is that people just don't know who to call when they have a problem, so they call the Governor. It's their right to do that.

In a free society the right to know often raises a delicate problem in determining the boundary line between the private and public affairs of a political figure. Where does the right to privacy as a citizen end and the obligation to be subject to public scrutiny begin? A free society implies that all its citizens should know all there is to know about their political leaders—their backgrounds, views, habits, hobbies, physical and mental health, family, and even extramarital life.

This is an ancient and difficult problem, as demonstrated in the discussion of the right to privacy (chapter 2). At the end of his classic novel, *The Red and the Black*, the French writer Stendhal wrote:

> The inconvenience of the rule by public opinion which, by the way, gives us *liberty*, consists of its meddling in matters it should not concern itself with; for instance, other persons' private life. Hence the sadness of the United States and England.[27]

It is interesting to note that this concluding remark is rarely found in the English translations. It seems to be censored by translators and publishers, not by government.

As a part of the constitutional ritual, most modern Communist constitutions also emphasize their citizens' right to know. The Yugoslav Constitution speaks of the right of people "to inform themselves through the media of information." The gap between the constitutional provision and the actual practice needs little elaboration. On the eve of the Prague Spring in 1968, the organ of the Slovak Communist party, *Pravda*, (Bratislava, October 26, 1967), dared to print the following comment on the reality of the constitutional "right to know":

> It is absolutely inexcusable to attempt to conceal facts from the people which—it is thought—might arouse criticism. . . . It is common knowledge that information on sensitive subjects is either refused by the authorities or obtained with greatest difficulty. . . . The "practice of concealment" is carried to the point of being ridiculous by some overzealous, super-cautious, or simply lazy officials. . . . In Košice [the capital of eastern Slovakia] the local national committee refuses to disclose the number of dogs in town.

The traditional American freedom of the press raised a far more serious issue than the number of dogs in town in 1971 (and again in 1972) when the *New York Times* and other newspapers decided to publish secret governmental documents obtained from allegedly disenchanted government officials. In 1972 the case involved the publication of secret documents related to the United States government decision-making process before and during the India-Pakistan war (1971) over Bangladesh. The case in 1971 concerned the so-called Pentagon Papers, a narrative history of the United States involvement in the war in Vietnam, which consisted of 47 volumes containing well over 7,000 pages and appended documents (an estimated total of 2.5 million words). These documents were Xeroxed by one of the co-authors of the history, Daniel Ellsberg, and offered to the *New York Times* for publication.

The *New York Times* began publishing a series of articles based on the secret documents on Sunday, June 13, 1971. After the first three installments appeared, the Justice Department obtained a temporary restraining order against further publication from the Federal District Court for the Southern District of New York. The government contended that if public dissemination of the history continued, "the national defense interests of the United States and the nation's security would suffer immediate and irreparable harm." The desire of the government to make the temporary restraining order permanent became the subject of a well-publicized legal battle fought through the courts for fifteen days. On June 30, 1971, the Supreme Court of the United States freed the newspapers to continue publication of their articles based on the Pentagon Papers.[28] The vote in favor of the media and against the government and its attempt at censorship was six to three.

The *New York Times* argued in its editorial of June 16, 1971:

> It is in the interest of the people of this country to be informed. . . . A fundamental responsibility of the press in this democracy is to publish information that helps the people of the United States to understand the processes of their own government, especially when those processes have been clouded over in a hazy veil of public dissimulation and even deception.
>
> As a newspaper that takes seriously its obligation and its responsibilities to the public, we believe that, once the material fell into our hands, it was not only in the interests of the American people to publish it but, even more emphatically, it would have been an abnegation of responsibility and a renunciation of our obligations under the First Amendment not to have published it. Obviously, *The Times* would not have made this decision if there had been any reason to believe that publication would have endangered the life of a single American soldier or in any way threatened the security of our country or the peace of the world.
>
> The documents in question belong to history. They refer to the development of American interest and participation in Indochina from the post-World War II period up to mid-1968 which is now almost three years ago. Their publication could not conceivably damage American security interests, much less the lives of Americans or Indochinese.

The dissenting minority of the Supreme Court challenged the newspaper's right, and its ability, to determine which government secrets were liable to threaten the national security. They also raised the question as to whether the events of the preceding three years, in the light of continuing military operations and diplomatic negotiations, could properly be viewed as "history." The "history" was only a few weeks old in the case of the Indian-Pakistani dispute in 1972.

Two separate constitutional and legal issues are involved in the case of the Pentagon Papers (as well as in the subsequent case concerning the India-Pakistan War papers).

First, the act of a governmental official who accepts the obligation to abide by the rules of secrecy but later changes his mind and takes documents from secret files and, motivated by idealism, vainglory, or money, transmits these documents to the mass media for publication is punishable—providing, of course, that his actions are clearly prohibited by a law whose constitutionality is not in doubt.

Second is the question of whether the mass media, which traditionally live on news leaks and indiscretion, can be prevented by government from publishing secret documents.

The case against the press and the assumption that it could legitimately determine questions of national interest and safety was expressed in three different opinions. One of them, presented by Justice Blackmun, read:

> I, for one, have now been able to give at least some cursory study . . . to the material itself. I regret to say that from this examination I fear that Judge Wilkey's statements[29] have possible foundation. I therefore share his concern. I hope that damage already has not been done. If, however, damage has been done, and if, with the Court's action today, these newspapers proceed to publish the critical documents and there results therefrom "the death of soldiers, destruction of alliances, the greatly increased difficulty of negotiation with our enemies, the inability of our diplomats to negotiate," to which list I might add the factors of prolongation of the war and of further delay in the freeing of United States prisoners, then the nation's people will know where the responsibility for these sad consequences rests.

Justice Black wrote one of the most eloquent opinions in favor of the press:

> In the First Amendment the Founding Fathers gave the free press the protection it must have to fulfill its essential role in our democracy. The press was to serve the governed, not the governors. The Government's power to censor the press was abolished so that the press would remain forever free to censure the Government. The press was protected so that it could bare the secrets of government and inform the people. Only a free and unrestrained press can effectively expose deception in government. And paramount among the responsibilities of a free press is the duty to prevent any part of the Government from deceiving the people and sending them off to distant lands to die of foreign fevers and foreign shot and shell. In my view, far from deserving condemnation for their courageous reporting, the New York Times, the Washington Post and other newspapers should be commended for serving the purpose that the Founding Fathers saw so clearly. In revealing

the workings of government that led to the Vietnam war, the newspapers nobly did precisely that which the founders hoped and trusted they would do.

The protection of the press against censorship and prior restraint, implicit in the First Amendment, has hardly been made crystal clear and absolute, even in the United States. The Supreme Court clearly reaffirmed[30] constitutional protections of the press against prior restraint, but the protection of the citizens' right to know and of the press against censorship still seems to be relative. Actually, the *New York Times* itself argued that the Pentagon Papers would not have been fit to print if they were current decisions and operational plans or if their publication could clearly threaten national security and American or Indochinese lives. Actually, the *New York Times* later seemed to applaud the extreme secrecy which cloaked Henry Kissinger's first trip to Peking to prepare a meeting between President Nixon and Chairman Mao.

In concluding this chapter, it is noted that the freedom of expression rightly occupies a privileged, highly elevated position in constitutional theory and practice. Yet, it is not elevated so high that it loses all the pulls of political gravity such as those highly controversial concepts of "national security," "preservation of lives," and "operational battle plans."

NOTES

1   Aleksandr Solzhenitsyn, author of *One Day in the Life of Ivan Denisovich* (the Nobel Prize winner in 1970), emphasized in his letter to the French daily *Le Monde* (May 31, 1967) that the Soviet Constitution of 1936 does not mention censorship and that censorship in the USSR was therefore illegal and should be abolished. Similarly, Vladimir Bukovsky, another Soviet writer, frequently quoted the Stalin Constitution during his secret trial in 1968 in the vain attempt to prove that his indictment and conviction were illegal. Soviet authorities have consistently treated such efforts—i. e., the contrast of revolutionary and constitutional promises with the present reality—as crimes, or, as in the case of intellectuals, writers, artists, and scientists, they are labelled as "obsessive reformist delusions." During the 1960s the number of Soviet dissidents committed to mental institutions by the authorities was significantly increased. The commitment of radical critics to mental institutions is not a Soviet invention, however; it was practiced under the Czars. See the article by I. F. Stone, "Radicals and Asylums in the Soviet Union," (*New York Times,* February 15, 1972). He labeled the "commitment of radicals to lunatic asylums in the Soviet Union . . . " an "international scandal."

2   In 1967, during a political trial in Yugoslavia, a persistent critic of authoritarian communism in his country and in the Soviet union, Mihajlo Mihaj-

lov, read several constitutional provisions in court in defense of his freedom of expression and his right to criticize Soviet realities. The Yugoslav judge interrupted his quotations of the bill of rights with impatience: " I know our constitution perfectly well. You don't have to read it to me." The accused Mihajlov replied: "But, excuse me, this is not our constitution I am quoting. It is the Soviet Constitution of 1936." He was sent to prison just the same (*New York Times,* April 20, 1967).

3 Václav Havel, "On the Subject of Opposition," *Literární Listy,* Prague, April 4, 1968.

4 Article 28 of the Turkish Constitution of 1961: "All individuals are entitled to congregate and march in demonstration without prior permission, so long as they are unarmed and have no intent to assault."

5 Alexander Meiklejohn, *Free Speech and Its Relation to Self-Government* (New York: Harper, 1948).

6 Fred P. Graham, "Is it Action or 'Symbolic Speech'?", *New York Times,* June 2, 1968.

7 Sirhan Bishara Sirhan, the murderer of Robert F. Kennedy, explained his act as a protest against the pro-Israeli policy of the United States and described his motivation as follows: "I was sick and tired of being a foreigner, of being alone. I wanted a place of my own, where they speak my own language, where they eat my own food, share my own politics. I wanted something I could identify as a Palestinian and as an Arab. I wanted my own country. I wanted my own land, my own city, my own business. I wanted my own everything, sir" (*New York Times,* March 5, 1969).

8 Charles S. Hyneman, "Free Speech at What Price?", *American Political Science Review* 56:4 (December 1962), p. 847.

9 Ibid., p. 848. Charles S. Hyneman's comment on the subject of the maximalist doctrine that considers the protection of the freedom of political expression absolute is both useful and challenging: "The absolute prohibition doctrine runs squarely into issues of reasonableness at three points. When you examine what Justice Black and Douglas have said from the bench and in addresses delivered in other places, you learn that one of them or both of them has asserted: first, that the First Amendment does not protect all kinds of verbal expression; second, that expression which the First Amendment does protect sometimes loses protection because it is inextricably mixed up with other action; and third, that statements which ordinarily are immune from restraint by government may be forbidden if the words can be said to be the efficient cause of certain punishable actions."

10 "Propaganda for war, that which offends public morals, and that for the purpose of inciting disobedience of the laws shall not be permitted"— Venezuela, 1961, Article 66.

11 "Any manifestation or propaganda of ethnic nature will be punished by law"—Chad, 1962, preamble. "All particularist propaganda of racial or ethnic nature" will be punished according to the constitution of Ivory Coast, 1962, Article 6. Similarly, the constitution of Senegal (Article 5) forbids "any regionalist propaganda that may threaten the integrity of the territory of the Republic."

12 A 1971 amendment to the constitution of Malaysia makes it an act of sedition, punishable by fine and imprisonment, to discuss any subject deemed "likely to arouse racial feelings and endanger racial peace in the country." This even applies to discussions in Parliament.

13 Slander is an oral statement that maliciously or falsely defames or injures another.

14 Libel is a written statement that maliciously or falsely defames or injures another.

15 Sedition is a vaguely defined crime, different from insurrection, rebellion, and treason. It generally means use of force and violence in opposition to the laws or conspiring to do so. It also means raising a commotion or a disturbance in the state.

16 Such skeptics argue, for instance, that the free election in Chile (September 4, 1970) in which a Marxist candidate, committed to Chile's socialist future, Salvadore Allende Gossens, obtained a plurality of votes may have been the first case in history in which a people, half knowingly, voted themselves into an ultimately one-party socialist system more akin to the Cuban than to the Scandinavian model. Allende was backed by a coalition of left-wing parties that had an organizational core in the Chilean Communist party.

17 The then-Communist leadership was headed by Eugene Dennis and included also his subsequent successor, Gus Hall.

18 Sections 2 and 3 of the Smith Act (54 Stat. 671, 18 U. S. C. par. 2385) provide as follows: "Section 2. It shall be unlawful for any person (1) to knowingly or willfully advocate, abet, advise, or teach the duty, necessity, desirability, or propriety of overthrowing or destroying any government [federal or state] in the United States by force or violence, or by the assassination of any officer of such government; (2) with intent to cause the overthrow or destruction of any government in the United States, to print, publish, edit, issue, circulate, sell, distribute, or publicly display any written or printed matter advocating, advising, or teaching the duty, necessity, desirability, or propriety of overthrowing or destroying any government in the United States by force or violence; (3) to organize or help to organize any society, group, or assembly of persons who teach, advocate, or encourage the overthrow or destruction of any government in the United States by force or violence; or to become a member of, or affiliate with, any such society, group, or assembly of persons, knowing the persons thereof. . . . "

"Section 3. It shall be unlawful for any person to attempt to commit, or to conspire to commit, any of the acts prohibited by the provisions of this title."

19 *Dennis* v. *United States,* 341 U.S. 494 (1951).

20 Ibid.

21 Ibid.

22 On April 19, 1967, Justice Lukić (Yugoslavia) sentenced a writer, Mihajlo Mihajlov, to jail for writing in opposition to the Communist party's political monopoly and for showing materials printed by Yugoslav anti-Communist

emigrés to his friends. Justice Lukić said: "Thoughts are freely expressed in our country but those that express hatred and an unconstitutional stand cannot be permitted freedom. We preserve the freedom of the press, but we safeguard against a use of the press so as to prevent the undermining of our system."

23 *Pravda* (Moscow), June 22, 1936.

24 The constitution of India (1949), Article 22(5): When any person is detained in pursuance of an order made under any law providing for preventive detention, the authority making the order, shall, as soon as may be, communicate to such person the grounds on which the order had been made and shall afford him the earliest opportunity of making representation against the order. Article 22(6): Nothing in clause (5) shall require the authority making any such order as is referred to in that clause to disclose facts which such authority considers against the public interest to disclose.

25 David H. Bayley, *Public Liberties in the New States* (Chicago: Rand McNally, 1964), p. 25.

26 In 1971 an American youth group called the "Silent Majority for a United America Organization" picketed the Columbia Broadcasting System in New York and distributed a leaflet which, in part, stated: "Boycott C.B.S. and advertisers who make it financially possible for C.B.S. to brainwash peoples' minds.—We indict C.B.S. and its officials and newscasters for a constant barrage of propaganda to destroy American Patriotism and Nationalism. . . . The Federal Communications Commission should re-examine C.B.S.'s franchise because we believe it is not in the interest of the true American public. . . . C.B.S. has put America on trial with its biased, slanted, unbalanced, pro-liberal broadcasting and opinion-forming programs. . . . We indict them on the following charges: For waging the greatest advertising campaign in history, selling leftist propaganda to our youth; for ridiculing pro-American personalities when they appear on talk shows (i. e. Al Capp's appearance on the Merv Griffin show); for giving tremendous favorable publicity to malcontent radicals such as Jane Fonda, Jerry Hoffman, Kunstler, etc; for exaggerating poverty and attacking our free enterprise system, which is the best when compared to all other political systems; for giving constant favorable publicity to liberal, pro-leftist public officials, while suppressing the opinions of the pro-government officials."

27 Stendhal, *Le Rouge et le Noir* (Paris: René Hilsum, 1931), p. 286. (By necessity, the quote was translated by the author.)

28 *The Pentagon Papers—as Published by The New York Times* (Bantam Books, 1971), contains a complete and unabridged series of articles on "The Secret History of the Vietnam War" as published by the *New York Times,* some of the key documents, the paper's editorials on that subject, and the Supreme Court decision of June 20, 1971.

29 The quote refers to a dissenting opinion of Judge Wilkey in the case involving the *Washington Post* and its decision to publish another portion of the Pentagon Papers. The District of Columbia Court ruled in favor of the

newspaper. Judge Wilkey objected and argued that documents scheduled for publication by the *Washington Post* could, if published, "result in great harm to the nation" and then proceeded to define "harm" to mean "the death of soldiers . . ." and so on as quoted by Justice Blackmun.

30 We refer to a 1931 case *(Near* v. *Minnesota)*. In reversing a lower court, the Supreme Court then said that prior restraints were abhorrent to the First Amendment but conceded that in certain "exceptional cases"—publication of the sailing dates of troopships or battle plans were mentioned—news articles could be suppressed.

CHAPTER 6

Participatory Rights:
Suffrage & Political Parties

If formulating and communicating demands for official action is often called the heart of politics, then, from the constitutional point of view, the basic participatory rights—the right to vote, the right to assemble and petition the government—are the blood vessels. Other specific rights have been derived from the fundamental participatory rights, such as the right to establish parties and the right to organize pressure groups to promote and defend particular interests by legitimate means, including a strike. The purpose of all political rights and means is the legitimate expression of individual and group interests to political authorities who convert them into binding decisions. Group demands are satisfied by either influencing or running the government.

THE RIGHT TO VOTE & BE ELECTED

Pre-twentieth-century constitutions give the impression that political authority is expected to be responsive and responsible to citizens as individuals rather than as organized political groups. The right to assemble peaceably suggests a town meeting in New England or a valley meeting in a Swiss canton, not organized political parties or mass rallies with loudspeakers and folk singers. The constitutional image evoked is that of individuals, endowed with inalienable rights and the right to vote (in the nineteenth century white men and taxpayers only), faced by governments with eminently useful coercive powers which are potentially dangerous when used unintelligently, irresponsibly, or excessively. Before the turn of the century constitutional texts rarely suggested there were other links between the citizen and his government, and between the voter and his representative assembly. The

191

group activities that figured prominently in the debates of constitutional assemblies were not translated into appropriate chapters and paragraphs in constitutional charters. Federal constitutions alone defined and described the functions of territorial interest groups, that is, the components of federal unions.

Like other constitutional guarantees, the basic right to participate in rule making by voting is not absolute. There are, invariably, age limitations. The United States Constitution left the matter to the states since the drafters in Philadelphia could not agree on national qualifications. Most other constitutions fix the voting age; more and more of them lower it to eighteen. The United States followed suit by adopting the Twenty-sixth Amendment in 1971.[1]

During the student riots in France (May 1968) it was suggested by some of the leaders that voting rights should be given 18-year-olds but withdrawn from those who retire from active life, and so become sensitive only to the past while continuing to shape the present and the future *(la république des vieillards)*. The young radicals argued that infantilism characterizes not only those under eighteen but also the very old. In other words, anybody over 65 cannot be trusted with the right to vote.

The denial of voting rights to criminals and the insane is also controversial. Perhaps fools and murderers should not have the right to representation in government, but political authorities may abuse allegations of "crime" and "insantity" by including political offenses, protests, and nonconformity. A nineteenth-century English law deprived clergymen, lords, lunatics, and bankrupts of the right to be represented in Parliment for a long time.

The constitution of Communist China excludes former propertyowners ("feudal landlords and bureaucrat-capitalists," Article 19) from voting pending their reeducation through labor. On the other hand, the constitution of Liberia requires the voter to own property; "in the Provinces of the hinterland of the Republic," says Article 1, Section 11, " 'possessing real estate' shall be construed to include possessing a hut on which he or she pays the hut tax."

Franco's Spain gave some Spaniards a limited right to vote after the constitutional change of 1966. The heads of families and their wives, unlike students and young workers, were expected to favor conservative stability. They can now elect about one-fourth of the members of the national legislature (*Cortes*). The other members are still selected by the political authorities, official trade unions, municipalities, etc.

Constitutional provisions governing the right of members of the armed forces and the civil service to vote oscillate between two extremes, from explicit recognition to complete denial. Article 138 of the

Soviet Constitution (1936) grants "Citizens serving in the Armed Forces of the USSR . . . the right to elect and be elected on equal terms with all other citizens." In Communist China the armed services elect deputies to the National People's Congress as do the provinces, autonomous regions, cities directly under central authority, and Chinese who live abroad (Article 23 of the constitution). The Algerian Constitution (Article 8) affirms the special role of the military:

> The national army is a people's army . . . it participates in the political, economic, and social activities in the framework of the party—National Liberation Front.

The Algerian founding fathers failed to foresee that the army would participate so well that it would support a coup d'état led by Colonel Boumedienne and take over the government, the party, and the country.

The opposite extreme was evident in many democratic European systems before World War II. It is also evident in some Latin American countries today. Members of the armed forces cannot engage in politics or vote in parliamentary elections. The constitution of Brazil (1967), Article 142, deprives privates of their right to vote but allows the following military personnel to register as voters: "officers, officer-candidates, the marines, sub-officers, sublieutenants, sergeants or students of military academies." The Cuban Constitution of 1959 which grants the right to vote to all Cubans over twenty years of age (Article 99) denies the right to vote to "individuals belonging to the Armed Forces or the police who are in active service" as well as "inmates of asylums, persons judicially declared mentally incompetent" and those "who are judicially disqualified because of a crime."

The Brazilian constitution has made the citizen's participation in electoral processes not only a right but an enforceable duty. This is not unusual. Many countries, especially in Europe, fine citizens who fail to vote if their excuse is inadequate. In Switzerland four cantons (Schaffhausen, St. Gallen, Aargau and Thurgau) make voting in federal matters obligatory under a threat of a fine.[2] When citizens have the legal duty to vote even if they are positively disinterested and consequently uninformed, the disadvantages of such a system seem obvious: although citizens dutifully perform the voting ritual, they pay no attention to the issues and persons involved and tend to cast a blank ballot or follow the advice of their friend, employer, or passer-by. Nevertheless some observers of the actual practice defend the laws which force citizens to vote and point to the fact that the legal duty to vote induces citizens to become interested and informed, since they must cast a ballot in any event. Laws which establish voting as a duty are not the first statutes to attempt a change in citizens' behavior; the assumption and hope of such laws are that, in the long run, a legally imposed obligation will become habitual behavior.

Universal suffrage came gradually in the Western democracies. The right to vote was originally reserved to the propertied and educated classes which were qualified to participate in politics by their payment of taxes. Negroes and women in the United States were not given the right to vote until 1890 (the Fifteenth Amendment) and 1920 (Nineteenth Amendment) respectively.[3]

The emerging countries apparently face a problem since they have suddenly granted the right to vote without requiring the voter to be literate. The extension of the right to vote in the Western democracies largely coincided with the elimination of illiteracy. It is, however, possible to err by assuming that education is a precondition for political wisdom. One quarter of the Nazi SS leaders had advanced university degrees; "the extremely anti-Semitic" Austrian Volkspartei was nicknamed the "professor party."[4] On the other hand, there is a substantial danger that the people's will can be rigged and distorted if the right to vote is given without preparation, regardless of literacy or familiarity with political processes, the celebrated Indian elections notwithstanding.[5]

EQUALITY OF FRANCHISE

An equality of franchise, which is a basic prerequisite for fair competition between parties, is generally guaranteed by most constitutions. The concept of "one man, one vote" has acquired three implied meanings, one of which forms the background for the system of proportional representation as adopted by several constitutions and electoral laws.

(1) First, the equality of franchise means that all adults should have the right to vote. Nobody should be denied this right on the basis of sex, race, tax bracket, education, class origin, or occupation. Exceptions to this general rule have already been noted.

(2) Second, "one man, one vote" means that no one should have more than one vote. Several countries formerly sanctioned plural voting by law or constitution. In Britain, until 1948, a voter could vote a second time in another constituency where he paid taxes on a business property, or as a university graduate voting with fellow graduates to elect a representative of their university in the House of Commons. In 1948, twelve university members remained in the British Parliament, representing Oxford, Cambridge, and other major schools. In Belgium a constitutional amendment in 1895 gave a second vote to voters who paid annual taxes of at least five francs or owned government bonds

with an annual yield of 100 francs. If such a voter also had a university education, he had a third vote. This system which was directed against workers and the socialist party, was maintained until the end of World War I to protect the propertied and educated groups against a rising tide of paupers and uneducated voters which constituted a majority in the population.

Some constitutional systems have deliberately introduced unequal weight of votes in order to ensure the federal principle of equal representation of unequal states; as a result, the value of votes is lower in larger states than in small states. In the United States, for example, a senator may represent as many as 3,728,864 votes (Robert F. Kennedy, New York, 1964) or as few as 66,907 (Howard B. Cannon, Nevada, 1964). In other systems there is an unequal weight of votes which deliberately enhances one class or economic interest at the expense of others. In the Soviet Union, for example, industrial workers (a minority for the first two decades after the revolution of 1917) were protected against peasant majorities by the constitutions of 1918 and 1924. City dwellers were constitutionally guaranteed overrepresentation (one deputy for 25,000 voters) whereas the rural areas were underrepresented (one deputy for each 125,000 voters). In the United States the shift of population and the inaction of state legislatures created a reapportionment problem (the so-called "gerrymander by default") opposite to that of the Soviet Union by underrepresenting the urban areas. The United States Supreme Court has dealt twice with unfair apportionment practices leading to inequalities in the franchise. *Baker* v. *Carr* (1962) dealt with the issue of gerrymander by default and *Reynolds* v. *Sims* (1964) dealt with apportionment for the purpose of election to a state upper house.

(3) The third, and most controversial, problem in providing an equality of franchise involves the question of whether the votes cast by a defeated minority should keep proportional weight after elections i.e., whether a minority should exert a continuing influence on policy making. "We are on a difficult ground," states a recent well-documented study, "when we define equality of franchise to require that everyone's vote should have the same weight or value."[6] A system of majority rule implies that the votes cast by a minority have an equal weight only before elections. Having lost an election, a minority presumably is reduced to a political nullity until the next election. Elections, after all, are supposed to produce victory and defeat. In the United States, for example, if the Democrats obtained a majority of one vote in all the 435 congressional districts, the Republicans would not seat a single representative in the House yet the difference nationally would amount to only 435 votes (e.g., 35,000,435 against 35,000,000).

The potential mathematical consequence of a majority system (which could be transformed into a one-party system in the national legislature between elections) is one of the most powerful arguments for proportional representation frequently heard in other countries.

A system of proportional representation guarantees proportional weight to minority votes after elections in theory but not entirely in practice. When a whole country becomes a single all-national constituency (as in the case of Israel), the proportional system may eliminate inequalities inherent in majority voting. However, some votes are bound to lose effect after elections in countries which are divided into several electoral districts or when a proportional system reduces the number of small splinter parties (e.g., by fixing minimum representation quotas).

> To assign to the vote a certain weight or values, is a sophistical exaggeration of the equality principle. No proportional representation system can guarantee an absolutely equal weight for each vote cast. . . . A voter who has cast his vote incorrectly has as little right to special consideration as does the person who comes up with the wrong solution to a puzzle.[7]

Nevertheless, one of the basic principles reflected in constitutions which decree proportional representation is the reduction of voting inequities which can be found in majority systems. Article 17 of the German Weimar Republic's constitution provided that every state legislature should be "elected in universal, equal, direct and secret elections by all male and female citizens in accordance with the principles of proportional representation." West Germany elects one-half of the representatives in the lower house by plurality in electoral districts, and the other half on the basis of proportional representation from state party lists of candidates (Federal Election Law of 1956). The constitution of East Germany (1949) prescribed proportional representation in the legislature and a proportional composition for the cabinet. The Communist totalitarian framework, in which non-Communist parties are satellites of the dominant Communist party, suggests that the provision for a coalition government in the East German constitution (Article 92) was a monument of constitutional hypocrisy:

> The Minister-President [prime minister] is appointed by the party with the greatest strength in the People's Chamber; he forms the Government [cabinet]. All parties having at least forty representatives in the People's Chamber are represented by Ministers . . . in proportion to their strength. Should one parliamentary party refuse to be included, the Government will be formed without it.

The Mexican Constitution, as amended in 1963, provides from five to a maximum of twenty special "party deputies" for each 2½ percent of the country's vote for each national party which has not obtained a majority in at least twenty electoral districts. The "party deputies" may be added to the number of deputies obtained by majorities in electoral districts. This amendment (Article 54) evidently was intended to soften the image of monopolistic rule by the Institutio:1al Revolutionary Party (PRI), which has dominated the Mexican political scene for more than three decades.[8]

NATIONAL CONSTITUTIONS
& POLITICAL PARTIES

During the eighteenth and nineteenth centuries national constitutions were drafted and transformed into living documents by political parties, yet those constitutions were silent regarding the existence and role of political parties and interest groups. That constitutional silence, in part, reflected the prevailing fear that parties and interest groups would split the national community by ruthlessly promoting selfish interests to the detriment of the collective national welfare. James Madison expressed that fear in the *Federalist Papers* (No. 10). The leaders of today's developing countries dread a fatal competition among factions, especially those based on ethnic, linguistic, tribal, or territorial differences, and condemn parties and factions in terms similar to Madison's. The former president of Pakistan, Ayub Khan, argued:

> In our case political party activities only divide and confuse our people and lay them open to exploitation by unscrupulous demagogues. So I believe that if we can run our politics without a party system, we shall have cause to bless ourselves—though I recognize that like-minded people in the legislative assemblies will group themselves together.[9]

They did and political parties were the result. One of them, the East Pakistani Awami League, finally became the symbol and instrument of Bangladesh secessionism.

By the end of the nineteenth century political parties and interest groups in Europe and America seemingly had proven their representative and democratic worth, but constitutions enacted during that period were still relatively silent on the subject of parties and pressure groups. By that time parties were as much a natural and essential part of constitutional democracy as breathing is of free speech. Presumably neither breathing nor parties need to be promoted by constitutional texts. The existence of parties was assumed and references to them were rather casual.[10]

In the twentieth century the success of Communist and Fascist parties created a new challenge to constitutional government; the old fears of excessive factionalism and the acceptance and approval of the role of political parties in the nineteenth century were replaced by a new fear that one well-organized party in control of government and national economy may eliminate all the other parties and thus constitutional democracy.

> The political party has been torn from its natural context in the system of democratic institutions in which it originated. It has suffered a triple change. It has been adjusted to the new cult of heroism: it has been turned into the mirror or focus of the new self-consciousness of national society; it has been made the planner or director of a newly nationalized system of economics.[11]

As a consequence, constitutions either began to ban antidemocratic parties and guarantee party pluralism, or constitutional charters were woven around a single party with a capital "P." Constitutional references to political parties became explicit instead of implicit as they had been in earlier documents. Provisions formerly found in electoral ordinances, legislative rules of procedure, or the by-laws of political parties began to be incorporated into constitutional texts. The constitution of Tanzania (1965) incorporates the rules of its only party, Tanganyika African National Union, into the national constitution (see Document 6.4). Those rules comprise one-third of the constitutional text.

RIGHTS & LIMITS
FOR POLITICAL PARTIES

Similar to other constitutional rights and liberties, the right to form political parties is relative, not absolute. Constitutions and laws based upon them limit the right to organize parties in terms of their goals, internal structure, and financing.

Modern constitutions that are committed to two or more parties understandably reflect a fear that a single party may seek to replace pluralism with a totalitarian one-party system. Such fears sometime lead to the interdiction of parties that have transnational links.[12]

Postwar constitutional provisions concerning undemocratic goals, methods, and internal organization of political parties clearly reflect the experience of West Germany and Italy with nazism, fascism, and communism. Article 49 of the Italian constitution (1947) guarantees all citizens the right "to freely form parties in order to contribute by democratic means to national policy." Article 17 forbids "secret associations and those which pursue political aims, even indirectly, by means of organizations of a military character." The constitution of West Germany (1949), Article 21/2, stipulates:

> Parties which, according to their aims and the conduct of their members, seek to impair or abolish the libertarian democratic basic order or to jeopardize the existence of the Federal Republic of Germany are unconstitutional. The federal Constitutional Court decides on the question of unconstitutionality. . . . Internal organization [of the parties] must conform to democratic principles. They must publicly account for the sources of their funds.[13]

Article 57 of the constitution of Turkey (1961) contains a rather elaborate provision dealing with political parties and their internal matters. The Constitutional Court of the Turkish Republic threatens parties which do not conform to constitutional standards with dissolution:

> The statutes, programs and activities of political parties shall conform to the principles of a democratic form of a democratic and secular republic, based on human rights and liberties, and to the fundamental principle of the State's territorial and national integrity. Parties failing to conform to these provisions shall be permanently dissolved.
>
> Political parties shall account for their sources of income and expenditures to the Constitutional Court . . . .
>
> Actions in law involving the dissolution of political parties shall be heard at the Constitutional Court, and the verdict to dissolve them shall be rendered only by this court.

These and similar constitutional provisions outlawed Communist parties in West Germany, Turkey, Venezuela, Brazil, Iran, the Philippines, most of the Central and South American republics, and many other countries. On the other hand, there are no constitutional proscriptions against the Communist parties of France and Italy—they are the largest parties in the opposition and they average 22 to 25 percent of the vote.

Some constitutions prescribe an internal democracy for political parties and require party leaders to be responsible and accountable to the members. Their drafters seemingly assume there is a direct correlation between undemocratic internal structures and undemocratic goals. It is, however, possible that political leaders could preside over an autocratic party structure yet observe, *outside* their own party, the democratic rules of the political game. In his classic treatise on political parties, Robert Michels argued that parties, regardless of their leaders' ideals and beliefs, are bound to become oligarchies—"who says Organization, says Oligarchy." Michels explains:

> Now, if we leave out of consideration the tendency of the leaders to organize themselves and to consolidate their interests, and if we leave also out of consideration the gratitude of the led towards the leaders, and the general immobility and passivity of the masses, we are led to conclude that the principal cause of oligarchy in the democratic parties is to be found in the technical indispensability of leadership.[14]

Some observers also argue that a multi-party system combined with proportional representation in a democracy makes oligarchic parties inevitable. Another writer suggests that "Proportional representation, more than any other electoral system, puts the actual exercise of political power into the hands of the party oligarchies and their bureaucracies, which are entirely beyond popular control."[15]

CONSTITUTIONAL COMMITMENTS
TO PARTY COMPETITION OR MONOPOLY

Modern constitutions variously commit themselves either to party pluralism or exalt a one-party system. These two broad alternatives require some refinement in the light of actual practice. Three party systems can be identified: (1) competitive multi-party, (2) two-party, and (3) one-party. The latter has four subcategories.[16]

> By far the most important aspect of any party system is and has always been the numerical relationship among the parties. This remains as true as ever at the crude level of distinguishing one-party (noncompetitive), two-party, and multiparty systems. . . . The number of players and the relative size largely define the nature of the game of electoral and parliamentary competition and coalition. The constant or fluctuating relationship between existing social groupings and voting patterns over a period of time gives the electoral and parliamentary game a time dimension and social perspective.[17]

(1) In a *competitive multi-party system,* three or more parties compete for votes. Usually it is impossible for one of them to command a majority of seats in the legislature.

(2) In a *two-party system* (a) not more than two parties have a genuine chance of gaining power at any time; (b) one party can win the requisite

majority and stay in office without help from a third party; and (c) the two parties are sufficiently matched in strength over a number of decades to allow them to alternate in power. Other parties are not real rivals.[18]

In a federation one system may prevail in the center with a different system in each of the states. For example, some states in the United States have had a one-party rule for decades. Many states in India are run by a coalition of parties, although the national government has been in the hands of the Congress party since India won its independence.

(3) In a *one-party system* only one political organization holds and exercises decisive, normally unchallenged power.

There are four variants in one-party systems:

(a) A dominant but competitive party. Other parties are permitted but over a number of decades have had no genuine chance to accede to power. Professor Robert Scalapino calls this a *one-and-a-half party system* and places the Liberal Democratic party's rule of Japan in this category. The dominance of the Congress party in India, the Democratic party in the American South (and the Christian Democratic Union under Konrad Adenauer in West Germany from 1949 to 1966) are examples of one-and-a-half party systems.

(b) A dominant, noncompetitive party, which permits relatively free articulation of nonpolitical interests outside the party, some discussion of political alternatives within the party, and severely limits political challenges to its rule. The Mexican one-party monopoly (PRI) belongs in this category.

(c) An authoritarian party permits a limited formulation of nonpolitical interests by leaving the family, the church, and purely private affairs mostly untouched. Franco's Spain is an example.

(d) A totalitarian party is similar to the authoritarian party except that it permeates the whole society to a greater degree—all through the party, all for the party, nothing against the party, nothing outside the party (to paraphrase Mussolini's dictum about his fascist state). The party, writes Crane Brinton, "pries and pokes about corners normally reserved for priest or physician or friend."[19] The totalitarian type of one-party system includes the Soviet Union and possibly the people's democracies, where the multi-party system is, in reality, a grouping of insignificant miniparties, directed and dominated by the Communist party.[20]

These categories are roughly sketched; they are not invariable. Party systems in practice gradually shade into one another so that hybrid types are more frequent than the "pure" typologies suggested above.

MULTI-PARTY CONSTITUTIONS

Constitutions which assume several parties seem to view them as aggregative agencies for transmitting demands to the political system. They are representative in that they seek "to incorporate divergent views in order to win the widest following and so political power."[21] In addition, as part of their representative function, such parties help the political authority to organize elections, select candidates, offer alternative programs of goals and action when in opposition, and run the government when in power (see Document 6.1).

Constitutional guarantees of party pluralism (e.g., the constitution of Turkey specifically sanctions the role of an opposition party) are intended to prevent the voters from voting themselves into a one-party tyranny. One essential feature of a truly democratic election is the guarantee that it will not be the last one. Note, however, that most one-party systems were not established by "last" or "suicidal" elections; rather they resulted from civil wars, wars of liberation, a revolution, or a coup d'état similar to Hitler's unconstitutional takeover of Weimar Germany.

When constitutions are silent on the subject of political parties (as in the case of many older constitutions) statutes regulate political parties. Statutory laws in those countries regulate party participation in elections, their financial and corporate responsibilities, and other duties and rights. The United States has numerous and elaborate statutes (both federal and state) to govern party primaries, campaign spending, the use of the broadcasting and television media, and many other aspects of party activities. Court decisions also affect the parties.

TWO-PARTY CONSTITUTIONS

The United States and England are classic examples of countries where two-party systems have developed extraconstitutionally. It has been maintained that the two-party system makes both the written constitution of the United States and the unwritten constitution of Britain work.

Colombia has the only known constitution (as amended in 1957) which provides for a two-party system. Following fifteen years of political violence, the two traditional Colombian parties, conservative and liberal, formed a coalition by neatly dividing political positions on an equal basis. The presidency was to alternate between the two parties until 1974, and all legislative and cabinet posts were to be divided between them. Voters were given a limited choice within the parties but

Document 6.1

CONSTITUTIONAL COMMITMENTS
TO MULTI-PARTY SYSTEMS

France, 1958
Article 4. Political parties and groups shall be instrumental in the expression of suffrage. They shall be formed freely and shall carry on their activities freely.

Cameroon, 1961
Article 3. [The] political parties and groups play a part in the expression of the suffrage. They shall be free to form and to carry out their activities within the limits established by law and regulations.

Morocco, 1962
Article 3. The political parties shall participate in the organization and representation of the people. There shall be no one-party system.

West Germany, 1949
Article 21. The parties shall participate in forming the political will of the people.

Venezuela, 1961
Article 114. All Venezuelans qualified to vote have the right to associate together in political parties in order to participate, by democratic methods, in the guidance of national policy.

Turkey, 1961
Article 56. Whether in power or in opposition political parties are indispensable entities of democratic political life.

could not vote for third-party candidates or alter the fifty-fifty division between the conservatives and the liberals. Colombia's constitutional guarantee of a two-party monopoly was supposed to protect the country against an excessive multiplication of parties that could make government impossible. In reality, it provided for a one-party system of sorts by guaranteeing each of its two "factions" half the political power. Article 93 of the constitution (1880), as amended in 1957, reads in part

> . . . In the popular elections that are held to elect public bodies up to 1968 inclusive, the posts corresponding to each electoral district shall be allotted, half-and-half, to the traditional parties, the liberal and the conservative. If there are two or more lists for the same party and there are more than two posts assigned to that party, the electoral quotient system shall be applied in allotting them, taking into account, however, only the votes cast for the lists of that party. . . .

The same fifty-fifty basis was applied (Article 120) to the composition of the cabinet. Article 114 provided for election of the president by a direct vote of the citizens for a term of four years, but for one candidate only. The constitution stipulates that the presidency would alternate, starting with a conservative in 1962, to be followed by a liberal in 1966, and so on. If these provisions read like a political deal more than a constitutional document it should be noted that constitutions are always an expression of a political agreement among those who matter.

Following the fall of Nkrumah's dictatorial regime in Ghana an effort was made to democratize and stabilize that country's internal situation in order to prevent a restoration of a one-party rule and inhibit the emergence of a multi-party system in which each party would represent a tribal or ethnic rather than political identity. An interesting document, written by Kwamena Bentsi-Enchill in 1968, suggested that "creative decisions about political parties in Ghana's new constitutional system should be taken *before* they emerge."[22]

In his tentative draft of the constitutional provisions for a two-party system in Ghana (see Document 6.2) the author condemned a one-party rule since a single party becomes undistinguishable from the state; he also asserts that "the claims that it is possible to have effective democracy within the one party have not been borne out by experience."[23] The controllers of the party get too powerful by their use of state coercive machinery. Bentsi-Enchill also condemned a multi-party system by simply stating: "If two are enough then it is merely distracting and complicating to have more than two."[24]

ONE-PARTY CONSTITUTIONS

Some constitutions endorse a one-party system by stressing its elitist nature and directive role. The primary function of the single party is not to articulate and aggregate the interests of the voters or to communicate those interests to the authorities. The party is the agency which transmits the inspirations and concrete orders of the ruling elite via the party members to the society at large. Constitutions in the one-party systems thus confirm the party as the principal instrument of coercive social mobilization and political recruitment. The goal of the one-party system is to ensure that the citizenry is responsive to the political authority—it is not to ensure that the political authority is responsive to the demands of the citizenry. The function of the single party is to articulate the party's orientation, directions, and goals.

However, the contrast between the authoritarian and totalitarian parties, and the two-way traffic typical of representative competitive

Document 6.2

A BLUEPRINT FOR THE PARTY GAME IN GHANA

(1) (i) There shall be *two* political parties in Ghana and no more.

(ii) No one shall be eligible to become a candidate for election to Parliament or to a local or regional council *unless* he is a member of one or other of the two national parties and has been selected by his party, as a candidate.

(2) (i) Each of the national parties shall be so organised as to contain and represent all the different peoples, shades of opinion and interests in the country.

(3) (i) The two political parties shall take turns in governing the country, each for the period of three years.

(ii) While one party governs the other party shall perform the political function of national custodian or watchman.

(iii) The rule of rotation shall be unalterable for 12 years, starting from the coming into operation of this part of the Constitution and may be continued for such periods thereafter as the nation may decide.

(iv) The decision as to which of the two national parties shall be the first to govern shall be made by tossing of a coin or the drawing of lots by their chairmen immediately after the first election.

(Proposed by Kwamena Bentsi-Enchill, dean of the Law School at the University of Zambia, in 1968 in a mimeographed document)

---

parties, is not always clear. The competitive parties also aim to inspire the masses, induce solidarity, and elicit continuing support for the system that the party administers. All political parties identify their own interests to those of the nation—totalitarian parties are not unique in that respect.

On the other hand, authoritarian and totalitarian parties are like democratic parties in that they need to know about public opinion, if for no other reason than to manipulate it. Consequently, even Fascist and Communist parties may serve as channels for transmitting occasional demands to the elite. Local party representatives may thus factually describe social discontent in their reports to the party leaders yet avoid the personal risks involved in analyzing its real cause and ascribing it to the system itself.

Since authoritarian and totalitarian parties also sift worthy local candidates for party, state administrative and managerial positions, local and functional interests influence party decisions to a limited extent.

The marginal changes that characterized the Communist systems in Europe, and Portugal, and Franco's Spain in the late 1960s were partly the result of overt challenges by students, intellectuals, and workers.

Those changes were also in response to the covert messages transmitted through party channels—messages which originated at the consumer foundations and passed through the managerial pillars to the top of the Communist and Fascist pyramids.[25]

Constitutions openly committed to a one-party system are necessarily ecstatic in describing the role of the party. The approach contrasts with constitutions that matter-of-factly describe parties in the plural as only one important configuration in a vast political firmament. One-party systems and the constitutions that reflect them are most prevalent in Communist and developing societies (see Document 6.3).

Several Communist states in Eastern Europe and the People's Republic of China pretend to be run by a coalition of several parties, some of which bear labels from the pre-Communist past. It is a master-slave coalition in which a few miniparties are allowed to orbit as docile satellites around the five-pointed star of the Communist party. In China this arrangement squares with Mao's concept that a joint dictatorship[26] and the people's democracy constitute a lower form of socialism. The concept that the Communist party exercises unchallengeable leadership yet is willing to cooperate with other organized groups was so central to the Chinese plans in 1954 that it found its way into the constitutional preamble:

> In the year 1949, after more than a century of heroic struggle, the Chinese people, led by the Communist Party of China, finally won their great victory in the people's revolution against imperialism, feudalism, and bureaucrat-capitalism and thereby brought to an end the history of oppression and enslavement they had undergone for so long and founded the People's Republic of China—a people's democratic dictatorship.... In the course of the great struggle to establish the People's Republic of China, the people of our country forged a broad people's democratic united front led by the Communist Party of China and composed of all democratic parties and groups, and people's organizations. This people's democratic united front will continue to play its part in mobilizing and rallying the whole people in the struggle to fulfill the general tasks of the state during the transition period and to oppose enemies within and without.

The last sentence seems to indicate that the concept of a united front may have no place in the final socialist and communist stages. A people's democracy is not a fully classless society and communist theory supposes that a political party is the organized expression of a class interest. Theoretically, several parties may exist in a multi-class people's democracy, and they do—or rather they vegetate. Their policies, size, public statements, even the circulation of their newspapers are[27] determined by an appropriate office of the Communist party. The satellite parties are encouraged to favor the central themes set by the Communist party in their public statements. The Christian Democratic parties in Eastern Europe have been known to make reference to the Holy Trinity and the Virgin Mary in praising a new Communist five-year plan.[28]

The prescribed role of miniparties in the Communist world resembles that of other organizations, e.g., trade unions and youth leagues which the party uses to manipulate the members of nonparty groups. The trade unions control the workers and the youth leagues orient the younger generation, whereas the satellite parties permit the Communist party to manipulate the members of former political parties. Many Kremlinologists and Maologists question why the Communist party insists on constitutionally embalming the pre-Communist political organizations—since the power of the Communist party has long been consolidated there is no longer a need to preserve the fiction by pushing dead bodies around.

Another inconsistency is the extreme sensitivity of the Communist leadership to the suggestion that a new party, committed to the same ideology, be accepted. Small non-Communist parties are permitted to exist but opposition Communist parties are not allowed. A former vice-president in Communist Yugoslavia, Milovan Djilas, was imprisoned for daring to suggest that two socialist parties be allowed to compete in more effectively administering Yugoslav socialism. He noted that two ideologically similar capitalist parties clash over the management of American capitalism. Djilas argued that the basic principles of socialism in Yugoslavia (as it is in the case of capitalism in the United States) would never be at stake.[29] Wherever a one-party system has ruled long enough to reveal its serious shortcomings in matters of social and economic progress, governmental efficiency, and popular controls, there is an echoing call for two parties. The Communist rulers admit the shortcomings of single-party rule but they have so far nipped attempts at legitimate socialist opposition in the bud.

While engaged in a polemic with Yugoslav Communists who recommended a two-socialist-party system, a leading Yugoslav theoretician (Dragomír Drašković) argued (*Gledista* [Belgrade, November 1967], pp. 1557–1566) that the weaknesses of a one-party system (weaknesses which he admits exists in Communist countries) "cannot be overcome by introducing a two-party system, that is, by the existence of . . . a legally organized opposition which would present minority views and which would have *normal* political dialogues with the majority party and would support a mutually accepted policy." Drašković claimed that if there were two socialist parties in a Communist country, that the mutual tolerance would soon disappear and different aims would appear.

Document 6.3

ONE-PARTY CONSTITUTIONS

USSR, 1936

Article 126. . . .The most active and politically conscious citizens in the ranks of the working class and other sections of the working people unite in the Communist Party of the Soviet Union (Bolshevik), which is the vanguard of the working people in their struggle to strengthen and develop the socialist system and is the leading core of all organizations of the working people, both public and State.

Nazi Germany (Law of July 14, 1933)

(1) The only political party in Germany is the National Socialist German Workers' Party. (2) Whoever attempts to maintain the organization of any other political party will be punished with imprisonment in the penitentiary or in jail from six months to three years, unless the offense calls for more severe punishment under other provisions.

Nazi Germany (Law on the Unity of Party and State, 1933)

I(1) After the victory of the National Socialist Revolution the National Socialist German Workers' Party has become the bearer of the German government and is inseparably connected with the State. (2) It is a corporation of public law. Its constitution is determined by the Führer . . . III(1) Members of the National Socialist German Workers' party . . . have, as the leading and moving power of the National Socialist State, increased duties toward the leader, the people, and the State.

Rumania, 1965

Article 3. In the Socialist Republic of Rumania, the leading political force of the whole society is the Rumanian Communist Party.

Article 26. The most advanced and conscious citizens from the ranks of the workers, peasants, intellectuals, and other categories of working people unite in the Rumanian Communist Party, the highest form of organization of the working class, its vanguard detachment.

The Rumanian Communist Party expresses and loyally serves the aspirations and vital interests of the people, implements the role of leader in all the fields of socialist construction, and directs the activity of the mass and public organizations and of the state bodies.

Yugoslavia, 1963

(6) The League of Communists of Yugoslavia, initiator and organizer of the People's Liberation War and Socialist Revolution, owing to the necessity of historical development, has become the leading organized force of the working class and working people in the development of socialism . . .

Under the conditions of socialist democracy and social self-government, the League of Communists, with its guiding ideological and political work, is the prime mover of the political activity necessary to protect and to promote the achievements of the Socialist Revolution and socialist social relations, and especially to strengthen the socialist social and democratic consciousness of the people.*

*In 1971 44.4 million persons belonged to Communist parties in fourteen Communist-ruled nations: USSR, China, Cuba, Albania, Bulgaria, Czechoslovakia, East Germany, Hungary, North Korea, North Vietnam, Mongolia, Poland, Rumania and Yugoslavia. Lenin's elitist concept of a vanguard party that leads the masses seems to be fully implemented on the international scale. Over 44 million Communists lead a bloc of fourteen nations, comprising over 1.18 billion people; an elite composed of about 4 to 5 percent rules over 95 percent of the people. In the non-Communist countries party membership in 1971 was approximately 2.8 million, or 5.9 percent of the world total.

Tibor Pethö, a leading political commentator in Communist Hungary of the daily *Magyar Nemzet* (March 1, 1967), categorically rejected the idea of a critical opposition party. "If the substance of opposition is criticism," argued Pethö, "then in Hungary everything is criticized where things do not proceed properly. And who is criticizing most sharply? The leaders of the Party and government. The Party and government fulfill the controlling and criticizing functions of an opposition." Pethö admitted that it was not easy for persons who "think in a bourgeois-democratic way" to understand that "the government in Hungary governs and at the same time is its own most severe critic."

One-party systems without legitimate opposition are found in many countries other than those dominated by Communists. Spain, Portugal, and Greece are good examples. Ten years after decolonization, in 1970, three-fourths of Africa's 345 million people either lived under a one-party political system or military rule. Only eleven of forty African nations ruled by blacks or Arabs had an opposition party. In that decade there were more than thirty coups[30] or abrupt, non-electoral changes of government. In Liberia, "True Whigs" have been in power since 1878. The opposition parties in the new African states during the 1960s (see Document 6.4) rarely had a chance, regardless of their constitutional provisions. Their leaders, as Gwendolen M. Carter noted, "were either in jail or in the government."[31] The Progressive party of Senegal and the African Rally of Upper Volta won all the legislative seats in elections. A similar "miracle" of total unanimity was recorded elsewhere; the leading parties in Tanzania, Malawi, and the Ivory Coast claimed 99 percent of the popular vote. Military coups in Algeria, the Central African Republic, both Congos (Brazzaville and Kinshasa, the latter now called Zaire), Ghana, Nigeria, Uganda, Upper Volta, Burundi, and

Document 6.4

AFRICAN ONE-PARTY CONSTITUTIONS

Central African Republic, 1962

Article 2. The people shall exercise its sovereignty freely and democratically within a single national political movement: The Movement for Social Evolution of Black Africa (MESAN).

Tanzania, 1962

Article 3. (1) There shall be one political Party in Tanzania.

(2) Until the union of the Tanganyika Africa National Union with the Afro-Shirazi Party (which United Party shall constitute the one political Party), the Party shall, in and for Tanganyika, be the Tanganyika African National Union, and in and for Zanzibar, be the Afro-Shirazi Party.

(3) All political activity in Tanzania, other than that of the organs of State of the United Republic, the organs of the Executive and Legislature of Zanzibar, or such local government authorities as may be established by or under a law of the appropriate legislative authority, shall be conducted by or under the auspices of the Party.*

Algeria, 1963

Article 23. The National Liberation Front is the single vanguard party in Algeria.

Article 24. The National Liberation Front shall define the policy of the nation and shall inspire the action of the State. It shall supervise the action of the National Assembly and of the Government.

Article 25. The National Liberation Front shall reflect the profound aspirations of the masses. It shall educate and form them; it shall guide them in the realization of their aspirations.

Article 26. The National Liberation Front shall achieve the objectives of the democratic and popular revolution and shall build Socialism in Algeria.

United Arab Republic, 1964

Article 3. National unity, formed by the alliance of the people's powers, representing the working people, being the farmers, workers, soldiers, intellectuals and national capital, make up the Arab Socialist Union, as the power representative of the people, driver of the Revolution's potentialities, and protector of sound democratic values.

*The Party Rules are part of the Constitution.

Dahomey have replaced the one-party rule of civilian leaders with military rule; both Burundi and Dahomey have experienced eight coups each in a decade. To sum up: the military became the party in a large portion of Africa. One exception is perhaps Upper Volta where, after five years of dictatorship, the military rulers made a brave attempt to phase themselves out and introduce free elections and three competitive political parties in 1972. Only the future can tell whether this isolated attempt will succeed.

ARGUMENTS AGAINST PARTY PLURALISM

Three somewhat modified theses of Marxism-Leninism run like a red thread through all African and Asian arguments favoring a one-party system.

(1) A political party is an instrument of class struggle; or as Stalin put it, "several parties—freedom of parties—can exist only in a society where antagonistic classes exist whose interests are hostile and irreconcilable."

(2) Imperialism, the highest stage of capitalism, has made the class struggle international. Oppressed and exploited nations are engaged in a struggle for liberation against the exploitation and oppression of imperialist powers. The external class struggle may temporarily obliterate internal class differences within a nation struggling for independence from colonial imperialism.[32] Such nations are actually one-class or classless communities.

The Leninist concept of imperialism combined with the notion that one class equals one party is explained by Julius Nyerere of Tanzania:

> The idea of class is something entirely foreign to Africa. Here in this continent, the nationalist movements are fighting a battle for freedom from *foreign* domination, not from domination by any ruling class of our own. To us, the other party, is the colonial power.[33]

Therefore, in the Asian and African context Stalin's argument that "there are grounds for only one party, the Communist Party, which boldly defends the interests of the workers and the peasants to the very end," reads "there are grounds for only one party, the nationalist party, which boldly defends its one-class nation against its external class enemy, that is, against colonialism or its return in the form of neocolonialism." This is the basic argument used by nationalist leaders to constitutionally sanction national liberation movements as permanent parties which preside over the modernization of various countries.

(3) A party is the vanguard force in the political struggle of the masses who alone can only "develop trade union consciousness. . . . Our task . . . is to combat spontaneity, to divert the labor movement from its spontaneous, trade unionist striving to go under the wing of the bourgeosie" (Lenin, *What Is to Be Done*). The Oxford- and Sorbonne-educated African elite which preside over under-educated tribalistic masses find Lenin's emphasis on elite leadership over backward masses even more appropriate in Africa than it was in Russia. The backward

tribal masses, left to their own devices, perhaps would not be able to protect themselves by spontaneous trade unionism. Under the rule of their chiefs, the tribal masses would adopt parochial and potentially secessionist attitudes.

The concept of democratic centralism[34] is closely related to the vanguard theory as the basis for the party's internal organization (see the Algerian Constitution, Document 6.4). In theory, democratic centralism is a good compromise between the need for leadership and the desire for democratic participation. Democratic discussion is free until a decision is reached, which is then binding without further discussion. In the Communist practice, however, democracy has yielded to monolithic centralism. In the name of "democratic centralism" decisions are transmitted from the top to lower echelons where they are to be "democratically" abided by—or else.

Two more arguments are often used to justify a preference for a one-party system. One concerns the international situation. Some leaders believe that multi-party systems are less immune to foreign infiltration and interference since one of the parties may become the tool of an enemy power. President Nasser rejected a proposal which would have permitted a nonsocialist party in Egypt in these words: "Once such a party is set up, the C.I.A. will infiltrate it the following day."[35]

The second argument favored by dictators is that "the country is not ready." They argue that the people must be tutored into democracy by a benevolent, enlightened leadership. Leadership is particularly necessary, according to the argument, during modernization and the slow progress toward literacy. Sun Yat-sen advocated a long tutelage in China to be followed by a general literacy and economic development which would allow a Western type of democracy and several parties to be introduced. Similarly, many Asian and African leaders argue that democracy and a multi-party system will be possible only when their people, and the tribes, are ready. The premature introduction of a multi-party system might contribute to localism, separatism, and secessionism, especially when party support coincides with ethnic or tribal boundaries.[36]

Arguments based on Marxism-Leninism, fascism, and tutelage are supplemented by another justification for the one-party formula. It is more reminiscent of James Madison and John C. Calhoun than of V. I. Lenin or Mao Tse-tung in that it questions the majoritarianism which implies defeat of minorities by the sheer weight of numbers. The wisdom of majoritarian rule was challenged by President Nyerere of Tanzania, who praised traditional African rule making by saying: "The elders sit under the big tree and talk until they agree. This talking until you agree is the essential of the traditional African concept of democracy." In Sukarno's Indonesia, the synthesis of views, a consensus known as *mufakat,* was to be discovered through extensive discussion (*musjawart*): the nature of the consensus is detected in a way "reminiscent of the Quaker 'sense of the meeting,' not through majority vote."[37]

The ability to perceive the "sense of the meeting" may be developed into a fine art by charismatic, authoritarian leaders who ensure that meetings always advocate what they personally wish, provided that political parties do not meddle. Sukarno of Indonesia did so until his fall. His speech in 1956 celebrating the anniversary of Indonesia's liberation from Dutch rule spoke of his "dream of a meeting of all the leaders of the political parties in Indonesia at which they will decide to bury the present political parties." Such dreams are presumably enjoyed by many leaders whose "detection of the sense" of their nation's wishes differs from that of political parties.

Long before Asian and African doubts about majority decisions were voiced, James Madison expressed a fear of selfish factions which could affect American nation building. John C. Calhoun later spoke of a need to find a way to unify groups divided by frighteningly diverse climates and racial, cultural, religious, and economic patterns. Calhoun concluded that every vital decision would have to be adopted by a *concurrent majority,* i.e., by unanimous or nearly unanimous agreement.[38]

Walter Lippmann once argued that vital human decisions should not be made by majority vote until the consent of the minority has been obtained. Similarly, the advocates of the filibuster in the United States Senate view it as a device which prevents transient majorities from acting tyrannically. Some Asian and African leaders note that the Western democracies dedicated to majoritarianism often abandon it in wartime or during national emergencies. The frequent call for bipartisanship in the United States during international crises also serves as a corrective for the majoritarian principle. "In Western democracies," wrote Nyerere, "it is accepted practice in times of emergency for opposition parties to sink their differences and join together in forming a national government. This is our time of emergency."[39]

Lippmann's "great decisions," Calhoun's "concurrent majority," Sukarno's "mufakat," and Nyerere's "talk under the tree until you agree," were all intended to prevent factions from wrecking the process of nation building and modernization. In that context the advantages of the one-party system cannot be dismissed lightly by outside observers, who cannot suggest concrete, feasible alternatives.

> The single-party system, or the military rule which has been imposed in several countries, has evident virtues where the people are sharply divided

among themselves and unity is the first requisite, where a new political, social and economic society must be brought into being, and where the hardships and disciplines of development must take priority over private preferences.[40]

The short-run advantages of a one-party system, however, must be balanced against long-run disadvantages. The evolution of systems which have no critical opposition may permit some rulers to hold power for its own sake, silence their opposition, and prevent the masses from being aware of possible alternatives. Regardless of its original justification, a one-party system may result in despotism of the worst kind. A lack of economic progress may be the ultimate result.

At this point it is fitting to conclude with a postscript written more than thirty years ago:

[This chapter] is devoted to the thesis that the political parties created democracy and that modern democracy is unthinkable save in terms of the parties [in plural]. As a matter of fact, the condition of the parties is the best possible evidence of the nature of any regime. The most important distinction in modern political philosophy, the distinction between democracy and dictatorship, can be best made in terms of party politics. The parties are not therefore merely appendages of modern government: they are in the center of it and play a determinative and creative part in it.[41]

The next chapter will show that the "determinative and creative" role of political parties under modern conditions ought to be supplemented by interest groups, free to organize and exercise pressure upon lawmakers, administrators—and political parties.

NOTES

1 The 26th Amendment enfranchised an estimated 11.3 million new voters; some 4 million are college students. In some communities a problem arose in determining whether college students could vote where they attended school or whether they had to register as voters at their home residences. It was feared that students in some small university towns would outnumber the local population and that the "dormitory concept" of politics would decide the political fate of the community. At Amherst, where about 25,000 students attend the University of Massachusetts, Amherst College, and Hampshire College the town's registered voters could be outnumbered by a ratio of more than two to one. The Massachusetts Attorney General, Robert H. Quinn, however, ruled (July 21, 1971) that voters under twenty-one years of age had the right to choose their place of residence for the purpose of voting. Several other states adopted the same rule.

2 On Pitcairn Island, a tiny British possession in the Pacific, every islander over eighteen must vote or pay a fine of one New Zealand dollar. A Pitcairn

election official noted, "Few people can stand that kind of fine, so we always have a full turnout" (UPI news item, January 1, 1972). There are 61 registered voters on Pitcairn.

3 Great differences in voting requirements imposed by various states in the United States still remained in the 1970s, resulting in voting limitations for which there are no bases in the constitution. Professor William J. Crotty enumerated several discriminatory practices in a letter to the *New York Times* (January 6, 1971): "In addition to state differences as to age and literacy qualifications, varying periods of residency (state, county, city, precinct) in virtually every state, institutionalization, certain types of crime, pauperism (strictly defined), 'bad character' provisions, improper lobbying, a dishonorable discharge and the like serve to disenfranchise prospective voters. In some states, those of Mongolian or Chinese ancestry, those living in "common law" marriages, Indians, those living on Federal lands, and, believe it or not, duelers are further restricted from the vote. Unlike her 49 sister states, North Dakota has no registration procedures. . . . How can such patently discriminatory practices be justified?"

4 Michael Curtis, *Comparative Government and Politics* (New York: Harper and Row, 1968), p. 52.

5 In India, since only about one-third of the Indian population is literate, symbols and images for party identification must be used so that the voters will be able to choose among alternatives. In 1969 thirty-two different symbols had to be officially recognized, reflecting a bewildering proliferation of splinter parties in India. A pair of bullocks, for instance, symbolizes the Congress party, a sickle and an ear of corn the Communist party, and symbols drawn from the traditional country and village scenes denote other parties: a hut, an oil lamp, a plough, or newer gadgets which an Indian villager aspires to, such as a pump or sewing machine. A multiple-ballot-box technique has been adopted: the Indian voter drops a ballot bearing his chosen party symbol into a box bearing the same. Illiteracy and unfamiliarity with representative democratic processes in the developing nations is not considered to be a serious obstacle in emulating Western multi-party or Soviet one-party elections.

6 John G. Lexa, "Equality of Franchise Under Proportional Representation," *The American Journal of Comparative Law* 15:3 (1967) 3, p. 482.

7 Lexa, "Equality of Franchise," pp. 482–83, quoting K. Braunias, *Das Parlamentarische Wahlrecht,* 1932.

8 In 1967, the PRI obtained 177 seats out of 178. The only seat gained by the conservative National Action party in one district of the Mexico City area resulted from a last-minute withdrawal by the PRI candidate.

9 *New York Times,* May 2, 1962.

10 The constitution of the Philippines (1935), Article VI/12, suddenly mentions parties seemingly out of a constitutional nowhere by providing for an Electoral Tribunal and a Commission of Appointments: "There shall be a Commission of Appointments consisting of twelve Senators and twelve Members of the House of Representatives, elected by each House, on the

basis of proportional representation of the political *parties* therein" (italics added).

Constitutions contain few references to political parties but national legislatures incorporate parties as primary movers and organizers of legislative work by including them in rules of procedure, bylaws, and organizational statutes.

11 Ernest Barker, *Reflections on Government* (Oxford: The Clarendon Press, 1942), p. 284.

12 The constitution of Rwanda (1962), Article 29, states: "All communist activity and propaganda are forbidden." The constitution of Peru (1933), Article 53, says: "The State does not recognize the legal existence of political parties of international organization. Persons who belong to such parties may not fulfill any political function."

13 On July 24, 1967, the West German Parliament enacted a law which proclaimed political parties to be "necessary ingredients of a libertarian democratic basic order" (Article 1). The law prescribed in detail the statutes and practices required of political organizations to qualify them as political parties in the constitutional sense; e.g., according to Article 11 party leadership must consist of at least three members elected every two years. That rule is intended to prevent a return to the *Führer-prinzip* and it sanctions collective leadership. The forty-one articles in the law cover, in detail, the rights and duties of party members, internal democracy, financing, and audit, and prohibit unconstitutional parties. "Gesetz über die politischen Parteien (Parteiengesetz)," *Sommelblatt* (August 18, 1967), pp. 1197–1204.

14 Robert Michels, *Political Parties* (New York: Dover Publications, 1959), p. 400.

15 Karl Loewenstein, "Reflections on the Value of Constitutions in our Revolutionary Age," in Arnold J. Zurcher, ed., *Constitutions and Constitutional Trends Since World War II* (New York: New York University Press, 1951), p. 213.

16 This short summary is based, with slight modifications, on Gabriel A. Almond and James S. Coleman, *The Politics of the Developing Areas* (Princeton: Princeton University Press, 1960), pp. 40–41.

17 Peter H. Merkl, *Modern Comparative Politics* (New York: Holt, Rinehart and Winston, 1970), p. 284.

18 The three criteria are identified in Leslie Lipson's study, "The Two-Party System in British Politics," *American Political Science Review* 47:2 (June 1953).

19 Crane Brinton, *The Anatomy of Revolution* (New York: Alfred A. Knopf and Random House, Vintage Book, 1965), p. 255.

20 The names of such Communist-led coalitions usually include the word "front"—an appropriate term indeed—with some variation in the adjectives: Fatherland Front, National Front, Regenerated National Front, United Front, National Liberation Front, or Patriotic Front.

21 Harry Eckstein and David E. Apter, *Comparative Politics* (New York: The Free Press, 1963), p. 330.

22 Kwamena Bentsi-Enchill, "A Blueprint for the Party Game in Ghana," p. 1. A mimeographed document, 1968.

23 Ibid., p. 36.

24 Ibid., p. 37.

25 "The workers . . . have been called upon to make good the succession of plans issued by the party . . . by surpassing the norms and raising the level of production. . . . Workers have simply turned a deaf ear to the demands for greater effort, putting into practice the slogan . . . 'the conscientious withdrawal of efficiency' . . . so effectively that the party planners have been forced to move on to new methods." "Editorial," *East Europe,* vol. 16, no. 12 (December 1967), p. 1.

   See also chapter 5 on the subject of sterile or productive freedom.

26 "The first step in, or stage of, this revolution . . . [will be] the establishment of a new-democratic society under the joint dictatorship of all Chinese revolutionary classes [including the anti-imperialist national bourgeoisie], headed by the Chinese proletariat." Mao Tse-tung, *Selected Works,* vol. III (New York: International Publishers, 1954), p. 115.

27 According to the *Handbook on People's China,* Peking, pp. 88–94, in 1957 eight parties had representatives among the 1,226 deputies of the National People's Congress: the China Democratic League (a leftover of the Third Force Movement of 1946–1948, mostly intellectuals), 80 seats; China Democratic National Construction Association (former business interests, the so-called "national bourgeoisie"), 63 seats; the Revolutionary Committee of the Kuomintang (defectors from Chiang's Nationalist party), 63 seats; the Chiu San Society (mostly intellectuals), 24 seats; the Chinese Peasants' and Workers' Democratic party (strangely, mostly doctors), 19 seats; the China Association for Promotion of Democracy (mostly teachers), 16 seats; the Chihkuntang (oldest of them all, for it claims its origin in the period of the Taip'ing Revolution of 1851–1864), 4 seats; and the Taiwan Democratic Self-Government League (defectors from Taiwan), 2 seats.

28 Each non-Communist party in Eastern Europe has its own daily and one or two weeklies. The eight satellite miniparties in China share one daily, *Kuang Ming;* An-p'ing, the editor of *Kuang Ming,* daringly attempted to alter the satellite status of the miniparties and suggested that the Communist party should not act as if it owned the people. During the brief period in which more than one flower was permitted to bloom in Mao's pasture, An-p'ing said: "There are twelve deputy premiers in the Cabinet, not one of whom is a non-Party man. Could it be that there is not a single person among the non-Party people [non-Communists] who can sit in a deputy premier's chair, or that none of them can be groomed to hold this chair?"

29 Incident to the draft of a new Czechoslovakian constitution in 1968 several non-Communist groups (see also chapter 5) sought recognition of the need for an opposition party under democratic socialism. The central issue was whether to create a new party or to revitalize the existing satellite parties to provide a suitable opposition.

Božidar Bogdanović, a Yugoslav Communist journalist, reported that several Communists in Czechoslovakia recommended a second party whose basis would also be Marxist. Bogdanović added: "In no book written in the classic of scientific socialism has it ever been said that only a single party can exist in a socialist country." *Politika*, Belgrade, November 15, 1967.

30 Professor Aristide R. Zolberg writes: "The coup can be viewed as an institutionalized pattern of African politics on statistical grounds, since in recent years it has become the mode form of governmental change. More significantly, however, the coup is a normal consequence of the showdown between a government and its opponents, who use force against each other in a situation where the force at the disposal of the government is quite limited. In Africa . . . there is some evidence that governments even prefer to dissolve themselves than to fight." From a paper delivered at the 1966 annual meeting of the American Political Science Association.

31 Gwendolen M. Carter, ed., *African One-Party States* (Ithaca, New York: Cornell University Press, 1962), p. 9.

32 The leaders of African systems, although heavily influenced by Communist theories and models, claim to be African socialists, not Communists. The prime minister of Senegal, Mamadou Dia, addressing Khrushchev in 1962, asserted that his country "was being developed on the basis of socialism" [which drew applause from the Soviet audience] but he quickly informed his hosts that "we do not pretend to be Marxist-Leninist" and then, almost adding insult to injury, ambiguously observed that "we are only people of good will." Zbigniew Brzezinski, *Africa and the Communist World* (Stanford: Stanford University Press, 1963), p. 224.

33 Paul E. Sigmund, Jr., *The Ideologies of the Developing Nations* (New York: Praeger, 1963), p. 198. Reprinted from *Spearhead*, Dar-es-Salaam, November, 1961.

34 The Algerian Constitution of 1963 (preamble) proclaimed: "Harmonious and efficient working of the political institutions established by the Constitution is assured by the National Liberation Front which mobilizes, guides and educates popular masses for the purpose of realizing socialism. . . . and whose organization and structure are based on the principle of democratic socialism."

35 *New York Times,* August 8, 1966. In the same statement Nasser also rejected the idea of setting up two socialist parties, which would deprive his Arab Socialist Union of its monopolistic position: "If I allow the creation of two Socialist parties, they would wreck one another and the reactionary elements in them would find a way to exercise their influence. Hence it is necessary to form one bloc for the sake of creating a society in which class distinction is eliminated."

36 Compare *Time's* report from Zambia (December 27, 1968, p. 28) which says: " If President Kenneth Kaunda fails to arouse the nation to vote his ticket overwhelmingly, he intends to eliminate other parties by parliamentary means . . . [by] a constitutional amendment abolishing all parties except his

own. Kaunda maintains that one-party rule is necessary because Zambia is being needlessly fragmented by the politics of 72 continually quarrelsome tribes." On December 13, 1972, a constitutional amendment transformed Zambia into a one-party state.

37 George McT. Kahin, *Major Governments of Asia,* 2nd ed. (Ithaca, N.Y: Cornell University Press, 1963), pp. 588–89.

38 See John Fischer's "Unwritten Rules of American Politics," *Harper's Magazine Reader* (Chicago: Bantam Books, 1953).

39 Sigmund, *The Ideologies of the Developing Nations,* p. 199.

40 Rupert Emerson, *Political Modernization: The Single-Party System,* The Social Foundation Monograph Series in World Politics, Vol. I, no. 1 (1964), p. 29.

41 E. E. Schattschneider, *Party Government* (New York: Holt, Rinehart and Winston, 1942), p. 1.

CHAPTER 7

Right to Influence:
Interest Groups

۞ The right of interest groups to organize for the purpose of influencing government is part of many modern bills of rights. Constitutional texts usually mention interest groups and political parties in a single breath—as though parties and interest groups cannot be clearly defined or distinguished from each other. Basically, they are not because interest groups and parties frequently overlap. Both are aggregates of individuals who have clustered around a material interest, an idea, or a combination of economic interests and ideologies. Indeed, material benefits may be justified in ideological terms and devotion to ideology may result in material gains.[1]

The *intended role* is one criterion that can help differentiate parties from interest groups. The political party is frequently defined as a group of leaders and followers, organized to obtain *direct control* of the political authority for the purpose of securing for themselves either material or ideological benefits. Interest groups, on the other hand, are organized to *influence* policy making and legislation and the way they are executed and adjudicated. In simpler terms—political parties want to be the government; interest groups want only to influence it.

There is an extremely thin line which separates control (which may be imperfect) from influence (which may be decisive). A political party, for instance, may run a national government which, in fact, is controlled by bankers or labor unions. Despite its occasional ambiguity, the criterion of intended goals seems more useful than the criteria frequently cited by texts on American government, i.e., size, frequency of activities, and special versus general interest.

Size is a useful criterion in comparing the two major political parties in the United States (which seem huge in terms of voters and sympathizers, but not members) to interest groups (e.g., the American Legion,

National Association of Manufacturers, National Organization of Women, Daughters of the American Revolution, and American Medical Association). But the criterion of size becomes quite misleading even in the context of American politics when the membership of an interest group such as the AFL-CIO is compared to that of the Black Panther party or when the National Audubon Society (American birdwatchers) is compared to the miniscule Communist party of the United States. The Trades Union Congress in Britain is much larger than both the Labour and Conservative parties. Political parties are usually much smaller than labor organizations in countries that have developed multi-party systems. For instance, the French Trade Union Congress (C.G.T.—Confédération Générale du Travail) has always had more members than any of the political parties which produced a prime minister. By definition and deliberate policy, political parties in Communist countries comprise a small ideological elite. The broad masses of people in those countries can or must join various functional organizations. e.g., labor, women, youth, and writers' groups and agricultural cooperatives. These mass organizations are directed by but are not part of the Communist party.

In some countries the *constant activity* of political parties contrasts with the occasional activities of interest groups alarmed by legislative or executive threats to their vital interests. This criterion hardly applies to the United States, where the two major parties are infrequently active on the national level except for the feverish activity which accompanies national elections every four years. The pressure groups and their lobbies in Washington, D.C., on the other hand, never rest.

The contrast between *general* (national) interest as opposed to *special* (subnational) interest is useful but it creates the self-evident problem of determining what interests are truly general and what are merely special. This is especially true since there is no special and selfish interest that cannot be appropriately dressed up to become a general (national) one. What is good for General Motors or labor is often claimed to be "good for the country." Similarly, the special interests of Jews, SDS, the blacks, farmers, construction workers, watchmakers, Irish-Americans, cities, students, Chicanos, Catholics, senior citizens and so on are claimed to be identical with "the national interest." Few parties or groups have ever been so foolish as to present their special claims as a singularly selfish interest. None have said, "I want my interest fully satisfied and I deny you the right of any satisfaction of your interest conflicting with mine." Usually the promotion of one interest at the expense of another is justified in terms of the collective interest of all.

England provides an illustrative case: at one time the British Labour party might have chosen to represent only the special interests of industrial workers. Workers in heavily urbanized and highly industrialized England constituted a numerical majority and could conceivably have disregarded the interests of the bourgeois minority. If industrial workers voted as a class (they did not, contrary to Marx's analysis, since workers have never constituted an undifferentiated monolith) their collective interest could have been presented, in accordance with the majoritarian principle, as a national interest. The consequent disregard for the interests of the defeated minority, however, would have been contrary to the English concept of democracy which admits majority rule with full consideration of minority rights and interests. Moreover, such a course would simply be politically unwise.

TYPES OF INTEREST GROUPS

Five major categories of interest groups have received either general or specific recognition and protection by national constitutions:

(1) *Territorial interest groups* are aggregates of individuals who define common interests in terms of territory and the need to promote and protect it. In other words, these are communities that perceive common interests in terms of ethnic origin, race, language, religion, tribe, a common history or common territorial programs for the future (e.g., "ideological secessionists" such as the thirteen American colonies in 1776, or the Southern states in 1860); in addition, these groups possess or identify these interests with a geographically delineated area. Such interest groups are, in fact, "stateless nations." In this context a nation state may be considered to be the largest viable territorial community, in other words a "national interest group."

Citizens are born into territorial communities rather than by paying membership dues or making declarations of adherence as required when joining other interest groups. People also become members of territorial communities by voluntary or forcible immigration (e.g., the slave trade).

Constitutional notice of territorial interest groups appears mostly in provisions concerning regional and local governments, especially within the framework of multilingual or polyethnic federalism, as noted in chapter 2.

(2) *Dispersed-ethnic groups* differ from territorial interest groups because they are incapable of endowing the promotion and defense of a common interest with a territorial dimension. They cannot sustain demands for territorial autonomy or threaten territorial secession. As noted in chapter 2, the constitutional recognition of dispersed-ethnic groups ranges from mere mention of their right to exist to specific guarantees of separate-and-equal status, cultural autonomy, or proportional quota representation.

Many ethnic groups, living in foreign national environments, defy neat categorization. The French are territorial in Québec but dispersed in other parts of Canada; the Kurds are partly dispersed and partly territorial in Turkey, Iraq and Iran; and Irish Catholics are partly territorial and partly dispersed in Northern Ireland.

(3) *Functional groups,* or, as they are sometimes called, associational[2] groups, are specialized structures for interest articulation, such as labor unions, farmers' cooperatives, manufacturers' associations, professional groups, chambers of commerce, etc. Such general categories are mentioned in many modern constitutions. Article 9/3 of the West German Constitution (1949) for example, states:

> The right to form associations to safeguard and improve working and economic conditions is guaranteed to everyone and to all trades and professions. Agreements that restrict or seek to hinder this right are null and void; measures directed to this end are illegal.

According to constitutional texts the dominant interest of such groups appears to be material but it is often presented in moral or ideological terms. Constitutions often grant these groups the right to organize, promote and defend their common interests and also, specifically, the right to bargain collectively, picket, and strike. The constitution of the United States makes no such specific provisions concerning pressure groups. The drafters dreaded the selfishness of all factions and did not, perhaps could not, anticipate their essential contribution to democratic pluralism. The freedom of speech and assembly and the right to petition government have, so far, been considered to be sufficient protection for the numerous pressure groups that have mushroomed in the "nation of joiners" which the United States has become.

(4) *Promotional groups* in this context are aggregates of men oriented toward general political, religious, ethical, and ideological goals. Such groups do not consider themselves to be political parties, (i.e., they do not aim at becoming government). Their creeds and dogmas are special interests vis-à-vis political parties and public authorities. They include pacifist groups, the Lord's Day Observance Society in England, associations for preventing cruelty to animals, churches, world federalists, veterans of foreign wars, former inmates of Nazi concentration camps, etc. All reflect the variety as well as the competition inherent in the various values, goals, and beliefs held by men. The term "promotional groups" was coined by Samuel H. Beer who analyzed "self-oriented" groups such as labor, business, and farmer organizations in contrast to "promotional" groups in his comparative study of groups in England and the United States.[3] Promotional groups, like political parties, are broadly aggregative and committed to promoting general and national rather than special or local interests. National constitutions extend pro-

tective umbrellas over such groups by the usual general provisions securing the basic freedoms of speech, assembly, religion, and the press and the right to petition the government.

Some functional and promotional groups have developed important transnational links with similarly organized and oriented groups abroad. In some cases they have formed permanent international organizations to coordinate bringing their respective pressures to bear on national governments. The World Federation of Trade Unions, International Chamber of Commerce, International Federation of Agricultural Producers, World Veterans Association, World Council of Churches, and many others are examples of international pressure groups (they are officially called "nongovernmental organizations," "NGOs"). The United Nations charter (Article 71) provides for consultation with "nongovernmental organizations which are concerned with matters within the competence" of the Economic and Social Council. The political aspects of such transnational links between interest groups are discussed later in this chapter.

Some analysts consider those functional and promotional groups whose activities cut across national boundaries to be good indicators that there is a growing awareness of an interdependent world. Marshall MacLuhan and others tend to see the world developing into a global village. The development of transnational links and activities is viewed with particular favor by the adherents of "functionalism,"[4] the functional approach to peace. In theory and practice functionalism attempts to shift international and national attention away from a preoccupation with national security and power politics toward the solution of problems that cut across the walls of national sovereignty. Functional activities therefore refer primarily to nonpolitical problems, such as economic cooperation and development, technical advancement, illiteracy, ill-health and violations of human rights. So far functional activities, undertaken in the hope of reducing or eliminating international conflict, have been themselves curtailed or eliminated by tension and competition among nations.

Nevertheless, the imperatives of interdependence and ecology may yet erode national sovereignties and accelerate the emergence of groups led by men having a primary allegiance and commitment to other than national goals. J. David Singer predicts:

> . . . the displacement of national entities by extranational associations of intra-national groups which are based more on such attributes as social class, ideology, profession (including managers, technocrats, etc.) and somewhat less on the accident of birth, ethnicity, and language. As the more natural associations become more integrated and influential via the gradual

assumption of many functions now handled by the national state (or not handled at all), they will develop into coalitions of Non-Governmental Organizations and begin to compete successfully for influence in pluralistic settings at the headquarters of the various emerging global institutions. Inevitably they will demand more than observer status and will begin to share with national governments the representative function in the various legislative bodies.[5]

Finally, it should be noted that international cartels and important national corporations with international responsibilities and operations (e.g., United Fruit, Standard Oil of New Jersey, IBM, ARAMCO, Royal Dutch, etc.) influence international politics by bringing effective and in some cases, decisive pressure to bear on national governments.[6]

(5) *Institutional groups.* These are groups composed of professionally employed personnel (e.g., managers, bureaucrats, and the military) having designated political and social functions *other than* the promotion and defense of common material or idealistic interests.[7] In the developing countries, they may be most important since they frequently either influence the government or run it as the political parties do. Lucian Pye's important study on "Armies in the Process of Political Modernization"[8] noted several advantages which armies may have in comparison with other functional, promotional, ethnic or tribal groups. He noted that armies maintain physical and organizational links with rural areas, discipline and esprit de corps, awareness of foreign models, acquaintance with modern technology (even though limited to weaponry), and a commitment to national rather than tribal values. In the case of China, it is difficult to determine whether the People's Army is the single most important interest group, a sector of the party, or a branch of the government. The Chinese Army traditionally combines political, economic, and military missions in the life of the nation.[9] One author commented on the political roles of modern armies by concluding: "What is an army? A kind of political party. What is a party? A kind of army."[10]

In the past constitutions did not treat the armed forces and other institutions as legitimate interest groups. Some modern constitutions ascribe important political roles to the military.

The preamble to the constitution of Algeria (1963) for example, proclaims: "The National Popular Army, yesterday the Army of National Liberation, has been the steel of the spear of the liberation struggle; it has remained in the service of the people. In the framework of the Party, it participates in political activities and building the new economic and social structure of the country." Article 8 repeats the constitutional guarantee for the army's participation in politics. The Algerian army is constitutionally a part of, and subservient to, the dominant party, but the constitutional hope that the army will remain within the party has not been fulfilled. A military coup in 1966 confirmed that the army is an institutional interest group and potentially a political party and government as well.

This discussion of interest groups should also note that *opposition parties,* even *national executives* are "interest groups" *sui generis.* Political parties which are in opposition, either temporarily or "permanently" (if they have no realistic chance of soon becoming the government, like the Communist party of the United States, the Liberal party in England, and the Socialist party in Japan) are similar to pressure groups in many ways. Opposition parties are thus *short-run pressure groups;* in the long run they are parties which hope eventually to run the government. This characteristic of the opposition party is especially evident when it challenges a ruling party in the hope of altering existing policies, not when it confines its activities to preparing a brief for the next election.

Almond's definition of an interest group applied to the national executive (cabinet or council of ministers) fits exactly. A national executive is "a group of individuals who are linked by particular bonds of concern and advantages and who have some awareness of these bonds."[11] The national leadership differs from other interest groups because of its legitimate right and capacity (often challenged in revolutionary situations) to have the last coercive word. Nevertheless national leaderships also "democratically" compete with the other categories of interest groups mentioned above. They promote and defend their own concept of the general (national) interest (including their own interest in political survival) and add that interest to the whirlpool of other interests also presented as being in the collective interest of the whole nation.

METHODS OF PRESSURE

Constitutional texts leave the methods of action largely to the imagination of interest groups and their leaders, and their imagination has proved to be quite fertile. The following is an incomplete list of the methods and devices used by pressure groups to make their wishes and complaints known to public authorities:

(1) *Publicity.* Pressure groups communicate their causes through posters, letters to the editor, paid advertisements, pickets, mass meetings, marches, strikes, sit-ins, and other forms of violence and disturbance. These activities may include deliberate riot, the taking of hostages for political blackmail, self-immolation, and fasting. Fasts are usually publicized as nonviolent personal sacrifices, but they nonetheless produce

political effects because authorities typically fear that riots and bloodshed will follow the death of a fasting leader. For example, the linguistically delineated state of Andhra in India was created following a fast-unto-death by a leader, followed by violent riots. The creation of a Sikh State in the Punjab was preceded by the fast of the Sikh leader (challenged, in turn, by a counterfast of a Hindu leader) and by violent clashes between Hindus and Sikhs in the area. Symbolic acts and expressions are usually protected as well as limited by bills of rights (see chapter 5 on the freedom of expression).

(2) *Lobbying.* Lobbying generally means the presentation of demands by experts to the legislative, executive, and judicial branches of government.[12]

(3) *Participation in elections.* This method of promoting group special interests may take different forms: (a) Promise of group support for political candidates; (b) Causing a pressure group's representatives to be elected within one or several political parties (current in England); (c) The partial merging of a group with a political party (or the group may itself become a political party).

In many countries parties and interest groups are intimately interlocked by design. Sometimes it isn't possible to determine where one begins and the other ends. The British Labour party extends the Trades Union Congress into the Parliament and the cabinet since most of the funds and membership of the Labour party come from the trade unions. The party's final accession to political power depends ultimately, however, on nonparty and nonunionized voters in general elections. In Western Europe and elsewhere, on the contrary, interest groups often extend political parties into the lives of workers, farmers, businessmen, youth, and womens' groups. The Communist party in France traditionally dominated one trade union congress, the socialists another, and the Catholic-oriented center a third.[13] This is also true in many other countries.

The mutual permeation of parties and interest groups has disadvantages:

.... when parties control interest groups they inhibit the capacity of interest groups to formulate pragmatic, specific demands; they impart a politico-ideological content to interest group activity. When interest groups control parties, they inhibit the capacity of the party to combine specific interest into programs with wider appeals.[14]

The interest group in a multi-party system, however small, pragmatic, self-oriented, and intermittently active it may be, can assume the name, structure, and methods of a political party. It can present candidates in general elections, have representatives elected to the legislature and selected for ministerial posts in coalition cabinets as many small peasant parties in Western Europe have done. Czechoslovakia before World War II had a small traders' party, an interest group disguised as a party. A member of that party held important ministerial portfolios in the coalition cabinets. Before Sukarno streamlined Indonesia's parliamentary democracy into a personal dictatorship, interest groups had representatives voted into Parliament. Indonesian minor "parties"[15] were strong despite their size, "primarily because no major party has ever commanded a majority."[16] Interest groups which aim not to dominate but merely to influence the government by their presence (whether disruptive or cooperative) in national legislatures and cabinets are sometimes decisive in special circumstances by making or unmaking coalition cabinets.

This potential role of interest group as party within the national legislature was, perhaps, in the mind of the founders of the Black Convention in the United States (see chapter 2 on "Israel and Liberia") when they began to speak of an all-black political party in 1972. Such a party could obviously not aim at ruling the country. It could make its presence felt throughout the legislative and executive branches of the federal government.

(4) *Soul-force.* Several groups in India, in true Gandhian spirit, have tried to exert pressure on the emotions of all men and thus, indirectly, on government. Vinova Bhave's land-gift movement (*Bhoodan,* largely a failure), the American Quakers and other similar movements belong to the soul-force category. Modern "hippies," especially the flower people of the 1960s and the "Jesus Freaks" of the 1970s, may be soul-force variants of sorts.

(5) *International links.* Subnational interest groups—territorial, dispersed-ethnic, functional, promotional, and institutional—sometimes try to increase their chance of success by establishing either open or secret links with similarly oriented groups or with foreign governments. As a consequence, many domestic conflicts are "internationalized" either partially or totally.[17] Governments may also initiate a link and cooperate with a subnational group which is active within the framework of a foreign nation state—thereby interfering in the domestic affairs of other nations. Interference and intervention have been practiced by nations since ancient Egypt and Greece, although many observers argue that the practice is more general today. The growth of interventionism can be explained by the nuclear stalemate (wherein the major powers tend to engage in the balancing process by proxy); by the ecological, economic, and technological interdependence of the world; rapid communications; global exchanges of goods, men, and ideas; and

because many subnational groups are generally receptive to supranational doctrines. If we are becoming a "global village," as Marshall MacLuhan suggests, we should note that neighbors in any village constantly poke their noses into other people's business.

The line between a legitimate neighborly concern and illegitimate interference is often blurred. Political leaders and political scientists have failed to agree on an acceptable definition of interference and intervention.[18] During the 1972 summit meeting in Moscow, for instance, the Soviet leaders apparently resented and therefore rejected President Nixon's interest in the future fate of the Soviet Jewry as an impermissible intervention in the Soviet Union's domestic affairs. The *New York Times* (May 27, 1972) quoted the following Soviet remark:

> Why did Henry Kissinger say the President would come here to raise the Jewish question? What would Nixon say if we raised the case of Angela Davis?

It should be stressed that the world is interdependent, and we are aware that it is—however, the world remains politically divided into mutually intolerant and highly suspicious nation states. In such a context transnational links formed by any subnational group, whether initiated by it or a foreign government, tend to be treated by national authorities as evidence of disloyalty or treason, especially if they are directed with the support of a foreign government against the policy and goals of the national government.[19] As recipients of foreign advice and support interest groups can be viewed as willing targets and instruments of foreign meddling. Thus, pacifist groups in the United States that demonstrate by displaying the Vietcong rather than the American flag, or those which have established open or confidential links with the government of North Vietnam have often been accused of disloyalty, collaboration with the enemy, or treason by their opponents.

The problems of double loyalty, to say the least, may be particularly acute in polyethnic or polytribal countries such as the Soviet Union, Nigeria, Zaire, and Canada. Many hyphenated groups in the United States—Afro-Americans, Hispanic Americans, Irish-Americans, American Jews, or Czech-Americans—may identify with, respectively, Zimbawe (the African term for the white-dominated South Africa), Chile, Eire, Israel, or Czechoslovakia more than with the United States. Such an identification may or may not be good for the United States. The former leader of Students for Non-Violent Action, Stokely Carmichael, suggested in 1972 that the double loyalty of the American blacks should be expressed by acquiring two passports, one American and the other African. This advice was part of Carmichaels' speech in which he promoted the idea of a Pan-African party for the American blacks (*New York Times*, November 21, 1972). Stokely Carmichael himself claims to have two citizenships, two homes and two passports, Guinean and American.

Internal unity in polyethnic Switzerland has been maintained by tradition and federal structure and also by Switzerland's neutral foreign policy. Neutrality was called by a Swiss political scientist "the cement of the Swiss unity . . . one of the requirements of their domestic equilibrium."[20] The unity of Switzerland could hardly have been maintained through the centuries if either its national government or its German, French, and Italian components had decisively taken sides in the constant wars and conflicts between neighboring Germany, France, and Italy. It may be that the capacity of the United States to act as a unit in international politics may be impaired by a future "unmelting of the melting pot" in which blacks, Hispanic Americans, Jews and Irishmen identify with political issues and conflicts in Africa, Latin America, the Middle East and Irish Dublin and Ulster. Would a neutrality à la Switzerland then be a solution? Can a superpower remain as neutral as a small, landlocked country whose neutral status is agreed upon by the major powers?

(6) *Co-administration.* In several socialist and non-socialist countries many labor and consumer interest groups are represented and participate in the administration of major national laws and economic and social institutions, e.g., nationalized industries and social security, welfare, and health systems.

Two forms of special interest promotion, *strikes* and *participation in administration,* have resulted in significant additions to modern constitutional texts. The following segments of this chapter deal with them specifically.

THE RIGHT TO STRIKE

Strikes are authorized in roughly one-third of today's constitutions.[21] The two most frequent limitations of the right to strike are the limitation of the right to interrupt work in the armed forces, essential services, and public administration; and limitation of the right to strike for noneconomic, political purposes. Article 123/16, as amended in 1960 and 1962, of the constitution of Mexico (1917) states:

> Both employers and workers shall have the right to organize for the defense of their respective interests, by forming unions, professional associations, etc.
>
> (17) The laws shall recognize strikes and lockouts as rights of workmen and employers.

(18) Strikes shall be legal when they have as their purpose the attaining of an equilibrium among the various factors of production, by harmonizing the rights of labor with those of capital. In public services it shall be obligatory for workers to give notice ten days in advance to the Board of Conciliation and Arbitration as to the date agreed upon for the suspension of work.

(19) Lockouts shall be legal only when an excess of production makes it necessary to suspend work to maintain prices at a level with costs, and with prior approval of the board of Conciliation and Arbitration.

Limitations of the Right to Strike

Constitutional limitations on the right to strike encounter two difficulties: strikes by public servants[22] and strikes with political overtones. All strikes may assume political overtones in countries that have nationalized some of their industries since strikes may be interpreted as a threat against the government and may involve many public servants. A strike in the nationalized coal mines of Britain necessarily has political aspects whether a Labour or a Conservative government runs the national economy. In a system that owns and manages a large portion of national production and services, people who work for the government, directly or indirectly, may represent two-thirds or more of the labor force. The right to strike in that case cannot logically be reserved to workers in the private sector. The denial of the right to strike to public and semi-public workers in nationalized industries deprives a majority of the labor force the essential right to effectively promote and protect its interests.

Communist constitutions do not grant workers the right to strike.[23] In the context of class struggle the argument is that strikes are needed only to defend the working class against exploitation by capitalists. Therefore, since capitalists have been expropriated in the socialist, one-class society, strikes have no place. Furthermore, the means of production have been nationalized so ownership and management have been transferred to the working class. Obviously, workers cannot strike against themselves (see Documents 7.1, 7.2 and 7.3). The argument, of course, is based on Marxist-Leninist theory. In practice Communist workers occasionally resort to strikes, picketing, and violence when they inevitably discover that a political authority having a monopolistic power over the national economy is even more demanding and deaf to the workers' needs than a capitalist employer in a competitive system where trade unions are free to organize and strike.

RIGHT OF CODETERMINATION

Although Communist constitutions deny to trade unions (and implicitly to collective farms) the right to strike, they do grant interest

THE RIGHT TO STRIKE UNDER COMMUNISM*

J. Chyský:

Although our legal system does not mention the right to strike in any of its provisions, this right cannot be simply passed over in silence as if it did not exist. This is all the more valid as strikes have in fact already occurred in this country, whatever the reasons and aims may have been, . . . This privilege is one of the social rights which is greatly emphasized by the workers in the capitalist states, as it is one of the most effective means of protecting and promoting the other economic and social rights of the workers, although it is only resorted to in extreme cases.

In the socialist states the right to strike has been and is still being passed over in silence. It is neither expressly prohibited nor permitted, and the question is circumvented in a variety of ways. In Czechoslovakia this has been done through the assertion that "the working people have become the manager of their country" (Article II of the preamble to the constitution of 1960), a phrase which, although not entirely lacking in substance, conceals the implied dogma that the workers do not and cannot have a reason to strike, However, the facts have proved the very opposite.

It has always been clear that, although not even the word "strike" has been uttered in connection with our internal conditions within the past 20 years, and although nothing has been written about strikes, the question of the right to strike has always been lurking somewhere in the background and that it would be brought out into the open at the first suitable moment. . . .

In the CSSR (just as in the capitalist states) the right to strike ought to be legally ensured either through being directly embodied in the new Czechoslovak constitution or through being expressly recognized in some other law (for example in the Labor Code) as a principle and as one of the fundamental social rights. . . .

Even under a socialist order a distinction must be made between the state as the representative of public power and as an employer. The state only represents the workers' class as a political and public power. This does not prevent a relationship of dependence from existing in economic relations. Where the workers are on the one side and the director of an enterprise as the representative of the state is on the other side, individual or mass labor disputes cannot be avoided. And if such disputes are prevented, this is not due to the fact that there are no reasons for them, but to the fact that they are suppressed by power-political intervention. . . .

In the socialist countries, the ban on strikes is an ideological and economic argument. The possibility of work stoppages cannot be reconciled with the plan ordered from above. Strikes and the plan, unless it is flexible, are contradictory phenomena and the interruption of production cannot be tolerated.

However, economic planning is also used in capitalist industry; there too strikes become a troublesome means of settling mass labor disputes. And certainly avenues will be explored to find a way in which the exercise of the right to strike can be avoided and the use of this weapon in mass labor disputes completely eliminated. It is obvious that this cannot be done through power means and that it will be necessary to co-ordinate political, economic, and legal instruments in order to make the right to strike practically superfluous. This could come about if, for instance, an absolutely impartial procedure of reconciliation or arbitration were guaranteed, whose results would, in addition, be subject to examination by an independent court.

*This is an excerpt of a lengthy monograph published by the Law Institute of the Czechoslovak Academy of Science, Prague: *Právník,* no. 7 (July 1969). It is of interest that the study was published *after* the Soviet takeover of Czechoslovakia in August 1968.

---

groups some status by assigning them various functions, including the right to codetermine rules and economic plans. Communist constitutions describe the new functions of their interest groups in detail. Interest groups help provide candidates for elections, recruit and indoctrinate candidates for party and state careers, and, above all, transmit, explain, and publicize plans, goals, and inspiration from the party elite to the nonparty membership of functional groups. They act as "the transmission belts."

The Communist systems emphasize making the members of mass organizations responsive to the state and the party. Messages in the mass organizations come down from the top in a powerful stream; demands reach the top from below in a trickle. Interest groups in Communist countries, in contrast to the Western concept, are not regarded as primary sources of demand impulses; rather they are considered to be targets for rule makers (see Document 7.5).

There is an assumed harmony of interests between employers (in the Communist case the state itself) and workers in those authoritarian constitutions influenced by the "guild" system of fascist Italy. That system was inspired by Catholic reformers before the turn of the twentieth century. The Italian fascist guilds (*corporazione*) aimed to ensure labor peace and to deny that the concept of class struggle was valid. They also existed to fragment the political community into narrowly oriented interest guilds. The guilds could formulate specific professional demands but they could not translate those demands into a political challenge to the ruling party or the dictator. The guild concept survives in Article 102 of the constitution of Portugal (1935), which deals with Portugal's Corporative Chamber, composed of representatives of different "social interests."

Codetermination practices are found in the democratic context in Western Europe, notably in Western Germany (*Mitbestimmungsrecht*). There federal legislation first made trade unions into "junior partners"

THE RIGHT TO STRIKE UNDER CAPITALISM

Thomas Kennedy:*

While the strike performs a valuable function in our free collective bargaining system, it is legitimate to question whether the costs are too great in relation to the benefits. Might some alternative to the strike, such as compulsory arbitration, serve the interests of the parties and the public better? To answer this question, let us begin by examining the costs of strikes. . . .

It is estimated that there are approximately 300,000 labor agreements in the United States. On the average, about 120,000 of these agreements terminate each year. Thus, across the country during an average year, 120,000 management bargaining teams sit across the table from 120,000 union bargaining teams and try to work out agreements on new contract terms. The issues which they deal with are wages, benefits, hours, and other important working conditions. These are matters which are extremely vital to the companies, the unions, and the employees. Despite the difficulties of these issues, the parties are successful in 96 percent or more of the negotiations. Only 4 percent or less of the negotiations result in strikes, and in most cases these strikes are short-lived. The problem is that a peaceful settlement is seldom front-page news, whereas a strike may be good for a number of headlines.

The Bureau of Labor Statistics estimates that the amount of working time in the total economy which was lost directly as a result of strikes in 1969 was only 0.23 percent. Moreover, the general trend has been down. From 1945 to 1949 the average time lost per year was 0.47 percent, compared with 0.26 percent from 1950 to 1959, and only 0.17 percent from 1960 to 1969. We have been losing far more time in coffee breaks than in strikes!

It has often been proposed that strikes in the private sector be made illegal. The managements of the railroads and the maritime industry openly advocate compulsory arbitration as a desirable alternative to free collective bargaining. There is reason to believe, . . . that unions in industries where automation has reduced the strike power will also move to that position. Suppliers and customers hurt by a strike are likely to mutter, "It should be outlawed."

Unfortunately, it is not a matter of eliminating strikes by devices which have no costs. The various compulsory settlement methods also are expensive, and it may be that managements, unions, and the public would find such costs more onerous than the costs of strikes. . . .

Finally, if government becomes involved in the determination of labor contract terms in order to avoid strikes, it may not be able to stop there. With our democratic political structure it would be impossible, I believe, to prevent compulsory settlement of wages for union members from leading to compulsory determination of *all* wages; that, in turn, would lead to government decisions concerning salaries, professional fees, and, finally, prices and profits.

So long as free collective bargaining is permitted, it forms an outer perimeter of defense against government regulation in other areas. If it fails, the possibility of more regulation in the other areas becomes much greater. It is worth noting that George Meany, the president of the AFL-CIO, stated several months ago that he would not be opposed to wage controls if similar controls were placed on salaries, prices, and profits. Meany's view of these relationships is one that many people might share.

I conclude that the right to strike is preferable to a compulsory settlement system. . . . Any broad prohibition of strike freedom would prove to be very costly in itself and also lead to major government controls over other parts of the economy. Free collective bargaining, which includes the right to strike and the right to lock out, constitutes the outer defense of the private enterprise system.

*This is a short excerpt from Thomas Kennedy's article, "Freedom to Strike Is in the Public Interest," *Harvard Business Review* (July-August 1970). The author is professor of business administration at the Harvard Business School and a member of the editorial board of the *Harvard Business Review*. Quoted by permission of the *Harvard Business Review* and Thomas Kennedy.

---

in the management of large coal and steel enterprises.[24] Later, they were given in a modified form, similar functions in all large enterprises. Codetermination in West Germany was intended as an alternative to nationalization of key industries and as a modification of private enterprise. A similar formula of labor representation in management was adopted by those West European countries that nationalized key industries in the wake of World War II. The West European idea of codetermination as a modifier of capitalism in Communist Yugoslavia became a vehicle for the democratic modification of centralized communism.

INTEREST GROUPS AS LEGISLATIVE ADJUNCTS

Several democratic countries have attempted to associate interest groups with the preliminary stage of law making by adding a "third" chamber to their bicameral parliaments. Peru (Article 182) provides for a National Economic Council to be composed of "representatives of the consuming population, capital, labor and the liberal professions." Italy (Article 99), has added a National Council of Economy and Labor to its bicameral parliament; the council is composed of "experts and representatives of the productive categories." And France introduced an Economic and Social Council in the Fourth Republic and kept it in the Fifth:

The Economic and Social Council, whenever the Government [the Executive, in the French context] calls upon it, shall give its opinion on the Government bills, ordinances and decrees, as well as on the Parliamentary bills submitted to it.

Document 7.3

A STRIKE v. A GREATER STAKE

George Meany, president of the AFL-CIO (in an interview
with labor reporters in Washington, D.C., reproduced in the
New York Times, August 31, 1970):

Our members are basically Americans, they basically believe in the American
system and maybe they have a greater stake in the system now than they had
15 or 20 years ago because under the system and under our trade policy, they
have become middle-class. They have a greater stake.

You can be quite radical if you were involved in a labor dispute where people
are getting 30 cents an hour because if you pull an honest strike, all you lose
is 30 cents an hour. But you have people who are making $8,000 or $9,000 a
year, paying off mortgages, with kids going to college, you have an entirely
different situation when you think about calling them on strike.

They have got obligations that are quite costly—insurance payments and all
that sort of thing. So this makes the strike much less desirable as a weapon.

Naturally we wouldn't want to give it up as a weapon but I can say to you
quite frankly that more and more people in the trade union movement—I mean
at the highest levels—are thinking of other ways to advance without the use
of the strike method.*

*Compare with the last paragraph in Document 7.1.

A member of the Economic and Social Council may be designated by the
latter to present, before the Parliamentary assemblies, the opinion of the
Council on the Government or Parliamentary bills that have been submitted
to it (Article 69).

The Economic and Social Council may likewise be consulted by the Government on any problem of an economic or social character or interest to the
Republic. . . . Any plan, or any bill dealing with a plan, of an economic or
social character shall be submitted to it for advice (Article 70).

President de Gaulle proposed, in 1968, a constitutional amendment
to merge the Economic and Social Council with the Senate. The new
chamber—*Sénat economique et social*—was to be a consultative chamber
whose opinion was not to be binding on the National Assembly but was
always to be sought and heard. The aim of the new Economic and Social
Senate was to express the new trend toward regional quasi-federal
decentralization which *Le Figaro* (August 31, 1968) labeled "a return to
the revolutionary ideas of 1789." At the same time, it was to assure that
modern nonterritorial functional interest groups such as labor, business,

Document 7.4

A STRIKE v. PARTY BOSSES*

An unemployed worker in the West can buy two to four times as many goods for his jobless benefits as our factory worker or office worker can buy for his working wage. . . . We have no socialism in our land! . . . How can there be socialism with 20 times as many spongers and bosses as there were in Czarist Russia? How can it be socialism if the workingman's average wage is 100 rubles and the income of a high official several thousand a month! . . .

How can it be socialism if the people are virtually deprived of their most elementary rights: freedom of speech, of the press, of the right to strike, etc! . . . And it is not toward Communism that we are going—that is all a lie! What we have is state capitalism, the worst and the most rapacious system of government! . . .

Respected citizens! Fight for your rights, for a better life. Defend one another, one for all, and all for one. Only through struggle can we achieve a change for the better. If we won't fight, we will turn more and more into the slaves of the Communist party's upper crust, into draft animals.

*A "Citizens Committee" underground appeal, circulated in Moscow in May and June 1972. It complains that the national wealth is being squandered both on a life of luxury among the privileged and on foreign aid for political purposes, mainly for the Arabs, Cuba, and North Vietnam. It recommends strikes and demonstrations for better living conditions as the Poles successfully did in 1970.

---

private and nationalized industries, agriculture, and universities were represented. The inclusion of universities was one of the consequences of the French student and labor ferment which led to a crippling 72-day strike in May 1968.

Interest groups have been added to parliamentary bodies primarily in Catholic countries due, obviously, to the influence of social doctrines expressed in the papal encyclicals (discussed in chapter 3). The concept of a "third chamber" or "lobby chamber" traveled from France to many African institutions.

Tricameral systems that transform interest groups into legitimate adjuncts of the rule-making mechanism (which has traditionally been based on territorial representation) have several theoretical advantages. They assure interest groups the right to formulate demands and to be heard as a matter of legislative routine. Furthermore, constitutions prescribe the composition of the "third chamber" so that unorganized, or loosely organized, groups (e.g., the aged, consumers, etc.), can get a hearing. The superior financial resources and organizational skill of

Document 7.5

SOVIET TRADE UNIONS

USSR, 1936

Article 126. In conformity with the interests of the working people, and in order to develop the organizational initiative and political activity of the masses of the people, citizens of the USSR are guaranteed the right to unite in public organizations: trade unions, cooperative societies, youth organizations, cultural, technical and scientific societies. . . .

Article 141. . . . The right to nominate candidates is secured to public organizations and societies of the working people: Communist Party organizations, trade unions, co-operatives, youth organizations and cultural societies.

Rules of the Trade Unions of the USSR (1959)*

The Soviet trade unions, which are a mass non-party public organization, unite, on a voluntary basis, workers and other employees of all occupations irrespective of race, nationality, sex, or religious beliefs.

The Soviet trade unions conduct all their activities under the guidance of the Communist Party of the Soviet Union, the organising and directing force of Soviet society. The trade unions of the USSR rally the masses of workers and other employees around the party and mobilise them for the struggle to build a communist society. . . .

The trade unions are working to secure a further consolidation of the socialist social and state system, whose basis is the unshakable union of the working class and the collective-farm peasantry, the indestructible friendship among the peoples of the USSR, and the moral and political unity of the entire Soviet society. The trade unions share actively in State, economic and cultural affairs, participate in the elections to organs of State power and in drafting laws on production, labour, living conditions and culture. They strive to strengthen the administrative and managerial apparatus and to improve its work.

The trade unions instill into their membership the spirit of Soviet patriotism and a communist attitude towards work and public, socialist property. . . .

*The rules of the Soviet Trade Unions implement the constitutional principle in a way which transforms even more clearly the mass labor organizations into agencies of state and party power.

labor and employer groups otherwise monopolize the attention of rule makers.

In theory the tricameral system is good; in practice it is disappointing. Constitutions make third chambers merely consultative assemblies; their advice is not mandatory. Members of third chambers are usually appointed and their deliberations are not public. They do not even have the power to influence public opinion by the publicity given their debates that the British House of Lords still enjoys. That is certainly not tricameralism in the true sense of the word. The French Fourth Republic alone gave its Economic and Social Council the right to discuss its recommendations in public.

Several African republics[25] copy the French model with slight modification.

The Swiss Constitution (1848) provides for consultation with important interest groups without creating a special organ:

> The Confederation takes the necessary measures. . . . for the welfare of the people and the economic security of the citizens (Article 31A, 1947).
> . . .The competent business organizations should be also consulted before the enactment of the laws of execution. They may be asked to cooperate in the execution of these measures (Article 32).

In Switzerland, interest groups may significantly influence economic and social policies by their use, or threat of using, legislative referenda to bring a controversial piece of legislation to a popular vote. In some cases referenda are obligatory. In others they may be initiated by either seven cantons or 30,000 voters. A well-organized interest group may gather the necessary signatures with relative ease. The record shows that Swiss voters usually reject rather than approve new laws in legislative referenda. Accordingly, Swiss legislators cannot lightly dismiss threats by an interest group to organize referendum initiatives.

The association of interest groups with rule making and rule implementation has developed extraconstitutionally in many countries. Samuel H. Beer's studies indicate the extent to which British labor unions and farmers' organizations have become responsible for the administration of the collectivist society. Price controls, materials allocations, the regulation of imports and the expansion of exports, agricultural programs, etc., could not be enforced without the direct participation of different interest groups. Those groups are often well organized; at other times they are motivated to get organized in the prospect of participation and influence. They are sometimes unorganized yet influential simply because they are composed of voters (e.g., social security beneficiaries).[26] In the past interest groups were usually established to prod political authorities. It may be sometimes the other way around in a welfare state—interests get organized as a result of prodding by the authorities:

> The greater the degree of detailed and technical control the government seeks to exert over industrial and commercial interests, the greater must

be [the interest groups'] degree of consent and active participation in the very process of regulation, if regulation is to be effective and successful.[27]

Interest groups in many countries have extended their traditional influence to the initiation, preparation and formulation of rules and policies, and they actively participate in the implementation of rules and policies. The causal connection with the welfare functions of a modern state is obvious.

Legislative bodies have been traditionally based on territorial representation. There is a new search, expressed extraconstitutionally and in constitutional texts, for a formula which will provide for participation and representation by nonterritorial, functional interests to complement legislative mechanisms.

A DUTY TO RESPOND?

As the preceding pages have demonstrated, constitutions guarantee the right of groups or citizens to influence or participate in decision making in a general way (e.g., as in the United States Constitution) or in a specific and detailed manner as in the most modern constitutions. Several constitutions describe and regulate the various forms in which the right of access to rule making may be exercised. These constitutional guarantees, descriptions, and regulations may be interpreted as a solemn constitutional commitment on the part of the political authority to receive social wants in terms of group-formulated demands (*inputs* into the political system), respond to them, and convert demands into policies and laws (*outputs*).

No constitution can promise, of course, that the authority pledged to listen will also be guided by everything it hears. A great many actions are initiated by governments themselves in anticipation of future, still unarticulated, needs or to implement a ruling group's commitment to specific political, economic, or ideological goals. Various demands have to be deliberately disregarded or reluctantly sacrificed in favor of others more justified. Some will be simply overlooked through negligence.

Many demands get a hearing, and action, because they have been presented with skill or represent a credible threat of violent consequences. Consequently, people often cannot oblige the government to listen to lesser grievances and unorganized complaints until they result in an explosion. No constitution, and not this book, can resolve that critical and continuing problem.

NOTES

1 This old truth has been expressed by a Viennese joke that describes a rich liberal saying: "Dealing in ideology I have accumulated a pretty penny." ("Ich hab' mir, bei der Ideologie, hübsch paar Gulden erspart.")

2 Gabriel A. Almond and G. Bingham Powell, Jr., *Comparative Politics* (Boston: Little, Brown, and Co., 1966), p. 78. The authors distinguish four types of groups: *associational, nonassociational* (e.g., status, ethnic, regional, or religious groups that articulate interests intermittently, without appropriate organization), *institutional,* and *anomic* (i.e., the more or less spontaneous penetrations of highly dissatisfied groups into the political system).

3 Samuel H. Beer, "Group Representation in Britain and the United States," *Annals of the American Academy of Political and Social Science,* vol. 319 (1958), p. 133.

4 For an early explanation of the functionalist hope see David Mitrany, *A Working Peace System* (London: National Peace Council, 1946). For a critical treatment of functionalism see Inis L. Claude, *Swords into Plowshares* (New York: Random House, 1964).

5 J. David Singer, "The Global System and Its Subsystems: A Developmental View," a paper presented at the meeting of the American Political Science Association, New York, 1966. Also reproduced in Ivo D. Duchacek, ed., *Discord and Harmony: Readings in International Politics* (New York: Holt, Rinehart and Winston, 1971), and in James N. Rosenau, *Linkage Politics* (New York: The Free Press, 1969).

6 For a scholarly analysis see Robert O. Keohane and Joseph S. Nye, Jr., eds., *Transnational Relations and World Politics* (Cambridge, Mass.: Harvard University Press, 1972).

7 Almond and Powell, *Comparative Politics,* p. 77.

8 Lucian W. Pye, "Armies in the Process of Political Modernization," in J. J. Johnson, ed., *The Role of the Military in Underdeveloped Countries* (Princeton: Princeton University Press, 1962), pp. 69–89.

9 Ralph L. Powell, "Soldiers in the Chinese Economy," *Asian Survey* 11:8 (1972), pp. 742–60.

10 Robert C. Fried, *Comparative Political Institutions* (New York: Macmillan, 1966), p. 82.

11 Almond and Powell, *Comparative Politics,* p. 75.

12 Some interest groups may not be formally organized, yet they are represented by lawyers. Such groups may thus succeed in producing significant inputs into the political system. A recent study notes that convicts are a group which has greatly contributed to society: "Convicts not only have no right to vote but are also not a very respectable constituency for any legislator. . . . Yet they have played an important role in creating safeguards in criminal law that protect all members of the society. Through their appeals, the Supreme Court has decided that searches and seizures must be carried

out with a proper warrant. . . . that all defendants must have the opportunity to have legal counsel, and that the prohibition against self-incrimination applies in state as well as federal courts." Herbert Jacob, *Justice in America* (Boston: Little, Brown, and Co., 1965), p. 33.

13 The Communist trade union conference is called CGT *(Confédération Générale du Travail);* the socialist CGT-FO *(Force Ouvrière,* "Workers' Force"); the Catholic conference was originally called CFTC *(Confédération des travailleurs chrétiens),* now it is CFTD (democratic instead of Christian). Similarly, in Italy, the Communists and the left wing of the socialists control CGIL *(Confederazione General Italiana del Lavoro),* the Christian Democratic influence prevails in CISL *(Confederazione Italiana dei Sindacati Lavoratori)* and democratic socialists lead the small UIL *(Unione Italiana del Lavoro).* In Holland the dividing line between trade unions is mainly religious: there is a Catholic Trade Union Center NKV *(Nederlands katholiek vakverbond)* and a Protestant Center CNV *(Christelijk nationaal vakverbond).* There is a third trade union federation that is secular; it is dominated by democratic socialists who have banned the Communists from membership.

14 Gabriel A. Almond, "A Comparative Study of Interest Groups and the Political Process," *American Political Science Review* 52:1 (March 1958), p. 276.

15 Some of the minor "parties" were the Saint John Ambulance Association, the Organization of Prosperous Peasants, the Retired Pensioner's Association, a small Lutheran Christian Party (Bataks in North Sumatra, Celebes, and South Moluccas), a small Catholic Party, etc. After the 1955 elections, 27 political parties, organized into 17 parliamentary alignments, were represented in Parliament. The subsequent dictatorship of President Sukarno (1956–1965) ended multi-party competition in Indonesia. In 1965, after an abortive Communist coup and a successful military counter-coup, Sukarno's successor, President Suharto, partly restored electoral competition. On July 3, 1971, Indonesia's first national elections since 1955 were held amidst the complaints of nine opposition parties against the financial expenditures and intimidation or pressure tactics of Suharto's own political organization, Sekber Golkar.

It is interesting to note that Holland, the former colonial master of Indonesia, seems to suffer from a similar plague of party proliferation. In the legislative elections held on April 28, 1971, twenty-eight political parties competed. A standing Dutch joke on their excessive number of political parties is: "Two Dutch people form a couple, three a religion, and four a party." That joke unfortunately applies as well to Indonesia. One can only wonder whether Indonesian party proliferation is a native tendency or based on a Dutch-imported model.

16 George McT. Kahin, *Major Governments of Asia,* 2nd ed. (Ithaca, N.Y.: Cornell University Press, 1963), p. 610. Also see Robert C. Bone, "Organization of the Indonesian Elections," *American Political Science Review* 49:4 (December 1955), pp. 1067–84.

17 On the inevitability of international linkages see James N. Rosenau, *Linkage Politics* (New York: The Free Press, 1969).

18 See *Journal of International Affairs* 22:2 (1968). The whole issue focuses on the problem of international intervention; essays by James N. Rosenau, Max Beloff, Oran R. Young and Andrew M. Scott are particularly useful.

19 This problem is treated in greater detail in Ivo D. Duchacek, *Power Maps: Comparative Politics of Constitutions* (Santa Barbara: Clio Press, 1973), chapter on "National Defense."

20 Jacques Freymond, "European Neutrals and Atlantic Community," in Francis O. Wilcox and H. Field Haviland, Jr., eds., *The Atlantic Community: Progress and Prospects* (New York: Praeger, 1963), p. 86.

21 The constitution of Turkey (1961) states in Article 47: "In their relations with their employers, workers are entitled to bargain collectively and to strike with a view to protecting or improving their economic and social status." Similar provisions may be found in the constitutions of France, Italy, and West Germany; in Latin America, in the constitutions of Bolivia, Brazil, Colombia, Costa Rica, Ecuador, Mexico, Panama, Uruguay and Venezuela; in Africa, Algeria, Central African Republic, both Congos, Dahomey, Guinea, Malagasy, Mali, Rwanda, Senegal, Somalia, and Togo. In Asian constitutions a direct reference to the right to strike is still rare but is implied, as in the South Korean Constitution of 1948 (Article 18): "Freedom of association, collective bargaining and collective action of laborers shall be guaranteed within the limits of the law." Since one finds identical wording in the constitution of Japan (1946), one assumes it was transferred to Korea by an American pipeline.

22 The Colombian Constitution of 1886 (as amended in 1936), Article 18: "The right to strike, except in public services, is guaranteed."

23 One exception was the first constitution of Communist Eastern Germany which, in Article 15, declared: "Recognized trade unions are vouchsafed the right to strike."

24 In coal and steel industries, for instance, a "labor director" now shares in the decision-making process alongside the other two members of the board of directors, the production manager and the business director. See also John H. Herz, "Problems of German Society," in Gwendolen M. Carter and John H. Herz, *Major Foreign Powers* (New York: Harcourt, Brace and Jovanovich, 1967), pp. 461–62.

25 Cameroon, Article 37; Chad, Article 37; Congo (Brazzaville), Article 74; Gabon, Article 64–66; Ivory Coast, Article 67; Niger, Article 67; Senegal, Article 88; Tunisia, Article 58; Upper Volta, Article 88. Other African countries have modified the French concept; a link with national planning is clearly present in the Algerian Constitution, which makes the director of the Economic Plan and the governor of the Central Bank members of the council along with the "representatives of the principal national economic and social activities." In Morocco, corporate functional interests are more clearly represented in the Senate, two-thirds of whose members are elected by the

Chambers of Agriculture, Chambers of Commerce and Industry, and Handicrafts, and the trade unions. Its "third chamber," the Supreme Council of National Development and Planning (Article 96), seems to be concerned only with the plan. Dahomey (Article 97) calls its council "Chamber of Reflection."

26 Samuel H. Beer, *British Politics in the Collectivist Age* (New York: Knopf-Random, 1966), p. 344.

27 E. Pendleton Herring, *Public Administration and the Public Interest* (New York: McGraw-Hill, 1936), p. 192.

Rights & Liberties: Conflict & Balance

Ø At the time this study is concluded many new constitutions and bills of rights are being drafted and promulgated. The drafting of new constitutions is one of the facets of contemporary social and political ferment all over the world. Many new nations have recently been established and men everywhere are in search of new political purposes and new forms of local, national, and international politics in the hope that a new balance between citizens' rights and duties can be achieved.

The constant need for constitutions and their manifest impermanence reflect contradictory traits in human nature. Man needs change, which results from new goals and values in a changing environment. He also needs stability, which is a reflection of his desire to enjoy what he has achieved. "Give me a fixed point," suggested Archimedes in another era and in another context, "and I will move the earth." Clearly, the wish has not come true either in physics or in politics. National constitutions and their bills of rights attempt to fix a point in their environment, but they only succeed in mirroring a relatively brief phase of the perpetual movement of the political universe. Times and men change—and their national charters with them.

ECUMENISM & PAROCHIALISM

In the twentieth century nations and men have been exposed to two simultaneous and conflicting pulls—ecumenism, universalism, and the trend toward supranational unity, and in opposition, parochialism, the assertion of separate identities of subnational groups.

Current appeals for supranational cooperation and global planning express the dreams of a few idealists and believers in a common destiny of mankind and the hard imperatives of modernity—an internationally interdependent economy, technology, nuclear armaments, mass communications and transports, space exploration, population explosion, and ecology.

Industrial pollution, for instance, is no longer the singular preoccupation of a few highly industrialized nations such as the United States, Japan, Germany, and the Soviet Union. It is also the concern of underdeveloped portions of Asia, Africa, and Latin America where national elites have committed themselves to rapid modernization and industrialization—initially without consideration of the human and environmental costs. The urgent call for Asian regional cooperation to check the contamination of rivers, seas, and atmosphere issued in April 1972 by Prime Minister Indira Gandhi of India, addressed to all neighboring countries engaged in modernization, illustrates the increasing worry of national leaders in that area.[1] A new project for recycling waste in Swaziland was begun in 1972 with the expectation that it would "end a pollution hazard that has plagued not only Swaziland but also the neighboring countries of South Africa and Mozambique." In discussing that project the report in a South African magazine continued:

> To the developing countries of Africa, the task of pollution control is an added headache in their efforts to bridge the gap between themselves and the developed world. All too often, the costs of controlling pollution to the satisfaction of Western standards can make the difference between the economic viability and failure of new industries.[2]

People of all nations and continents were bound to realize that industrial pollution of the air, water, and land—like a malaria-bearing mosquito—crosses national boundaries without passport or visa. Sovereign nations cannot solve the problem of transnational pollution alone; they need the cooperation of others. The first United Nations Conference on the Human Environment, held in Stockholm in June 1972, made that message clear—the environmental problem of any nation is a problem for the whole international community. A *New York Times* editorial (June 4, 1972) stated: "Nature's limits and man's activities are forcing the planet toward a unity that a millenium of idealism could not achieve."

On the other hand, within the established nation states today many alienated groups—racial, ethnic, religious, lingual, and ideological—press for a recognition of their separate cultures and identities. They sometimes glorify their ghettoes, demand decentralization, and specifically ask for community controls, quota proportional systems, self-government, or threaten to secede. Secession, in turn, produces a new nation state, more often than not an unviable mini-state even less in tune with ecumenic appeals. Thus, fragmentation within existing nation states complements the fragmentation of humanity into sovereign nations—and that the universalists deplore.

Internal fragmentation produces a novel situation in which some nation states (especially those where there is freedom of speech) speak with many internally and externally conflicting voices. The strident dissonance of these multiple voices is entirely audible on the international scene and they affect international rivalries and the general practice of interference. The process of fragmentation within various nation states has a counterpart in the process of imperfect integration of many newly established states. Arnold Wolfers noted in 1961 that the process of consolidation and integration in some of the new states is so poor "that other states must deal with parts rather than a fictitious whole, if diplomacy is to be effective."[3]

The nation state today is too weak and ill-equipped from an ecumenic point of view to cope with interdependence and the attendant problems which seem to require that separate sovereignties be first merged into regional and then global cooperative pools.

From the point of view of subnational groups and individuals the modern nation state has become a monster. Thus, paradoxically, nation states in the 1970s appear to be too small or too vast. The individual citizen of service states with their big governments, huge budgets, and growing bureaucracies, unions, factories, cities, computers, and pollution experiences a feeling of impotence and insignificance. In Erich Fromm's words,

> The individual became more alone, isolated, he became an instrument in the hands of overwhelmingly strong forces outside himself; he became an "individual," but a bewildered and insecure individual.[4]

Because identification with the nation and state has become difficult, various ethnic, racial, ideological, and religious communities have become refuges—identity nursing homes of sorts—for bewildered and insecure individuals. Assertion of a separate identity and culture and self-rule on the part of such subnational groups is not only a response to past injustice and discrimination but also a reaction to the uncontrollable dimensions of modern societies, cities and industries.

These cravings and protests are being translated into new rights and liberties; the right to be informed, the right to participate directly in decision making, the right to community control and self-rule, the rights of youths and the right to a clean environment are being incorporated into new constitutions. The constitution of Montana, adopted on June 6, 1972, includes, for example, the "right to know," "rights of

persons not adults," and lists the "right to a clean and healthful environment" first among the inalienable rights guaranteed the citizen of Montana. These rights, in one form or another, will presumably find their
way into national constitutions and bills of rights.[5]

For nearly a decade a group of scholars at the Center for the Study
of Democratic Institutions in Santa Barbara, California, have been engaged in redrafting the United States Constitution, including its bill of
rights. Thirty-six drafts were prepared between 1961 and 1970, and the
37th was published in 1970 to stimulate thinking about the shortcomings of the American constitutional system in this era of profound
domestic and international change by presenting an alternative plan for
public debate. The drafters "did not attempt to settle the question
whether the United States needed a new constitution" nor did anyone
think "for a moment that a constitution drawn up at the Center would
be adopted by the people."[6]

The published draft provided for the existing fifty states to become
twenty republics delineated by more rational territorial boundaries. It
provided that the president of the "United Republics of America" be
directly elected, and it recognized five separate branches of government:
regulatory, planning, electoral, judicial, and legislative. The draft
changed the term of the House of Representatives to three years and
made the Senate an appointive body. The argument for a new constitution was expressed by Robert M. Hutchins on behalf of the Santa
Barbara Center:

> The Constitution [of 1789] says nothing about the principal concerns
> of the present day. It does not mention technology, ecology, bureaucracy,
> education, cities, planning, civil disobedience, political parties, corporations,
> labor unions, or the organization of the world. It does not contemplate the
> conquest of the moon. Its references to communications, like its conception
> of the common defense, are primitive in the extreme. Meanwhile, the subject
> that necessarily preoccupied the framers, the government of territory, has
> lost its significance, because with modern communication and transporta-
> tion, geographical considerations no longer amount to much.[7]

A counterargument was offered by Ramsey Clark, the former United
States Attorney General, who urged increased "liberty, curiosity, and
doubt" instead of constitutional revision as the better way to political
and social change. He said:

> The failure has been us, not the Constitution. . . . Words are not self-
> executing. Let us not ask too much of constitutions and words. Let's ask a
> lot more of ourselves.[8]

SEPARATISM INTERNATIONALIZED?

Paradoxically, many subnational separatists are internationalist at heart. Various groups and individuals alienated from nation states having overcentralized systems advocate international cooperation, planning, and world government. We may yet see such slogans as "All Secessionists of the World Unite" or "All Individualists Merge Into a World Nation, One and Indivisible." If subnational parochialism frequently represents an understandable and justified reaction to big, distant, and inaccessible national systems it would appear that supersystems such as a United Europe, United Africa, United Asia, or a United World might appear even more unapproachable to the bewildered individual. Evidence of a popular lack of interest or an actual fear of supranational systems is suggested in the high abstention rate (over 39 percent) experienced in the important French referendum of April 23, 1972, which was to express French approval of the admission of Britain, Norway, Denmark, and Ireland into the European Economic Community. It was one of the highest abstention rates in the French history of voting. Even though the abstentions may be interpreted as a disapproval of the Pompidou leadership and government, the fact remains that only 36 percent of the total French electorate approved their country's participation in the enlarged European community. A few months later a similar popular referendum took place in Norway. The majority of Norwegians voted against Norway's participation in the enlarged European community.

It is conceivable that supranational ecumenism and subnational parochialism may be ultimately reconciled and that regional or continental political systems will result from partial fragmentation of the present nation states—not from their precipitous federalization. Nations may have to be fissioned in order to be fused.

The trends toward unification or fragmentation may also converge, thereby giving a new lease on life to the melancholy Westphalian[9] formula which produced medium-size territorial nation states. Medieval Europe once experienced manorial and city parochialisms which were in conflict with Catholic universalism. As a result, instead of finally establishing a united continent, European leaders splintered Europe into territorial compartments. Instead of forming a supraterritorial spiritual community, men became citizens and soldiers of their respective territorial states. This pattern of political territorial organization remained basically unaltered until the present. Again, the sovereign territorial state may appear preferable to any other alternative since it is a barrier against further internal fragmentation or engulfment by potentially oppressive supranational systems, especially if they are dominated by a superpower. Despite external and internal challenges the nation state may remain "the most extensive community to which men give their effective allegiance . . . with which they most intensely and most unconditionally identify themselves."[10] And it might be added, for which men diligently and passionately continue to produce national constitutions and bills of rights.

LINCOLN ONE CENTURY AFTER

The new constitutions may differ from the old in style, ideological commitment, form of political institutions, and social priorities but the core goal of all of them is fundamentally the same as that expressed by Abraham Lincoln in 1863—government of the people, by the people, and for the people. That appealing and succinct formula still does not determine who are the people—a majority or all of us? Nor does it suggest a reliable way of determining what the people want.

The collective noun "people" is often written with a capital "P," but neither people nor nation implies monolith. The people and the nation will always suggest a mosaic of individuals and groups with conflicting goals and differing concepts of how to attain them. Even when men agree on such general goals as the "pursuit of happiness," they are likely to disagree on their precise meaning and how best to pursue them. The conflicts which result pit individuals against individuals, groups against individuals, and groups against each other. Constitutions are primarily political documents which reflect the core meaning of politics by identifying conflicting values and interests and provide for their solution by compromise or coercion.

Similar conflicts and inner tensions develop in the hearts and brains of individuals. They often desire mutually exclusive values simultaneously and search for an acceptable balance between them. For example, most men desire to be individually free and yet have a sense of direction. The individual needs to be left alone and yet to belong; to achieve material comfort without spiritual poverty. Man must doubt and question everything and yet believe in something.

The major conflicts in fundamental goals have been the subject of the preceding chapters. These conflicts usually appear as familiar pairs: each component is desirable but, at least partly, in conflict with the other. These pairs include, for instance, individual liberty v. social equality; free speech v. public order; privacy v. public interest; diversity v. unity; majority rule v. minority rights; and a simultaneous need for change and desire for stability. This era of messianic ideologies also produces idealistic programs for future generations v. a pragmatic concern for the well-being of the present generation. One hundred years ago a Russian revolutionary, Alexander Herzen, warned against messianic commit-ments to a future ideal that would transform the present generation into caryatids supporting "a floor for a future generation some day to dance upon."[11]

Bills of rights create, rather than resolve, dilemmas by listing conflict-ing rights and liberties and promising constitutional protection for all of them. Consequently, the search for appropriate compromises and balance among desirable yet conflicting values is left to the subsequent

Drawing by Ed Fisher; © Punch, London.

"Are you kidding?"

working and evolution of a given national system. Therefore, bills of rights, either explicitly or implicitly, treat rights and liberties as relative, not absolute.

Despite its revolutionary fervor, the French Declaration of the Rights of Man and Citizen, 1789, a prototype of constitutional bills of rights, treated the liberties proclaimed as relative. It suggested a formula for the limitation of liberty:

> Liberty consists in the power to do anything that does not injure others; accordingly the exercise of the natural rights of each man has no limits *except* those that secure to the other members of the society the enjoyment of these same rights (italics added).

This comparative study has illustrated that there is hardly any liberty or right that does not require balancing with other rights and liberties or subordination to collective interests such as order, peace, and national security. Free speech conflicts with the right of other persons not to be hurt by it (libel, slander, obscenity, or false commercial claims) and with internal order and external security. The right of the individual to manage his property as he sees fit includes the implied right to fire and hire at will. These constitutionally protected rights therefore clash with another right, protected by the same constitution—the right of the individual to protect his job by union action pushed to an extreme may make property rights illusory. If property rights are interpreted to include the right of a proprietor to refuse transportation, room, and food to a particular group he dislikes, that right obviously conflicts with the right of the group to use public accommodations. Even more fundamentally, the right of the group to be spared humiliation and its right to human dignity are endangered.

The process of constitution making over the past two centuries has seen the pendulum swing back and forth between conflicting rights and liberties. Rights and liberties are valued differently according to the period and the political cultures involved. During the nineteenth century bills of rights were primarily concerned with individual liberties and political rights. The emphasis shifted in the twentieth century to social and economic collective interests. But, in reaction to totalitarianism under communism and fascism, the basic quest again seeks individual liberty and political rights.

The use of the term "balance" to describe the search for an acceptable compromise between conflicting rights and liberties is politically correct but mathematically misleading. "Balance" suggests equilibrium, a search for some center of gravity. In reality the acceptable point of balance is usually found closer to one pole than to the other. Moreover, the point of acceptable balance has been constantly shifting in response to new social, political, and environmental challenges. This is, of course, the primary reason why the process of drafting or amending bills of rights has been continuous. Therefore, the term "balance" should simply suggest the need to be aware that no component of these conflicting pairs of rights and liberties can be realized absolutely without absolutely destroying its opposite. Absolute equality might lead to Orwellian totalitarianism, and absolute freedom could lead to anarchy and survival of a selfish few.

The French revolutionary motto, "Liberté, Egalité, Fraternité," added brotherhood to the primary yet conflicting pair, freedom and equality. The French political trinity may thus view the brotherhood of man as a missing link in the balanced evolution of rights, duties, and liberties, i.e., not a goal of itself but a precondition for the realization of the first two. To date constitutions and their bills of rights, instead of brotherhood, have been expected to provide that delicate balance. On the other hand, it may be argued that if men were really brothers they could do without governments or constitutions. Brothers seldom find it necessary to translate their unselfish relationship into written documents.

Finally, in this nonlegal context, constitutions and their bills of rights appear to be simply comments on human nature. Paraphrasing Emerson, constitutions are the lengthened shadows of men. Therefore they are bound to continue and constantly change to reflect the individual and collective needs of human communities.

NOTES

1 *India News,* April 28, 1972, p. 1.

2 "Swazis Re-Cycle Waste," *To the Point* 1:10 (May 20, 1972), p. 46.

3 Arnold Wolfers, *Discord and Collaboration: Essays on International Politics* (Baltimore: The Johns Hopkins Press, 1962), p. 21. Note also several violent conflicts between regional and tribal groups within several African states, such as the secessions of Katanga from the Congo, secession of Biafra from Nigeria, the long war between the Arab North and the black South in Sudan, and the inter-tribal bloody conflict in Burundi. In the latter case it was estimated that in the conflict between the ruling aristocracy of Tutsi (Watusi) tribesmen and the Hutu peasant majority 50,000 to 120,000 people were killed (*New York Times,* June 3, 1972).

4 Erich Fromm, *Escape from Freedom* (New York: Holt, Rinehart and Winston, 1941), p. 120.

5 *Constitution of Montana,* adopted June 6, 1972, "Declaration of Rights," Section II/3: "Inalienable Rights: All persons are born free and have certain inalienable rights. They include the right to a clean and healthful environment and the rights of pursuing life's basic necessities, enjoying and defending their rights and liberties, acquiring, possessing, and protecting property, and seeking their safety, health and happiness in all lawful ways."

Section 8 of the same article grants the *right of participation:* "The public has the right to expect governmental agencies to afford such reasonable opportunity for citizen participation in the operation of agencies prior to the final decision as may be provided for by law."

Section 9 describes the *right to know:* "No person shall be deprived of the right to examine documents or to observe the deliberation of all public bodies or agencies of state government and its subdivisions, except in cases in which the demand of individual privacy clearly exceeds the merits of public disclosure."

Section 16, entitled *Rights of Persons Non-Adults,* states: "The rights of persons under 18 years of age shall include, but not be limited to, all the fundamental rights of this article unless specifically precluded by laws which enhance the protection of such persons." The right of any person "to keep or bear arms in defense of his own home, person, and property," guaranteed by Section 12, evidently shall not include the right of five-year olds to purchase machine guns.

See also A. E. Dick Howard, "State Constitutions and the Environment," *Virginia Law Review* 58:2 (February 1972), p. 193.

6   The *Center Magazine,* 3:5 (September/October 1970), pp. 8–9.

7   Ibid. The philosophy of the new draft was stated in its introduction as follows: "It has been assumed in the course of this constitutional exercise that the time might come when the American people exasperated by the obstructionism of their Congress, the unwarranted assumption of legislative powers by their Supreme Court, and the unbearable load of duties under-tɛ ken by the President might decide that new institutions are necessary to fulfill their reasonable expectations of progress."

Compare also Leland D. Baldwin, *Reframing the Constitution: An Imperative for Modern America* (Santa Barbara, Calif.: Clio Press, 1972). The book is "dedicated to that group of men who met in Philadelphia in the Spring and Summer of 1787 and wrought better than they knew." It suggests that "many of our social and political problems arise from the defects in our Constitution or have been fostered by our constitutional system." These defects and the proposed remedies are the subject of the book that focuses on the need to renovate the party system to make the separation of powers effective; it also proposes the creation of larger and more viable states since they have now ceased to be viable and have become "antiquated, clumsy, antipathetic to each other, and no longer capable of performing their functions." The boundaries and the names of the new territorial components are indicated as New England, New York (city), Alleghenia, Appalachia, Savanna, Erie, Chicago, Mississippi, Texas, Missouri, Deseret (including Utah, Arizona, and New Mexico), Oregon, Sierra (including northern California), and California (including Los Angeles).

8   *New York Times,* "Hutchins and Clark Debate the Constitution," November 12, 1970.

9   The Peace of Westphalia in 1648 is generally considered to be the birthday of the territorial-national state as we know it today. Europe, split by the

religious conflict between Catholicism and Protestantism, was pacified at the cost of its territorial fragmentation.

10 Rupert Emerson, *From Empire to Nation* (Cambridge, Mass.: Harvard University Press, 1960), p. 95.

11 "Do you truly wish to condemn all human beings alive today to the sad role of caryatids . . . supporting a floor for others some day to dance on? . . . This alone should serve as a warning to people: an end that is infinitely remote is not an end, but, if you like, a trap; an end must be nearer. . . . Each age, each generation, each life has its own fullness." Quoted by Daniel Bell, "The Passing of Fanaticism," in M. Rejai, *Decline of Ideology* (Chicago/New York: Aldine/Atherton, 1971), p. 44.

Bibliography & Index

Selected Bibliography

This selected bibliography is composed of two segments. The first contains source and reference books, mostly annotated anthologies of national constitutions and other fundamental documents.

The second segment of the bibliography contains general comparative and analytical works. Only a few single-country sample studies (especially with reference to England and the United States) have been included. Standard textbooks on comparative government that focus on specific areas in Europe, Asia, Africa, and Latin America have been omitted; they may be consulted with profit since they all refer, directly or indirectly, to the relationship between constitutional guarantees of rights and liberties and extraconstitutional realities.

SOURCE BOOKS & ANTHOLOGIES

Abernathy, Glenn M. *Civil Liberties under the Constitution.* New York: Dodd, Mead, 1972.

Ahmad, M. B. *Select Constitutions of the World.* (Prepared for presentation to the Constituent Assembly of Pakistan.) Karachi, 1951.

Andrews, William G., ed. *Constitutions and Constitutionalism.* Princeton: Van Nostrand, 1963.

Bedau, Hugo A. *The Death Penalty in America: An Anthology.* Chicago: Aldine, 1965.

Braham, Randolph L., ed. *Documents on Major European Governments.* New York: Knopf-Random, 1966.

Chaffee, Zachariah. *Documents on Fundamental Human Rights.* New York: Atheneum, 1963.

Dodd, W. F. *Modern Constitutions.* 2 vols. Chicago: University of Chicago Press, 1909.

Duverger, Maurice. *Constitutions et Documents Politiques.* Paris: Presses Universitaires de France, 1957. (Contains all French constitutional documents since 1789.)

Elton, G. R., ed. *The Tudor Constitution.* New York: Cambridge University Press, 1960.

Emerson, Thomas I.; Haber, David; and Dorsen, Norman. *Political and Civil Rights in the United States.* 2 vols. Boston: Little, Brown, 1967.

Fitzgibbon, Russell H. *The Constitutions of the Americas*. Chicago: University of Chicago Press, 1948.

Foreign Office. *Constitutions of All Countries*. Vol. I, *The British Empire*, 1938; Vol. II, *Continental Europe and their Dependencies*, planned but not yet published. London: H. M. Stationery Office, 1938.

Gaind, D. N., and Sharma, R. P. *Main Constitutions of the World*. Agra: Ratan Prakashan Mandir, 1963.

Hanham, H. J., ed. *The Nineteenth Century Constitution, 1815–1914*. New York: Cambridge University Press, 1969.

Irish Free State. *Select Constitutions of the World*. (Prepared for presentation to Daile Eireann by order of the Irish Provisional Government.) Dublin: Stationery Office, 1922.

Kenyon, J. P., and Grant, G. F., eds. *The Stuart Constitution, 1603–1688*. New York: Cambridge University Press, 1966.

Konvitz, Milton R., ed. *Bill of Rights Reader: Leading Constitutional Cases*. Ithaca: Cornell University Press, 1968.

McBain, H. L., and Rogers, L. *The New Constitutions*. London: Doubleday Page, 1922.

Mirkine-Guetzévitch, B. *Les Constitutions Européenes*. Paris: Presses Universitaires de France, 1951.

Muller, Steven, ed. *Documents on European Governments*. New York: Macmillan, 1963.

Newton, A. P. *Federal and Unified Constitutions*. London: Longmans, 1923.

Peaslee, Amos J. *Constitutions of the Nations*. New York: Justice House, 1956/1967.

Philippine Islands National Library. *Planes constitucionales para Filipinas (coleccion de textos constitucionales antiguos y modernos para información de los membros de la Asamblea constituyente)*. Manila: 1934.

Sharma, Indra D. *Modern Constitutions at Work*. New York, Bombay: Asia Publishing House, 1962.

Shiva, Rao B. *Select Constitutions of the World*. Madras: Law Journal Press, 1934. (Includes the constitutions of Switzerland, Austria, Finland, Mexico, Denmark, Norway, Sweden, Belgium, Yugoslavia, Czechoslovakia, Estonia, Australia, Canada, and the South African Union in addition to those of Germany, USSR, France, and the United States.)

Tanner, J. R. *Constitutional Documents of the Reign of James I, A.D., 1603–1625*. New York: Cambridge University Press, 1952.

Triska, Jan F., ed. *Constitutions of the Communist Party States*. Stanford: Stanford University Press, 1968.

Wight, Martin. *British Colonial Constitutions*. London: Oxford University Press, 1951.

Williams, E. Neville. *The Eighteenth Century Constitution: 1688–1815*. New York: Cambridge University Press, 1968.

Wuest, John J., and Vernon, Manfred C. *New Sources in Major European Governments*. Cleveland: World, 1966.

ANALYTICAL & COMPARATIVE WORKS

Abernathy, Glenn M. *The Right of Assembly and Association*. Columbia: University of South Carolina Press, 1961.

Abraham, Henry J. *The Judicial Process: An Introductory Analysis of the Courts of the United States, England, and France*. New York: Oxford University Press, 1968.

Almond, Gabriel A., and Coleman, James S., eds. *The Politics of the Developing Areas*. Princeton: Princeton University Press, 1960.

————, and Powell, G. Bingham, Sr. *Comparative Politics, A Developmental Approach*. Boston: Little, Brown, 1966.

————, and Verba, Sidney. *The Civic Culture, Political Attitudes and Democracy in Five Nations*. Boston: Little, Brown, 1965.

Anson, William R. *The Law and Custom of the Constitution*. New York: Oxford University Press, 1935 (first published in 1892).

Asher, Robert E., et al. *The United Nations and Promotion of Welfare*. Washington, D. C.: The Brookings Institution, 1957.

Bagehot, W. *The English Constitution*. New York: Oxford, 1931.

Baldwin, Leland D. *Reframing the Constitution: An Imperative for Modern America*. Santa Barbara: Clio Press, 1972.

Barker, Sir Ernest. *Essays on Government*. 2d ed. London: Oxford University Press, 1951.

————. *Reflections on Government*. London: Oxford University Press, 1942.

Bayley, David H. *Public Liberties in the New States*. Skokie, Ill.: Rand McNally, 1964.

Beer, Samuel H. *British Politics in the Collectivist Age*. New York: Knopf, 1966.

Blondel, Jean. *An Introduction to Comparative Government*. New York: Praeger, 1969.

Bruce, Maurice. *The Coming of the Welfare State*. New York: Schocken, 1966.

Bryce, James. *Modern Democracies*. New York: Macmillan, 1924.

————. *The American Commonwealth*. New York: Macmillan, 1910.

Brzezinski, Zbigniew. *Between Two Ages: America's role in the Technetronic Era*. New York: Viking, 1970.

————, and Huntington, Samuel P. *Political Power, USA/USSR, Similarities and Contrasts, Convergence or Evolution*. New York: Viking, 1964.

Bunn, Ronald F., and Andrews, William G., eds. *Politics and Civil Liberties in Europe: Four Case Studies*. New York: Van Nostrand, 1968.

Burmeister, Werner, ed. *Democratic Institutions in the World Today*. New York: Praeger, 1958.

Butler, David E., ed. *Elections Abroad*. New York: St. Martin's, 1959.

Campbell, Angus; Converse, P. E.; Miller, W. E.; and Stokes, D. E. *Elections and the Political Order*. New York: Wiley, 1966.

Carter, Gwendolen M., ed. *Politics in Africa: Seven Cases*. New York: Harcourt, Brace, Jovanovich, 1966.

————, and Herz, John H. *Government and Politics in the Twentieth Century.* New York: Praeger, 1965.

————, and Westin, Alan F., eds. *Politics in Europe: Five Cases in European Government.* New York: Harcourt, Brace, Jovanovich, 1965.

Castberg, Freda. *Freedom of Speech in the West: A Comparative Study of Public Law in France, the United States, and Germany.* London: Allen and Unwin, 1961.

Castles, Francis G. *Pressure Groups and Political Culture: A Comparative Study.* London: Routledge, 1967.

Chaffee, Zachariah. *Free Speech in the U.S.* Cambridge, Mass.: Harvard University Press, 1941.

Coleman, James S., ed. *Studies in Political Development.* Princeton.: Princeton University Press, 1965.

Corwin, Edward S. *Total War and the Constitution.* New York: Knopf, 1947.

Currie, David P. *Federalism and the New Nations of Africa.* Chicago: University of Chicago Press, 1964.

Curtis, Michael. *Comparative Government and Politics: An Introductory Essay in Political Science.* New York: Harper and Row, 1968.

Dahl, Robert A. *Modern Political Analysis.* Englewood Cliffs, N.J.: Prentice-Hall, 1963.

————. *Polyarchy.* New Haven: Yale University Press, 1970.

————, ed. *Political Opposition in Western Democracies.* New Haven: Yale University Press, 1968.

David, René. *Major Legal Systems in the World Today: An Introduction to the Comparative Study of Law.* London: Stevens, 1968.

Deutsch, Karl W. *The Nerves of Government.* New York: Free Press, 1966.

Dicey, A. V. *The Law of the Constitution.* 10th ed. London: Macmillan, 1959.

Duchacek, Ivo D. *Comparative Federalism: The Territorial Dimension of Politics.* New York: Holt, Rinehart, and Winston, 1970.

————. *Power Maps: Comparative Politics of Constitutions.* Santa Barbara: Clio Press, 1973.

Duverger, Maurice. *Party Politics and Pressure Groups: A Comparative Introduction.* New York: Crowell, 1972.

————. *Political Parties: Their Organization and Activity in the Modern State.* New York: Wiley, 1954.

————. *The Study of Politics.* New York: Crowell, 1972.

Easton, David. *A Framework for Political Analysis.* Englewood Cliffs, N.J.: Prentice-Hall, 1965.

————. *A Systems Analysis of Political Life.* New York: Wiley, 1965.

Ehrmann, Henry W., ed. *Democracy in a Changing Society.* New York: Praeger, 1964.

————, ed. *Interest Groups on Four Continents.* Pittsburgh: University of Pittsburgh Press, 1958.

Emden, C. S. *The People and the Constitution.* New York: Oxford University Press, 1956.

Emerson, Thomas I. *Toward a General Theory of the 1st Amendment.* New York: Random, 1966.

Epstein, Leon D. *Political Parties in Western Democracies.* New York: Praeger, 1967.

Ernst, Morris I., and Schwartz, Alan U., eds. *Privacy: The Right to be Let Alone.* New York: Macmillan, 1962.

Fagen, Richard R. *Politics and Communication.* Boston: Little, Brown, 1966.

Fellman, David. *The Defendant's Rights.* New York: Holt, Rinehart and Winston, 1958.

————. *The Limits of Freedom.* New Brunswick, N.J.: Rutgers University Press, 1959.

Field, G. Lowell. *Comparative Political Development: The Precedent of the West.* London: Routledge, 1968.

Finer, Herman. *The Theory and Practice of Modern Government.* London: Methuen, 1961.

Finer, S. E. *Comparative Government.* New York: Basic Books, 1971.

————. *The Man on Horseback: The Role of the Military in Politics.* London: Pall Mall, 1962.

Fogarty, Michael P. *Christian Democracy in Western Europe, 1820–1953.* Notre Dame: Notre Dame University Press, 1957.

Francis-Williams, Edward. *The Right to Know: The Rise of the World Press.* London: Longmans, 1969.

Fried, Robert C. *Comparative Political Institutions.* New York: Macmillan, 1966.

Friedrich, Carl J. *Constitutional Government and Democracy: Theory and Practice in Europe and America.* 4th ed. Waltham, Mass.: Blaisdell, 1968.

————. *The Impact of American Constitutionalism Abroad.* Boston: Boston University Press, 1968.

————. *Transcendent Justice—The Religious Dimension of Constitutionalism.* Durham, N.C.: Duke University Press, 1964.

————. *Trends of Federalism in Theory and Practice.* New York: Praeger, 1968.

————, and Brzezinski, Zbigniew K. *Totalitarian Dictatorship and Autocracy.* 2d ed. New York: Praeger, 1966.

Fromm, Erich. *Escape from Freedom.* New York: Holt, Rinehart, and Winston, 1941.

Gellhorn, Walter. *Ombudsman and Others, Citizens' Protectors in Nine Countries.* Cambridge, Mass.: Harvard University Press, 1967.

Greaves, H. R. *The British Constitution.* London: Allen and Unwin, 1955.

Hamilton, Alexander; Jay, John; and Madison, James. *The Federalist Papers.* New York: Mentor Paperback, 1961.

Hawgood, J. A. *Modern Constitutions since 1787.* New York: Macmillan, 1939.

Heckscher, Gunnar. *The Study of Comparative Politics and Government.* New York: Macmillan, 1957.

Hennig, Stanley, and Ander, John, eds. *European Political Parties.* New York: Praeger, 1970.

Hoch, Paul. *Academic Freedom in Action.* London: Sheed and Ward, 1970.

Howe, Mark de Wolfe. *The Garden and the Wilderness: Religion in American Constitutional History.* Chicago: University of Chicago Press, 1965.

Huntington, Samuel P. *Political Order in Changing Societies.* New Haven: Yale University Press, 1968.

Jennings, William I. *The British Constitution.* New York: Cambridge University Press, 1961.

————. *The Law and the Constitution.* London: University Press, 1959.

Kanowitz, Leo. *Women and the Law.* Albuquerque: University of New Mexico Press, 1966.

Kelsen, Hans. *General Theory of Law and State.* Cambridge, Mass.: Harvard University Press, 1930.

Kirschheimer, Otto. *Political Justice.* Princeton: Princeton University Press, 1961.

Kolarz, Walter. *Communism and Colonialism.* New York: St. Martin's, 1964.

Konvitz, Milton R. *Expanding Liberties: Freedom's Gains in Postwar America.* New York: Viking, 1966.

————. *Fundamental Liberties of a Free People: Religion, Speech, Press, Assembly.* Ithaca: Cornell University Press, 1961.

Kornhauser, William. *The Politics of Mass Society.* New York: Free Press, 1959.

La Palombara, Joseph, and Weiner, Myron, eds. *Political Parties and Political Development.* Princeton: Princeton University Press, 1966.

Laski, Harold J. *A Grammar of Politics.* London: Allen and Unwin, 1938.

————. *The Rise of European Liberalism.* London: Allen and Unwin, 1936.

Lasswell, Harold. *Politics: Who Gets What, When, How.* New York: World, 1971 (1936).

Lauterpacht, H. *International Law and Human Rights.* London: Stevens, 1950.

Lewis, Anthony. *Gideon's Trumpet.* New York: Knopf, 1964.

Lindsay, Alexander D. *The Modern Democratic State.* New York: Oxford University Press, 1943.

Lipset, Seymour Martin, ed. *Party Systems and Voter Alignments: Cross-National Perspectives.* New York: Free Press, 1967.

Livingston, William S. *Federalism and Constitutional Change.* New York: Oxford University Press, 1956.

————, ed. *Federalism in the Commonwealth.* London: Cassell, 1963.

Loewenstein, Karl. *Political Power and the Governmental Process.* Chicago: University of Chicago Press, 1957.

Lorwin, Lewis L. *The International Labor Movement: History, Policies, Outlook.* New York: Harper and Row, 1953.

McIlwain, Charles H. *Constitutionalism, Ancient and Modern.* Ithaca: Cornell University Press, 1940.

————. *Constitutionalism and the Changing World.* New York: Cambridge University Press, 1939.

MacIver, Robert M. *The Web of Government.* New York: Macmillan, 1947.

MacMahon, Arthur W., ed. *Federalism Mature and Emergent.* New York: Doubleday, 1955.

Macridis, Roy C. *The Study of Comparative Government.* New York: Random, 1955.

————, ed. *Political Parties: Contemporary Trends and Ideas.* New York: Harper and Row, 1967.

————, and Brown, Bernard E. *Comparative Politics: Notes and Readings.* Homewood, Ill.: Dorsey, 1972.

McWhinney, Edward. *Judicial Review.* 4th ed. Toronto: University of Toronto Press, 1969.

Mayer, J. de, et al. *Elections in the Countries of the European Communities and in the United Kingdom.* Bruges: De Tempel, 1967.

Meiklejohn, Alexander. *Free Speech and Its Relations to Self Government.* New York: Harper and Row, 1940.

————. *Political Freedom: The Constitutional Powers of the People.* New York: Harper and Row, 1960.

Merkl, Peter H. *Modern Comparative Politics.* New York: Holt, Rinehart, and Winston, 1970.

————. *Political Continuity and Change.* New York: Harper and Row, 1967.

Mill, John S. *Representative Government.* London: Basil Blackwell, 1946.

Miller, John D. *The Politics of the Third World.* New York: Oxford University Press, 1967.

Milnor, Andrew. *Elections and Political Stability.* Boston: Little, Brown, 1969.

Morley, Felix. *Freedom and Federalism.* Chicago: Regnery, 1959.

Morris, Richard B. *Fair Trial: Fourteen Who Stood Accused from Anne Hutchinson to Alger Hiss.* New York: Harper and Row, 1967.

Murphy, Walter F. *The Constitutional Right of Association.* Chicago: University of Chicago Press, 1962.

————. *Wiretapping on Trial.* New York: Random, 1965.

Myrdal, Gunnar. *An American Dilemma: The Negro Problem and Modern Democracy.* New York: Harper and Row, 1944.

————. *Beyond the Welfare State, Economic Planning and its International Interpretation.* New Haven: Yale University Press, 1960.

Neumann, Sigmund, ed. *Modern Political Parties, Approaches to Comparative Politics.* Chicago: University of Chicago Press, 1956.

Pfeffer, Leo. *Church, State, and Freedom.* Boston: Beacon, 1967.

————. *The Liberties of an American: The Supreme Court Speaks.* Boston: Beacon, 1963.

Pye, Lucian W. *Aspects of Political Development: An Analytic Study.* Boston: Little, Brown, 1966.

————, ed. *Communications and Political Development.* Princeton: Princeton University Press, 1963.

————, and Verba, Sidney. *Political Culture and Political Development.* Princeton: Princeton University Press, 1965.

Rae, Douglas W. *The Political Consequences of Electoral Laws.* New Haven: Yale University Press, 1967.

Riker, William H. *Federalism: Origin-Operation-Significance.* Boston: Little, Brown, 1964.

Ross, Murray G., ed. *New Universities in the Modern World.* New York: St. Martin's, 1966.

Rossiter, Clinton L. *Constitutional Dictatorship: Crisis Government in the Modern Democracies.* Princeton: Princeton University Press, 1948.

Rowat, Donald C., ed. *The Ombudsman: Citizens' Defender.* London: Allen and Unwin, 1965.

Schwartz, Bernard, ed. *American Constitutional Law.* New York: Cambridge University Press, 1955.

————, ed. *The Code Napoleon and the Common-Law World.* New York: New York University Press, 1956.

Siffin, William J., ed. *Toward the Comparative Study of Public Administration.* Indiana: Indiana University Press, 1957.

Silone, Ignazio. *The School for Dictators.* London: Cape, 1939.

Spicer, George W. *The Supreme Court and Fundamental Freedoms.* New York: Appleton-Century-Crofts, 1959.

Spiro, Herbert P. *Government by Constitution.* New York: Random House, 1959.

Strong, C. F. *A History of Modern Political Constitutions: An Introduction to Comparative Study of Their History and Existing Form.* New York: Capricorn, 1964.

Truman, David B. *The Governmental Process: Political Interests and Public Opinion.* New York: Knopf, 1951.

Van Dyke, Vernon. *Human Rights, The United States, and World Community.* New York: Oxford University Press, 1970.

Wallace, Graham. *Human Nature in Politics.* London: Constable, 1948.

Westin, Alan F. *Privacy and Freedom.* New York: Atheneum, 1967.

Wheare, K. C. *Federal Government.* 4th ed. New York: Oxford University Press, 1964.

———. *Modern Constitutions.* New York: Oxford University Press, 1963.

Wolf-Phillips, Leslie. *Constitutions of Modern States.* London: Pall Mall, 1966.

Zimmerman, Joseph F. *The Federated City: Community Controls in Large Cities.* New York: St. Martin's, 1972.

Zimmern, A. E. *The Greek Commonwealth.* New York: Oxford, 1961.

Zolberg, Aristide R. *Creating Political Order: The Party States of West Africa.* Skokie, Ill.: Rand McNally, 1966.

Zurcher, Arnold J., ed. *Constitutions and Constitutional Trends since World War II.* New York: New York University Press, 1955.

Index

This index is composed of references to national constitutions. Italicized page numbers refer to verbatim quotations.

267